DATE DUE

MAY 1 1 2007	
NOV 2 6 2008	
NOV 1 2 2009	
MAR 2 2 2012	
MAR 0 8 2018	

BRODART, CO.   Cat. No. 23-221-003

EXECUTED ON A TECHNICALITY

EXECUTED ON A TECHNICALITY

Lethal Injustice on
America's Death Row

DAVID R. DOW

Beacon Press · Boston

BEACON PRESS
25 Beacon Street
Boston, Massachusetts 02108-2892
www.beacon.org

Beacon Press books
are published under the auspices of
the Unitarian Universalist Association of Congregations.

09 08 07 06 05 8 7 6 5 4 3 2 1
This book is printed on acid-free paper that meets the uncoated paper
ANSI/NISO specifications for permanence as revised in 1992.
Text design by Isaac Tobin.
Composition by Wilsted & Taylor Publishing Services.

LIBRARY OF CONGRESS CATALOGING-IN-PUBLICATION DATA

Dow, David R.
  Executed on a technicality : lethal injustice on America's death row /
David R. Dow.— 1st ed.
    p. cm.
  Includes bibliographical references and index.
  ISBN 0-8070-4420-2 (cloth : alk. paper)
  1. Capital punishment—United States. 2. Criminal justice,
Administration of—United States. I. Title.

  KF9227.C2D69 2005
  345.73'0773—dc22   2004025758

CONTENTS

A DEATH PENALTY SUPPORTER
BECOMES A DEATH PENALTY LAWYER

When I started representing death row inmates in 1988, I was not opposed to the death penalty. I was somewhere between agnostic and mildly in favor of capital punishment. Frankly, the death penalty was not an issue I had spent much time thinking about. The question of capital punishment was, to me, an abstraction, far away from my own life. I had known two murder victims, but I did not know any murderers. I did not know how the system works.

That is no longer true. Now I know many murderers, and most of them will be executed. They will be executed not so much for what they have done, but because their lawyers failed them or because the courts refused to get involved. They will be executed not simply because they committed murder, but for technical reasons, reasons that I thought were not supposed to matter. That is the first lesson I learned as a death penalty lawyer.

This book is not a book about *the* death penalty; it is a book about *our* death penalty. Back in the days when the death penalty was still an abstraction to me, in the days before I had to prepare my clients and their families for death, I imagined that death row was populated with characters like Charles Manson and Hannibal Lecter. But Hannibal Lecter is fictional, and Charles Manson is not on death row at all. The actual inmates on death row ordinarily do not conform to the stereotype. When I realized that, the idea for this book began to grow; it developed out of a gradual recognition that my perception of the death penalty, and my perception of death row, did not even remotely resemble the reality. After the idea took shape, there was a single moment when I decided to write it.

It happened in Livingston, Texas, on a sweltering summer day in 2002. Livingston houses the Polunsky unit of the Texas Department of Criminal Justice, otherwise known as Texas's death row. The city of Livingston is on the edge of the big thicket, in East Texas. The land is fecund, crossed with rivers and creeks, and dense with cypress and pine. To get to the prison from my office at the University of Houston, I drive about seventy-five miles to the north-northeast. I see logging trucks hauling timber and farmers selling fresh produce on the side of the road, but no liquor stores: Death row sits in a dry county.

During the nearly two hours that it takes me to drive to the prison, I rehearse the conversations I will soon be having. A death penalty lawyer is part lawyer and part therapist. Every lawyer has to advise his or her client about the likelihood of prevailing, but when a death penalty lawyer tells the client that he or she will probably lose, it means that the client will be executed. Law school does not train you to have that conversation. I tell all my clients that they will probably be executed because in all likelihood they will be. Unlike a medical patient, for whom attitude might play a role in his or her recovery, my clients' fate is not affected by their good cheer. If they remain sanguine and hopeful, I do not try to talk them out of it. But I don't encourage it either, because I don't want to lie to them.

To see my clients, I pass through four electronic gates and two chain-link fences topped with rolls of razor wire. I hear a pack of dogs yapping in their kennels; they are trained to hunt down any escaped inmate (since death row was moved to its current location, no inmates have escaped). When my clients come out to see me, they are escorted to their places by a pair of guards. Their hands are shackled behind them. They sit in a cage, behind thick bulletproof glass. The guards lock the door behind them. My clients then squat on their haunches, like catchers behind a home plate, so that the guards can reach through a slot into the cage and uncuff their hands. We converse on a phone.

Across the visiting room sit vending machines with sodas, sandwiches, chips, and candy bars. If you want to buy food for the inmate you are visiting, you put coins in the machine, and a guard then puts the food into a paper bag, which she then passes to another guard, who passes it to the inmate through the same slot that was used to unshackle him. Visitors cannot touch the food or use paper money to purchase it. Only coins are permitted. The floors have eggshell-colored linoleum. The chairs are made of folding metal. There are two bathrooms, one for women and one for men, with doors that do not lock. The area is sterile and not particularly comfortable.

During the week, visiting hours last until 5 p.m. On Saturdays, death row inmates have evening visiting hours, from 5 until 9 p.m. Fridays are busy, because families can drive to Livingston for the weekend and visit their loved ones for two consecutive days without having to miss much work. On Friday afternoons, pickup trucks with camper tops crowd the parking lot, and the motels are full. In the death row visiting area, dozens of young children run around. They are the sons and daughters, brothers and sisters, of the more than four hundred people on Texas's death row.

I decided to write this book on a Friday. I try to avoid the Polunsky unit on Fridays because I do not want to see the families.

But on one particular Friday in 2002 I had to be there, and what struck me was the children. I had seen them before, of course, but never really noticed them. The toddlers were playing, as toddlers do, oblivious of what was around them. Some of the older children were crying softly. I spoke briefly to an inmate who was scheduled to be executed the following week and asked whether there was anything my office could do. He said that there was not. He was a so-called volunteer, a death row inmate who does not want any appeals filed on his behalf because he would rather be executed than spend his life in a sixty-square-foot cell. At his trial, he had been represented by a lawyer who had come to the courtroom drunk and snorted lines of cocaine in the bathroom during breaks in the testimony.

As I handed the phone to his mother, I finally apprehended the chasm between reality and my previous perceptions. This man had committed a murder, but he had been remorseful from the very moment that he had done so, and he had never been violent in prison. Undoubtedly, he had done something terrible, but he did not remotely resemble the stereotypical murderer; and he was on death row not so much because of what he had done, but because the lawyer that the state had appointed to represent him was a drunk and incompetent. I handed the phone to his mother, then I watched him say good-bye, first to her, then to his fourteen-year-old son. He could not hug them or kiss them because contact visits are not allowed on death row. That was the day I decided to write this book.

People have opinions about the "big" issue: whether capital punishment is moral or immoral, whether the state should or should not be in the business of executing its citizens. But that big issue is not really relevant, because the death penalty that people debate is not the death penalty we have. The abstract questions are too big and too disconnected from reality. In this book, I focus on something smaller. I focus on individual cases because even though the abstractions are too big, we can understand the individual cases, and once we do, we can think about what they mean.

I understand—and I appreciate—the arguments for the death penalty. As I mentioned, I used to support it myself. When I stopped supporting it, it was because I realized that the death penalty is applied unfairly. There is no room to dispute that, and I hope this book will illuminate this unfairness. Some of the people I write about in this book have committed horrible crimes, but that is not why they were executed. They were executed because the police or prosecutors were corrupt, because their own lawyers were inept, or because the judges did not do their jobs. You might think there is such a thing as a just death penalty, and perhaps there is, but even if there is such a thing in theory, our death penalty system does not come close to fitting the bill.

The difference between who I am now and who I was when I started representing death row inmates is the difference between knowing just an inmate's name and knowing an inmate, between knowing how the system is supposed to work and how it actually works. In this book, I tell you how the system actually works. I introduce you to some of the cases—and some of the people—that have changed my views. You will learn how a death penalty agnostic became convinced that the only defensible position regarding the death penalty is to abolish it.

BEYOND INNOCENCE

In the modern death penalty debate, everyone is obsessed with innocence. People wonder: Why do innocent men end up on death row?[1] How many have there been? How many have been executed? What can we do to make sure this does not happen again? The death penalty debate, such as it is, is not about the death penalty at all. It is about how to perfect the death penalty.

The current attention to innocence began in earnest when then-governor George W. Bush was running for president. Bush defended the pace of executions during his gubernatorial administration in Texas by insisting that he was 100 percent certain that everyone who had been executed was guilty as charged. Considering that more than ten men have been moved off death row in Texas after their innocence was established—including two during Governor Bush's term—Bush's bravado proves that he is either naive or dishonest, if not both. In January 2000 a different Republican governor, George Ryan of Illinois, had the courage to look around. He saw that during the period in which Illinois had carried out twelve executions, the state had released thirteen people from death row because they were innocent. When a state gets it wrong more often than it gets it right, even a committed proponent of capital punishment might balk, and balk Ryan did. As he was leaving office, Ryan commuted the sentences of all 170 residents of Illinois' death row to life in prison. Next, Governor Mitt Romney of Massachusetts, somewhat chastened by Ryan's Illinois experience, announced that he wanted to reinstate the death penalty in his state if he were confident that the legislature and courts could devise a procedure that would ensure that no innocent person would be executed.

Despite the differences in their approach and their ultimate conclusions, Bush, Ryan, and Romney typified the modern death penalty debate. All three focused on innocence. Bush had no qualms about the death penalty because he believed that no one on death row was innocent. Ryan, by contrast, had grave qualms because he believed numerous death row inmates were innocent. And Romney, midway between them, believed that Ryan was probably right but that implementing certain procedures could bring about the state of affairs that Bush believed we already had. None of the governors talked about the morality of executions, and none talked about the arbitrariness with which the death penalty is applied. The contemporary death penalty debate largely follows their script. Virtually no one discusses whether the state ought to execute; almost no one focuses on the wrongful application of the punishment, on how people are executed *not* because of what they *did*, but because prosecutors lie, defense lawyers are inept, or judges do not do their jobs. The only question in the current discourse is how we can be absolutely certain that the person sentenced to death is guilty.

I suggest that we are fixating on the wrong issue. Although the subject of innocence receives all the attention, ultimately it is a distraction. Innocence disguises something else. If you support the death penalty but are worried that innocent men are being executed, then you are really worried about something else: injustice. And injustice, as I show, is quite common.

Typically when politicians and the media use the phrase "legal technicality" to decry a decision that results in a new trial for, or the release of, a convicted offender, what they mean is that a criminal who did in fact commit a crime has been released for a trivial reason. It is worth noting, however, that these so-called technicalities can also—and at least as often do—prevent people who did not commit a crime from proving that they are innocent. These "technicalities" prevent people who should not be on death row from getting off.

In the United States, twenty thousand homicides occur every year. In a busy year for executioners, one-fourth of 1 percent of murderers will be executed. These men are not like Saddam Hussein or Charles Manson. The tiny handful that we execute is almost never the worst of the worst. Instead, people are executed because eyewitnesses make mistakes, police lie, defense lawyers sleep, and judges do not care. Further, a handful of people on death row are actually innocent. But even the guilty are not executed for what they have done; they are executed due to "technicalities," because even though their rights were violated, the courts are unwilling or unable to grant them relief. It is precisely this lethal injustice—not the question of innocence—that renders our system of capital punishment arbitrary and unsound.

A few readers might recall that our current innocence-centered debate differs markedly from that of previous decades. Indeed, a generation ago, during the early 1970s, another death penalty debate took place in America; that debate concerned the death penalty itself.

In 1972, in the case of *Furman v. Georgia*,[2] the Supreme Court struck down the death penalty for reasons that had nothing to do with innocence. To be sure, it is difficult to articulate a single principle that led to the ruling in *Furman* because each of the nine justices wrote his own opinion. Five supported the decision to strike down the death penalty (Justices William Douglas, William Brennan, Potter Stewart, Byron White, and Thurgood Marshall), and four opposed it (Chief Justice Warren Burger and Associate Justices Harry Blackmun, Lewis Powell, and William Rehnquist). Together, the opinions take up more than 230 pages in the official report of the case. Yet it is possible to identify one reason that the Court acted as it did: the justices perceived that the death penalty was *arbitrary*. In this context, *arbitrary* means unreasonable, or unreasoned. The death penalty was arbitrary—and hence, unconstitutional—because it was not being reserved for the most heinous crimes or the most despicable criminals. People who had committed less vicious acts were executed, and others who had committed truly monstrous crimes were not. To describe this state of affairs, Justice Potter Stewart wrote that being sentenced to death in America was like "being struck by lightning":

> For, of all the people convicted of rapes and murders in 1967 and 1968, many just as reprehensible as these, the petition-ers are among a capriciously selected random handful upon whom the sentence of death has in fact been imposed. My concurring Brothers have demonstrated that, if any basis can be discerned for the selection of these few to be sentenced to die, it is the constitutionally impermissible basis of race.... But racial discrimination has not been proved, and I put it to one side. I simply conclude that the Eighth and Fourteenth Amendments cannot tolerate the infliction of a sentence of death under legal systems that permit this unique penalty to be so wantonly and so freakishly imposed.[3]

The debate among the justices in *Furman* was not about in-nocence but about the permissibility of carrying out executions even when the guilt of the death row inmate was not in question.

The Court, in my view, arrived at the right answer; but more important, it asked the right question.

Yet the Court overplayed its hand. Several passages in the various opinions of the justices who voted to strike the death penalty down exuded an almost haughty sense that the Court had at last dealt a decisive blow to a barbaric punishment. Justice Douglas called the death penalty regime "pregnant with discrimination."[4] Justice Brennan characterized the death penalty as uncivilized,[5] and he concluded: "Today we reject public executions as debasing and brutalizing to us all."[6] Justices Brennan and Marshall appear to have believed that the Court was finishing what others had started—that the Court's decisive action was simply a culmination of a process that a grassroots abolitionist movement had begun.[7] Seldom has a judicial sensibility been further from the truth. The Court did not complete a process; it instigated one.

Decisive judicial action can lead to one of two consequences in the popular culture. At times, the Court's radical action almost instantaneously can come to be seen as so obviously and indisputably correct that challenging it, either in litigation or through political channels, becomes inconceivable. For example, when the Supreme Court decided *Brown v. Board of Education* in 1954,[8] it radically upended the social order, yet its judgment was unquestionably sound. The Court in *Brown* rejected a practice—racial separation—that was older than the nation itself, yet once it had done so, the principle of racial equality became unchallengeable. The Court's action did not inspire retrenchment; instead, by giving content to the constitutional ideal of equality, the Court catalyzed the movement to achieve racial desegregation.

Brown was of course a unanimous opinion, but the Court can inspire social change even when its decisions are not unanimous. Thus, in *Griswold v. Connecticut*,[9] the Court, by a vote of six to three, struck down a state law that prohibited married couples from obtaining contraception. In doing so, the Court identified a constitutional right of privacy that had not previously been articulated. The Court held that there are certain intimate human decisions over which the government may exercise no control. Despite the fact that the Constitution does not even contain the word *privacy*, the central idea of *Griswold* grew immediate roots; the notion that Americans possess a right of privacy that shields their intimate decisions from government intrusion was again so obviously right and true that it immediately became unassailable.

Both *Brown* and *Griswold* articulated radical ideas—equality and privacy. Yet the Court succeeded in rooting these radical ideas in a constitutional and moral foundation so solid that it was impregnable to question or doubt.

But not all radical decisions command such instantaneous and widespread support. Reactionary consequences to a decisive judicial act are also possible, as the 2003 decision of the Massachusetts Supreme Court to legalize same-sex marriage has shown.[10] In the end, the debate over same-sex marriage in America will validate the decision of the Massachusetts court, but the immediate point is that unlike *Brown* and *Griswold*, which effectively ended any debate, this decision prompted one. The Supreme Court's decision in *Furman* was more like the same-sex marriage case than it was like *Brown* or *Griswold*. Unlike *Brown* and *Griswold*, the Court's decision in *Furman* did not strike the nation as immediately obvious or even correct. And unlike *Brown* and *Griswold*, the Court's decision in *Furman* did not usher in a new era. Instead, the Court's decision in *Furman* inspired frenzied efforts to return to days of yore. Immediately after the Court declared the death penalty invalid, legislatures in more than thirty states began to draft new death penalty laws specifically designed to address the flaws that the Court had identified in the earlier statutes. Popular support for the death penalty soared, with some surveys showing that more than 80 percent of Americans supported capital punishment.[11] Legislatures passed new death penalty laws with uncharacteristic alacrity precisely because people overwhelmingly wanted them to. The Court's decision was promptly subverted, and its sense of popular opinion was exposed as an absurdity.

States began sentencing defendants to death under the newly enacted laws, and eventually these new laws began to reach the Supreme Court. At last, in 1976, the death penalty was resuscitated. The Court examined cases from five states, upholding three of the laws and striking down two.[12] Thus, whereas the 1972 decision striking down capital punishment had been one-dimensional—it focused on whether the death penalty was allowed—the 1976 cases introduced nuance. Some death penalty statutes would survive, and others would fail. There was no simple or unequivocal rule. The 1976 decisions therefore made it clear that the Court was not prepared to rule that the death penalty is inherently unconstitutional.

The war was over. Abolitionists had lost. As a result, death penalty opponents, and particularly death penalty lawyers, had to shift their focus. Hundreds of little pictures replaced the big one. The war had been lost, but individual battles could still be won. Death penalty lawyers would not be able to empty death row in one fell swoop, but they might still prevail in individual cases. The Court had ruled out abolition, but it had also demanded fairness. Fairness became the terrain on which death penalty lawyers worked. They would have to save their clients one inmate at a time by showing that a particular case was unfair. Justice Stewart had written that the death penalty is unconstitutional if it is arbitrary. It is arbitrary if being sentenced to death is akin to being struck by lightning. Death penalty lawyers would therefore prevail if they could prove that, in the case of their individual client, lightning had struck.

As it happened, although more than thirty states had reinstated the death penalty, arbitrariness was still the norm. The ultimate penalty was being consistently applied in a wrongful and arbitrary fashion. Consequently, over a period of two decades, beginning with the resumption of capital punishment in 1976, death penalty lawyers succeeded in their appeals at an astonishing rate. According to Professor James Liebman's definitive study of all death penalty cases from 1976 though 1995,[13] death row inmates prevailed on their appeals in federal court *more than half the time.* That is a stunning statistic that bears repeating: In half of all death penalty cases over a twenty-year period, a federal court reversed either the conviction or the sentence or both. In no other area of law are reversals the norm.

The overwhelming success of death penalty lawyers in obtaining relief for their clients on death row prompts a simple question: Why? Why did they win so often? What is it about the death penalty that leads to such a high error rate? How is it that the courts were finding harmful and serious constitutional errors in half of the cases? The answer to this question is that "death is different."

When the Supreme Court reinstated the death penalty in the 1976 case of *Gregg v. Georgia,*[14] three Republican-appointed, moderate-to-conservative judges—Justices Stewart, Powell, and Stevens—observed that "the penalty of death is different in kind from any other punishment imposed under our system of criminal justice."[15] It is different both qualitatively and in its finality. Justice Stewart, who had coined the phrase "struck by lightning" four years earlier, now embraced the view that the most promising method for avoiding arbitrariness was to demand heightened procedural safeguards in capital cases precisely because death is different. Consequently, beginning with *Gregg* in 1976, the Court began to craft special rules for death penalty cases, devising a death penalty jurisprudence that led appellate courts to review death penalty cases more carefully.[16] The key insight that underlay the developing death penalty jurisprudence was that we cannot tolerate injustice when a life is at stake. Police and prosecutors must be especially fair, defense lawyers must be especially good, and judges must be especially cautious. If we are going to have a death penalty, according to this developing jurisprudence, we must be especially vigilant as a society in ensuring that we are not executing people for the wrong reasons.

Whether these special rules succeeded in constructing a fairer system is debatable. But one thing is certain: Because of these special rules and the especially assiduous federal review that they required, death row inmates won with great frequency.

And thus arose a great irony. The "death is different" doctrine led to special rules for death penalty cases, which in turn led to an especial rate of success in death penalty appeals, which ultimately created increased popular support for the death penalty. Rather than focusing on the fact that the regularity of legal victories for death row inmates meant that the police and prosecutors were routinely violating federal constitutional law, people tended to focus on the fact that convicted murderers were getting new trials, were being removed from death row, or were being released from prison altogether. Demagogic politicians could blame the federal courts—unelected, unaccountable federal judges—for being more concerned with the rights of murderers than the rights of the murdered. Even some judges began to view death penalty lawyers as terrorists bent on subverting the will of the people and using the courts to coddle nefarious criminals.[17] This climate produced the so-called victims' rights movement and made possible the infamous Willie Horton ad during the 1988 presidential election (in which George H. W. Bush suggested that his opponent, Massachusetts governor Michael Dukakis, was weak on crime because during Dukakis's term as governor inmates, like Horton, who had been paroled committed violent crimes upon their release). Eventually, the death-is-different doctrine culminated in the most severe restriction on the right of criminals to gain access to the federal courts in American history when President Clinton signed the Antiterrorism and Effective Death Penalty Act of 1996, known as AEDPA.

We can summarize the period from 1972 to the present in the

following terms: The Supreme Court struck down the death penalty in 1972 because it was being wrongly applied. Four years later, in 1976, the Court permitted the states to reinstate the death penalty, but it basically conditioned that permission on the implementation of special rules designed to ensure that the penalty would no longer be wrongly applied. Federal courts discovered, however, that the penalty was *still* being wrongly applied, and so more than half of the people sentenced to death prevailed in their appeals. This time, however, the Supreme Court did not strike down the death penalty; it did not conclude that the experiment in achieving a fair death penalty had been a failure. Instead, fairness was deemed dispensable. Whereas in 1972 the Supreme Court ruled that if fairness and the death penalty could not coexist, the death penalty would be struck down, by 1996, politicians had opted for a different choice: If fairness and the death penalty conflicted, they would sacrifice fairness.

Roughly speaking, James Liebman's study examined the success of death row inmates in attacking either their conviction or their sentence during a period that began with the enunciation of the death-is-different doctrine and ended with the enactment of AEDPA. Since then, the rate of successful death penalty appeals has plummeted. Nationally, death row inmates now prevail less than 10 percent of the time.[18] This profound change in the rate of appellate success for death row inmates did *not* result from the implementation of a fairer death penalty system. As this book shows, the system is as unfair as it was more than a generation ago, when Justice Stewart coined the "struck by lightning" metaphor. The lives of racial minorities and the poor are still treated more cheaply than the lives of whites and the wealthy. Defense lawyers are still frequently incomprehensibly incompetent. Police and prosecutors still lie and withhold evidence. State court judges, who owe their status as judges to the electorate, still ignore compelling legal claims, because to grant relief to death row inmates on the basis of those claims results in a significant likelihood that they will lose their jobs come the next election. Federal judges ignore the rights of death row inmates because AEDPA compels them to, and because they are temperamentally inclined to do so anyway. In short, what did not change was the fairness of the system; what did change was whether death row inmates whose rights were violated would prevail in their appeals. They rarely prevail anymore. Lightning is still striking, but few people seem to care.

The reason, I think, for the lack of concern is twofold. First, as I have already suggested, the debate over innocence has diverted our attention from what truly matters. Second, and relatedly, the grisly details of horrific crimes tend to overwhelm our commitment to our constitutional values and the rule of law. We get distracted by innocence, and we get distracted by gory details that are irrelevant, yet luridly arresting. These irrelevant facts intrude on death penalty cases as a matter of course. Thus, in decisions involving the death penalty, Supreme Court opinions (and lower court opinions as well) routinely describe in meticulous detail the crime committed by the murderer, even when the details of the crime have nothing to do with the legal issue raised by the case. Even in cases that revolve around arcane legal issues, we invariably learn the gruesome details of the vicious crime.

Consider, for example, the recent case of *Atkins v. Virginia*,[19] which the Supreme Court decided in June 2002. In *Atkins*, the Court held that the Eighth Amendment to the Constitution precludes the states from executing murderers who are mentally retarded. The Court had last confronted this same question a mere decade earlier, in the case of *Penry v. Lynaugh*.[20] In *Penry*, the Court had reasoned that there was no national consensus against executing the retarded. Consequently, the Court concluded that it was not cruel and unusual punishment for the states to execute the mentally retarded if they so chose.

In deciding whether a punishment is cruel and unusual, however, the Court takes into account the "evolving standards of decency."[21] The basic idea of the "evolving standards of decency" inquiry is that the content of the cruel and unusual punishments clause of the Eighth Amendment is not static; its meaning is not fixed. Rather, the content of the clause changes as society changes. As a result, a punishment that might not have been cruel and unusual in 1790 could become so two hundred years later. The punishment does not change, but society's attitude toward it does. The Supreme Court's job, therefore, in cases that raise an "evolving standards" question, is to see whether some erstwhile permissible punishment has become impermissible, to ascertain whether society's norms have changed in such a way that a punishment once thought to comport with the Constitution now in fact violates the Eighth Amendment.

Hence, in *Atkins*, the Court's task was to determine whether changes in society had undermined its conclusion in *Penry*. And the Court did in fact conclude that the legal landscape had changed significantly since the time it decided *Penry* in 1989, meaning that a punishment that was constitutionally permissible in 1989 had become constitutionally forbidden by 2002. The analysis the Court used to answer the legal question was doctrinal and historical. It focused largely on what judges, juries, and legislatures had done over the immediately preceding decade in order to see whether those actions demonstrated that executing the mentally retarded had become "cruel and unusual." The precise legal issue the Court was confronting, and the analysis it employed to resolve that issue, had nothing to do with what the defendant, Daryl Atkins, had done, or even with whether Atkins was retarded. The Court simply stated that if he was retarded, the state of Virginia was barred from executing him.

Justice Scalia wrote a caustic dissent. Part of his opinion took issue with the Court's methodology. In particular, Justice Scalia objected to the Court's mode of ascertaining a so-called national consensus, and he continued his assault on the "death-is-different" strand of death penalty jurisprudence. Those strands were clearly germane to what a majority of the Court had said and done. But Justice Scalia's opinion was not limited to a doctrinal debate. He began his opinion by describing in close detail the murder of Eric Nesbitt, which Daryl Atkins had carried out. It was a horrific murder, as nearly all murders are. But why did Justice Scalia use these facts as a sort of a trope? Why did these facts, which had nothing to do with the legal issue presented to the Court, intrude themselves into Justice Scalia's opinion?

Two reasons present themselves, one noble and the other rather less so. The noble reason is that although law is fundamentally nothing more than the rules that govern human interaction, in discussions of legal rules we at times appear to lose sight of the fact that human beings are affected directly, and often significantly, by what courts do. In criminal cases in general, and death penalty cases in particular, it is easy to forget that a human being was murdered, often brutally. It is also easy to forget that the murdered human being was a father or mother, a brother or sister, a daughter or son. We may forget that the murder victim was loved and loved others. Murder victims are human beings who had goals and aspirations and accomplishments, and they were robbed of their lives wantonly. In the dry transcript of a legal proceeding, in the arcane language of law, it is easy to overlook that. It is easy to overlook that the case is not just about an abstraction. It is about a person. Principles are abstractions, and abstractions can distract us from the reality that these principles have profound effects on human lives. Death penalty cases are not academic exercises. They are human tragedies.

That is the noble reason why the facts sometimes intrude themselves into recondite analyses of constitutional questions. That is the noble reason why Justice Scalia told us about the suffering that Eric Nesbitt endured: because we should not permit an inquiry into the evolving standards of decency to obliterate the memory of Eric Nesbitt. But there is a more sinister reason as well, a reason that is essentially the obverse: The facts intrude not simply to humanize the murder victim—to make us remember that the case of *Atkins v. Virginia* grew out of the murder of Eric Nesbitt—but also to dehumanize the murderer. Justice Scalia wants us to see Eric Nesbitt as a human being, but he also wants us to see Darryl Atkins as an animal, as not fully human, someone we ought not to care about. Judges who want to deny a murderer certain constitutional rights deploy the facts of the murder as a distraction, as a justification for ignoring the rule of law. Why should we assiduously enforce the right against self-incrimination when we all know that the person who was convicted committed the murder, and when the murder was unspeakably cruel? Why should we care whether the police coerced a confession or suppressed evidence as long as we believe that they got the right guy? Why should we care whether the Constitution forbids the execution of the retarded, or whether Daryl Atkins happens to be retarded, after what he did to Eric Nesbitt? Why should we care about the rights of a savage animal when that savage animal was so callously indifferent to the rights of his victim?

It is, in short, easier, if not easy, to execute something that is not even human. If Daryl Atkins is a cockroach, then the state can do to him what it will. If we can, in general, avoid thinking of death row inmates as human beings, then we need not confront the moral question of whether killing human beings is something the state ought to be doing. If we can succeed in characterizing murderers as inhuman, then we need not be troubled by the machinations we employ to deny them their constitutional guarantees. Maybe the death penalty is wrongly applied, but if we can focus on Eric Nesbitt and forget Daryl Atkins, then we need not be concerned with fairness.

Perhaps the reason I care about fairness—and I want you to care about fairness too—is that I am a lawyer, and lawyers care about rules. But I think there is a second reason as well. Just as murder victims have human faces, so do murderers. I keep on my desk a death certificate for a death row inmate I represented. He was executed in 1995. On his death certificate, there is a space where the physician who declared my client dead was required to indicate the cause of death. The physician listed the cause of death as homicide.

Unlike the word *murder*, which is a technical legal term of art, the word *homicide* is simply the sum of its parts: *homi* from *homo*, meaning man; *cide* from *cidere*, meaning to kill or slay. What a murderer does when he murders is commit homicide; what the state does when it executes is commit homicide. Both are killing. There is a moral dimension to the issue of whether the state ought to kill that cannot be avoided by obscuring the identity of the murderer.

Let me be absolutely clear about my position: The murdered and the murderer are not morally equivalent. People who do not kill are better, I believe, than people who do. But people do not stop being human beings with inherent dignity even when they do something bad, even if what they do is very bad indeed. When parents teach their children that two wrongs do not make a right, they teach them that the fact that someone does something bad does not free us to do something bad in return. The moral rules that govern our behavior do not evanesce, and do not cease to have relevance, when someone else violates them. One of the reasons that the abuses at the Abu Ghraib Prison in Iraq caused us so much anguish, I think, is that our soldiers seemed to have forgotten this basic moral precept. The state does not gain license to abrogate the rule of law when one of its citizens commits a crime.

Of course, there are degrees of evil, and so it would be a mistake to suggest that the act of executing Timothy McVeigh was as wrongful as Timothy McVeigh's act of murderous terror. But the fact that something is not as wrongful as something else does not mean that it is not wrong.

Unfortunately, the current death penalty debate willfully ignores the continuing unfairness of the application of the death penalty—and does not even begin to consider whether the perfect death penalty regime would be morally wrong—because the modern debate has come to focus almost single-mindedly on the issue of innocence. To those with even the most fleeting familiarity with the criminal justice system, any debate that turns on the question of whether innocent people have been or will be executed is truly inane, for the answer is obvious. Of course innocent people have been executed, and of course they will be in the future, because the justice system is made up of human beings, and human beings err. If we can be certain of anything in life, it is that human institutions will at times fail. That fact is obvious, yet it is also irrelevant.

My objective in this volume is to illuminate principles by talking about human beings. Although I argue that innocence is irrelevant, I also believe that the fact that people do care about innocence ultimately discloses a deep commitment to principles and the rule of law. I hope to show how these two ideas are connected. If you believe that, given a conflict between fairness and the death penalty, we as a society must choose fairness, then I believe this book should cause you to reject the death penalty. I aim to show that our system is not fair. It is not even close to being fair.

There is some risk in approaching the subject in the way I have chosen, for the danger in talking about discrete individuals is that some readers may assume that their cases are aberrational. Nevertheless, I have used this approach because I believe that the sheer volume of disturbing cases demonstrates that they are, in fact, not aberrational, and because it is vital to continue acknowledging that when we do execute, we kill human beings. Although they may have committed heinous acts, these individuals have not ceased to be human. It is deeply tragic that a human being named Eric Nesbitt was murdered in Virginia in 1996. But it is a grave wrong to pretend that his murderer, Daryl Atkins, is not human too.

Because I supported the death penalty even as I represented inmates on death row, it is difficult for me to condemn as unreasonable anyone who still advocates capital punishment. And so I will not consider this book a failure if it does not persuade a death penalty proponent to become an abolitionist. I have a more modest goal: to illuminate that lightning is still striking in America, and that it is striking human beings.

CHAPTER ONE

THE EXECUTION OF CARL JOHNSON

I'm not the sort of lawyer who takes a lot of notes.

JOE CANNON

Eight minutes after the state of Texas began to inject poison into his veins, Carl Johnson died.[1] Like almost every inmate executed by the state, Johnson coughed twice before ceasing all other movement. Unlike most other execution victims, however, Johnson's eyes never closed but stared up lifelessly as the doctor checked his vital signs before declaring him dead at 12:24 a.m. on September 19, 1995. Johnson thus became the 99th person to be executed by the state since Texas had resumed the infliction of death as punishment in 1982. A hundred years from now, "Harold Joe Lane" will be the answer to a trivia question, for Lane was the state's 100th execution victim. Earl Heiselbetz was number 200, and Keith Bernard Clay number 300. Carl Johnson is long forgotten. He died a month too soon; a hundred years from now Johnson will be what he already is: a historical footnote.

Johnson was my client. I began representing him in October

I

1988. I had previously declined several requests to represent condemned inmates, but when I went to Texas's death row to meet several inmates at the invitation of another lawyer, Johnson was among them. My host told me that the state of Texas planned to execute Johnson in two weeks. He also informed me that Johnson's lawyer had quit the day before. Johnson found this out because his lawyer wrote him a letter telling him so. At the time, no petition for writ of habeas corpus (the device used to challenge the legality of a death sentence) had been filed. I thought it would be wrong for the state to execute a man who had no one representing him, so I agreed to handle the case. Johnson was my client for nearly seven years.

Whereas most of my clients are quite a bit younger than I am, Johnson was four years older than I. We were contemporaries. During one of our first nonlegal conversations, we talked about music. He struck me as someone I could have met at my high school reunion. I had expected death row inmates to look like murderers, but Johnson looked ordinary. He was slender, dark-skinned, and extremely soft-spoken. I met him at the old death row, before phones were needed to converse with inmates, and I had to ask him to speak up over and over again. On the day I met him, he seemed already resigned to his death. Unlike many men I have since represented, Johnson had no suggestions at all about how I could help him. I told him what I planned to do, and he simply nodded, asking no questions. When I asked him if there was anything he wanted to ask me, he shook his head. He seemed to sense that we were just going through the motions. Death penalty lawyers need to believe that they can win. Death row inmates, however, see others leave their cells, never to return. They have no illusions. Johnson was polite, and when I told him that he should write to me anytime he wanted to see me, to talk about his case or anything else, he said that he didn't think he'd need to do that.

*   *   *

In the last few years, the public, which has supported the death penalty by significant margins, has become increasingly hostile to legal claims raised by convicted murderers. This political sensibility has, regrettably, permeated the judicial sphere. Judges as well as politicians have grown weary of the law. Writing in the *New York Times*, for example, Judge Alex Kozinski of the United States Court of Appeals for the Ninth Circuit expressed the view that lawyers handling death penalty appeals get rich and that far too many appeals are filed.[2] Judge Edith Jones of the Fifth Circuit has likewise expressed the view that appeals linger too long.[3] Even Supreme Court Justices, notably Antonin Scalia and Clarence Thomas, have expressed exasperation at the appellate process.[4] They, like Judge Jones, have accused lawyers of abusing the system by prolonging appeals.[5]

I did not receive a penny for representing Johnson.[6] I frankly do not know a single lawyer who has gotten rich by representing murderers. Nevertheless, I do think it is fair to say that the universe of death penalty lawyers is like the universe of all other specialists: It includes practitioners who are unethical. So does the universe of tax lawyers, of law professors, of prosecutors, and even of federal judges. Ridding any profession of its unethical practitioners is a desirable goal. The problem, however, is that death penalty lawyers stand accused of being unethical simply because they are death penalty lawyers. Having served as a death penalty lawyer for more than fifteen years, I know that the vast majority of specialists in this very specialized universe care deeply about the law and the integrity of our legal system. To be sure, and not the least bit surprisingly, the overwhelming majority of lawyers who handle death penalty appeals for a living are opposed to capital punishment (if not when they begin their careers, then certainly by the end of them). Yet they are therefore excoriated, in demonic rhetoric,[7] for taking advantage of a legal mechanism —habeas corpus appeals—to pursue a political goal: namely, the abolition of the death penalty. Justice Antonin Scalia of the Supreme Court has referred to death penalty lawyers as guerrillas. Judge Edith Jones has compared a lawyer to his murderous client. Yet what these lawyers do is exactly what lawyers are supposed to do: They represent their clients zealously. Their clients may be unpopular, and even notorious, like tobacco companies or asbestos manufacturers; but unlike their counterparts who represent corporate clients, lawyers who represent murderers are chastised for doing what lawyers take an oath to do.

My aim in this chapter is to demonstrate exactly what death penalty lawyers do when they represent death row inmates in their habeas corpus appeals. I do so by describing the process of Carl Johnson's death penalty appeals and my representation of him. In certain respects, Johnson's case is unusual, yet in most regards it is fairly ordinary, which means that the general themes of this case also run through the typical death penalty case. My larger aim is simply to show, by relating the case of Carl Johnson, how in America we go about putting convicted murderers to death.

A death penalty case has three distinct phases. The responsibilities of the lawyers differ dramatically from one phase to another. Many myths surround the application of the death penalty in America, and one of these is that defendants receive a dozen or more appeals, so it is important at the outset to be clear about how the system works.

The first stage is the trial. A death penalty lawyer who is a trial lawyer has three principal tasks. The first two involve investigation. The third is picking the jury. If the lawyer does not pay attention when picking the jury, the case is already lost. But no matter how good the jury is, the case is lost if the lawyer has not performed an investigation. The investigation has two unrelated objectives: first, to challenge the state's claim that the lawyer's client has committed murder (this investigation might involve hiring DNA or ballistics experts or experts in eyewitness identification), and second, to learn *everything* about the client's character and background—how he grew up, the relationship between him and his parents and between him and his children, his education, his job history, his hobbies and church attendance and medical history—in short, everything. Most capital murder defendants have committed the crime the state has accused them of committing. This means that as a practical matter, the defense lawyer's client will ordinarily be convicted. The trial lawyer's job is to persuade the jurors who have convicted her client to spare her client's life, which means that the lawyer must convince the jury of the defendant's humanity. The lawyer cannot do that if she does not know her client as a human being.

Most capital defendants are convicted and sentenced to death.[8] In every state, they are entitled to an automatic appeal. This second stage of the process is known as the direct appeal. Death row inmates have a constitutional right to receive legal assistance during the direct appeal. The direct appeal takes place in the state court system, not in the federal courts. At the end of the direct appeal, a death row inmate can ask the U.S. Supreme Court to review the case, but the Court rarely does so. At this point, the case is said to be "final," and death row inmates no longer have a constitutional right to counsel.

Once the case is final, it has entered the third stage: habeas corpus appeals. States are not constitutionally required to provide death row inmates with an additional habeas corpus appeal, but all of them do as a matter of state law. Under federal law, death row inmates are entitled to one habeas appeal in federal court, but, as we will see in later chapters, the claims that death row inmates may bring in federal court are severely limited. In addition, Congress places significant limitations on the power of federal courts to grant relief to death row inmates.

After the death row inmate has passed through the third stage, his case is, for all intents and purposes, over. He may ask a state or federal court to address a new issue he has thought of, but, as we will see in later chapters, even if the inmate's lawyer asks, the courts will almost never listen. Hence, once the death row inmate has completed the third stage, the execution is almost inevitable.

Contrary to popular myth, the death row inmate will spend the remainder of his life in spartan conditions. Death row inmates in Texas, for example, live in a sixty-square-foot cell and remain there for twenty-three hours a day. For one hour a day, they may be allowed solitary exercise—they are moved from their private cell to a larger cell, called a day room. They do not have TVs. Most do not have radios. They do not have exercise equipment. Their cells have four solid walls. The cell's door has a slot, like a mail slot, through which the guards pass food. The cells have an opaque Plexiglas window. Life on death row is neither comfortable nor easy. One might think that that is as it should be, that convicted murderers are not entitled to anything better. I leave this argument alone until later. The point at present is to be clear about the reality. The reality is that death row inmates do not live in luxury; nor do they receive layer upon layer of appeals. As we will see, they actually receive two appeals, one in state court and the other in federal court. Once they lose, they spend their days awaiting execution in conditions that are solitary and brutish.

At around the same time that I met Carl Johnson I began teaching a seminar on substantive death penalty law. This seminar grew out of a course I had taught on federal jurisdiction. Federal jurisdiction deals with the types of cases that the federal courts are permitted to hear, and a subset of the subject is habeas corpus doctrine. Over the last decade, some of the most important cases in the area of habeas corpus have tended to be death penalty appeals,[9] and so through an interest in habeas corpus law I backed into an interest in substantive death penalty law. Unlike many death penalty lawyers, I did not start handling death penalty appeals out of some unequivocal opposition to capital punishment. Indeed, the first time I was asked to handle a death penalty appeal I answered by saying that I was uninterested because I supported the death penalty. The lawyer who approached me emphasized that I should take the case anyway because the only people who are executed are the poor. I replied that the solution to that problem would be to execute more rich people.

The transcript of the Johnson case opened my eyes to a phenomenon to which I suspect that the O. J. Simpson trial opened millions of pairs of eyes: America has two justice systems, one for wealthy defendants and another for the poor. As I suggest in later chapters, race matters in the death penalty system, but socioeconomic status matters even more. Wealth matters because in many cases trial outcomes depend less on what really happened than on an advocate's skill. It is a chilling irony that the public's sudden attention to this obvious fact derives not from publicity surrounding the causes of those defendants who have been wrongfully convicted, but from cases where the public perceives that a defendant has been wrongfully acquitted.[10] Of course, the former phenomenon is far more injurious to our justice system, and far more common.

Data unmistakably indicate how crucial the lawyer's role is. In the area of death penalty prosecutions, a lawyer's skill is the most important factor determining whether a defendant is sentenced to death or to life in prison.[11] For example, in cases where the federal government seeks the death penalty, the defendants are represented either by privately retained counsel or by federal public defenders, who are among the most talented death penalty lawyers in practice. That is why federal capital juries have rejected the death penalty for 20 of the last 21 defendants who have faced potential execution, and 38 of the last 43 since 2000. The significance of a lawyer's skill is equally apparent in the criminal context generally.[12] For example, criminal defendants in Texas who can afford to retain private counsel are three times more likely to be acquitted than are indigent defendants who rely on court-appointed lawyers; and, of those defendants who are convicted, indigent defendants are three times more likely to be sentenced to prison than defendants with sufficient resources to retain private counsel.[13]

In Carl Johnson's case, the ineptitude of the lawyer who represented him at trial jumps off the printed page. The transcripts indicate that during long periods of jury voir dire, while the state was asking questions of individual jurors, Johnson's lawyer said nothing at all; the transcripts give the impression that Johnson's lawyer was not even present in the courtroom. Upon investigation, it turned out that he was in fact present; it's just that he was asleep. Which is not to say that an awake lawyer would necessarily have done a better job or obtained a different result. It is simply that Johnson's lawyer was literally sleeping on the job.[14]

Johnson did have a second lawyer, a tyro less than a year out of law school who had never tried a capital case. He did not fall asleep. His burden was not incompetence but inexperience.

The mere fact that Johnson's chief lawyer slept during portions of the trial is not necessarily of any legal moment. An indigent capital defendant has a constitutional right to counsel, and that right has been construed to mean a right to effective counsel. The test used to determine effectiveness, however, is not especially rigorous. A defendant who challenges the competency of his lawyer must prove that the lawyer's performance fell below a certain standard and that except for the lawyer's error(s), there is a reasonable probability that the outcome of the trial would have been different.[15] The standard is onerous and rarely satisfied. Lawyers who show up at trial drunk, who have sexual affairs with the spouse of the defendant they represent, who go through entire trials without raising a single objection, and who file one-page appellate briefs from city drunk tanks have all been deemed constitutionally competent.[16] The courts may be willing to assume that a lawyer who sleeps through portions of the trial has not performed in accordance with professional standards, but the same courts tend to conclude that the defendant would probably have been convicted anyway.

Johnson was tried in 1979. He had left the army, returned to Houston with a heroin habit, and moved back into the bleak inner-city neighborhood in which he had grown up. In October 1978, a friend named Carl Baltimore proposed that he and Johnson rob a small grocery store, the Wayne's Food Market, to obtain cash for drugs. Johnson agreed to the plan but said he had no weapon. Baltimore provided him with one, a .38 revolver. They entered the Wayne's Food Market together. Baltimore held a gun to the owner's head, and then the details get murky. Johnson said that an elderly security guard named Ed Thompson started firing and that he fired back in self-defense. No one contradicted his version of events, but only Johnson knew whether it was true. Thompson, who was nearly seventy-five years old at the time, was shot in the head and killed. Johnson and Baltimore were arrested several days later.

Johnson had been arrested once before, for unlawful possession of a weapon (an offense, incidentally, for which half the population of Houston can be arrested at any given moment). When he was arrested for the robbery-murder at the Wayne's Food Market, Johnson made the crucial mistake of proclaiming his innocence. That gave Baltimore an opportunity to roll over first, which he did. He pleaded guilty in exchange for a forty-year sentence, of which he served eight before being paroled.

Johnson, who was indigent, had two lawyers appointed to represent him. One, as noted, had been out of law school for less than a year. He had never tried a capital case. The other had tried many capital cases. Every single one of his clients had ended up on death row. Indeed, at one point in the early 1990s, one in five members on death row whose cases had come out of Harris County had been represented by a single lawyer: the one representing Johnson.[17]

This lawyer did as bad a job as one can imagine. In addition to sleeping during jury selection and portions of the testimony, he neglected to interview witnesses prior to placing them on the stand, which led to an entertaining spectacle because he did not know in advance what his own witnesses planned to say. Although Johnson had given a confession, this lawyer put on a defense proclaiming Johnson's innocence. Johnson was quickly convicted.

During the second phase of a trial, the goal of the defense lawyer is to persuade the jury to spare his or her client's life. The jury hears the prosecution introduce evidence that the defendant is a bad person and—if the defense lawyers do their job—it hears evidence about the defendant's good qualities; it may also learn how the defendant came to the point of committing the horrible deed of which he is accused. Then the jury decides, in view of this evidence, whether the defendant should live or die. In Texas, it does so by answering what are called special issues. At the time of Johnson's trial, the first special issue required the jury to determine whether the defendant's actions had been deliberate; the second required the jury to determine whether there was a probability that the defendant would commit violent acts in the future. (A third question was not asked of the jury because Johnson's lawyer did not request that the judge issue it; if the third question had been asked, the jury would have been called upon to determine whether Johnson's decision to fire his weapon was a reasonable response to provocation.) If the two questions are answered affirmatively, the death sentence is automatically imposed.[18]

At the punishment phase of the trial, Johnson's lawyer called three witnesses. The first, Johnson's father, testified that he had abandoned Carl at an early age. The second, Johnson's former common-law wife, testified that he was basically nonviolent.

Only the third witness was unrelated to Johnson; he was the Reverend Shelvy Brown, the minister of a neighborhood Baptist church who knew Johnson and his family. He had approached Johnson's lawyer about testifying on Johnson's behalf, and Johnson's lawyer had the good sense not to turn him away. The essence of what Brown had to say was that Johnson's character was essentially good, that the violence he had committed was aberrational, and that he could list a variety of good deeds Johnson had performed in the community and for his family.

For technical reasons, which were probably ill founded legally,[19] the state objected to Brown's testimony. Johnson's lawyer, for unknown reasons, did not fight the state's objection. The trial judge instructed the jury to disregard the reverend's testimony.

During its deliberations, the jury sent the trial judge a note. The note read: "Can we consider rehabilitation in determining the answer to the second charge [that is, the one concerning whether Johnson would be dangerous in the future]?"[20] The trial judge should have said, "Yes, of course you can." Had the judge made clear to the jury that it could take the possibility of rehabilitation into account, the jury might have decided that Johnson would not pose a danger in the future, which would have translated into a life sentence rather than a lethal injection. Instead the trial judge said neutrally, "I can only refer you to the evidence you have heard and the charge of the court."[21] Johnson's lawyer, for unknown reasons, did not complain about this answer.

The Supreme Court's view has long been that rehabilitation is patently relevant to the determination of who should receive the death penalty; the Constitution therefore requires that the jury must be permitted to take a defendant's potential for rehabilitation into account when deciding who should be sentenced to death.[22] The Court has viewed the Texas question concerning future danger as one that allows the jury to consider rehabilitation potential, thereby satisfying the constitutional requirement.[23] The problem, of course, is that the leeway presumably offered by the Texas statute is not always evident to the jurors themselves, as was clearly the case with Johnson's jury. Simply put, a jury that knows it can take the potential for rehabilitation into account does not ask a trial judge whether it may do so.

The jury answered both special issues affirmatively, so Johnson automatically received the death penalty. A new lawyer was appointed to file a direct appeal. The appellate brief was approximately twenty pages long, which is rather short. It raised fewer than ten issues, even though at least twice that number were available. The Texas Court of Criminal Appeals, the highest court for criminal matters in the state, voted to affirm Johnson's conviction; but in spite of the thinness of the appellate brief, two judges on that court were persuaded that Johnson's conviction was problematic, and they voted to grant him a new trial.[24] Johnson's appellate lawyer did not ask the Supreme Court to review the case, so the trial court set Johnson's execution for July 28, 1982.

Once a criminal conviction is final, the legal device available to attack it (or the sentence) is the petition for writ of habeas corpus.[25] Habeas corpus literally means "you have the body"; this form of legal proceeding is even older than the Magna Carta, which was issued in 1215. The function of the writ is to prevent the government from interfering unlawfully with someone's liberty. In the death penalty context, the writ can be used to challenge the legality of either the underlying conviction or simply the sentence of death.

Under federal law, a habeas petitioner cannot proceed directly to federal court but must first give state courts an opportunity to correct any legal errors. This aspect of habeas corpus procedure is called the exhaustion requirement,[26] which refers to the need to exhaust state avenues for relief before pursuing a federal remedy. It is not an arcane element of habeas corpus law. Quite the contrary; it is a principle that is deeply rooted and firmly established in modern law.

The lawyer who filed Johnson's direct appeal filed a petition for writ of habeas corpus in federal district court in July 1982 even though he had not proceeded through the state courts. The federal court granted a stay of execution and then, nearly a year later, in May 1983, realized that Johnson had not exhausted his state court remedies. At that point the federal court dismissed the habeas petition without prejudice (meaning that the dismissal was not a comment on the merits of the petition's substantive arguments). For unknown reasons, however, neither Johnson nor the lawyer who filed the federal habeas petition was notified of the dismissal until 1987. During the intervening four years, the state took no action. It took no steps to notify Johnson that the date of his execution would be set unless he pursued his appeal. Finally, the state set Johnson's execution for October 10, 1988. In late September Johnson's lawyer resigned. I went to the prison on October 1, met Johnson, and was asked that afternoon whether I would represent him. On October 7 I asked the state court for an emergency stay so I could study the case and file a habeas petition in state courts. The stay motion was granted.

The following summer was a volatile period in Texas's death penalty law. In July the Supreme Court of the United States decided *Penry v. Lynaugh*,[27] which involved a challenge to the Texas statute by a retarded death row inmate who asserted that the Texas death penalty law did not provide the sentencing jury the opportunity to give mitigating effect to evidence of child abuse and mental retardation, as the Constitution requires.[28] The Supreme Court agreed with Penry, but it was not immediately clear how far-reaching the impact of the *Penry* decision would be. The language of the opinion appeared broad indeed: The Court explained that the Texas statute, by asking the jurors such specific questions at the punishment phase of the trial, did not provide them an opportunity to give effect to mitigating evidence. For example, an inmate like Penry might argue that the fact that he is mentally re-tarded means that he should not be sentenced to death. The jury, however, had no opportunity to give effect to that argument, be-cause all the jury does at the punishment phase is decide whether Penry's conduct was deliberate, and whether he will be dangerous in the future. Indeed, the evidence of mental retardation that Penry hoped would lead the jury to spare him from execution might actually increase the likelihood of his being sentenced to death, because it might make jurors more inclined to answer the future dangerousness question affirmatively. Thus, by recogniz-ing that the Texas statute did not protect Penry's constitutional rights, the Supreme Court seemed to imply that it did not protect the rights of scores of other death row inmates as well. Lawyers representing death row inmates in Texas almost uniformly con-cluded that their cases were helped by *Penry*. Finally, even the Texas Court of Criminal Appeals, a court with a well-deserved reputation of being most unfriendly to death row inmates, recog-nized the importance of the *Penry* decision and ruled that death row inmates could raise a claim under *Penry* for the first time on appeal (even though ordinarily inmates must raise a claim at trial if they want to be able to raise it later).[29]

Johnson's case remained in the state courts for nearly six years, as the law pertaining to so-called *Penry* claims percolated. Dur-ing those six years, several decisions amplifying the *Penry* hold-ing were handed down, by both the Supreme Court and the Fifth Circuit Court of Appeals. As the rule of *Penry* was increasingly refined—some would say eviscerated—I filed briefs on behalf of Johnson in the state court emphasizing the relevance of these de-velopments to his own case.

While Johnson's case was simmering in state court, the fed-eral landscape was changing dramatically. In addition to the grad-ual narrowing of *Penry*, the Fifth Circuit, the federal circuit with jurisdiction over Johnson's case, was becoming exasperated with death penalty appeals. Throughout the 1980s, a death row inmate pursuing federal habeas corpus appeals at some point could count on having an opportunity to introduce evidence that his trial lawyer had been ineffective. If a death row inmate did not get to introduce evidence in state court—to show, for example, that his confession had been coerced or that his lawyer had been incompetent—he would be able to do so in federal court. However, in the 1989 case of *McCoy v. Lynaugh*,[30] a capital defendant who had never received an evidentiary hearing as part of his first federal habeas petition—meaning that no court had ever considered evidence concerning his allegations—was speedily executed during his first trip through the courts. No court, neither state nor federal, gave McCoy an opportunity to introduce facts that would establish that his constitutional rights had been violated. This had never happened before. The *McCoy* case signaled that death row inmates would no longer be assured an opportunity to present live evidence establishing that their representation had been ineffective or that any other constitutional errors vitiated their conviction or sentence.

Throughout the 1980s the Fifth Circuit granted death row petitioners the opportunity to have oral argument before that court whenever it determined that reasonable minds could disagree about the merits of the legal arguments raised by the petitioner. But in the case of death row inmate Johnny James, whom I represented as co-counsel, the Fifth Circuit, for the first time in its history, issued a certificate of probable cause to appeal—meaning that James's case presented arguable issues—but then nonetheless disposed of the case on the summary calendar,[31] without providing James with oral argument.[32] In short, the Fifth Circuit had grown tired of death penalty cases.

Finally, in June 1993, the state trial court denied Johnson relief and set his execution for January 4, 1994. Six months later, on December 15, 1993, the Court of Criminal Appeals (CCA) adopted the trial court's determination in an unpublished order.[33] The case was finally ripe for federal court review. The order of subsequent events was as follows:

- Johnson filed a federal habeas petition (his first, excluding the petition from 1982, which should never have been filed in federal court in the first place) on December 23, 1993, barely one week after the CCA denied him relief and a week and a half before his scheduled execution.

- On January 3, a day before the execution, the federal district court granted a stay.

- More than nine months later, in September 1994, the district court ruled against Johnson. Johnson appealed to the Fifth Circuit.

- In March 1995 the Fifth Circuit set a briefing schedule and ordered that Johnson's brief be filed in May 1995.

- Following the issuance of the Fifth Circuit's briefing schedule, the state ordered that Johnson be executed on September 19, 1995.

- In May Johnson filed his brief in the Fifth Circuit, as ordered. In July, after receiving an extension, the state filed its answer.

- On September 11 the Fifth Circuit had still not decided the case, so Johnson filed a stay motion. (The execution was scheduled for the 19th.)

- The next day, on September 12, less than one week before his scheduled execution, the Fifth Circuit ruled against Johnson.

- Also on September 12, the clerk of the United States Supreme Court called to ask whether I would be filing any appeals with that Court. I said I would file a petition seeking a writ of certiorari along with a stay application on Sunday the 17th.

(A petition for a writ of certiorari is the legal device used to request that the Supreme Court review a lower court's judgment.)

- At 6 p.m. on Sunday the 17th a three-issue petition for a writ of certiorari was sent by facsimile to the Court. Johnson's execution was scheduled to occur in eighteen hours.

When exactly Johnson would be executed was a matter of some confusion. The Texas legislature had recently amended the law dictating the hour of executions.[34] Under the old statute, executions occurred between midnight and dawn. In one famous case, the appeal to the Supreme Court literally took all night, and by the time the Court ruled against the habeas petitioner the sun was rising in central Texas, and so the inmate, who had been strapped to the gurney since midnight, was taken back to his cell, to be executed six months later.[35] In Johnson's case, prison officials originally said that he would be executed under the new law, which provides that executions occur after 6 p.m. (between 6 and midnight). That meant that Johnson would be injected after 6 p.m. on Tuesday the 19th. But on Wednesday, September 13, when the clerk of the Supreme Court called me to ask when and if I planned to filed a stay application in the Supreme Court, she informed me that prison officials had determined that Johnson would be executed under the old statute, that is, eighteen hours earlier. In the meantime, guards on death row had told Johnson that he was going to be executed at 6 p.m. on Monday the 18th. Nobody was exactly sure when Johnson would die.

The stay application and certiorari petition were filed with the Court on Sunday the 17th, but they lacked an in forma pauperis (IFP) affidavit. Federal courts waive the filing fees for indigent litigants, but a waiver requires one to file an IFP affidavit attesting to one's indigency.[36] To file the affidavit, I needed to get Johnson's notarized signature.

The day of the scheduled execution was a beautiful Texas summer day. Huntsville, where the death row prison was located at the time,[37] lies about seventy miles north-northwest of Houston. The city is nestled next to the East Fork of the Trinity River, in a fertile area just to the east of the mouth of the San Jacinto River. Sam Houston camped nearby on his way south to fight in Texas's war of independence; the drive up from Houston takes you by the Sam Houston National Forest. The land's sheer physical beauty is stunning.

I drove into Huntsville at around 1 p.m., stopped by the motel at which I was registered to see if any messages had arrived, then drove out to the prison. I parked my truck in a parking lot full of other pickups. My shotgun rested in the gun rack visible through the truck's rear window. I approached the guard tower and told the guard my name and whom I was there to see. Then I waited. I looked at my watch, and then at the guard, and then again at my watch. After I had stood outside the razor-wire-topped fence for eight minutes and forty-five seconds under the scorching Texas sun, the prison guard took a break from her crossword puzzle to unlock the gate and let me into the prison.

There are no contact visits for death row inmates in Texas. A wall, with thick, wire-laced bulletproof glass, separates the inmates from their visitors. When I got to the visiting area, Johnson's wife, Barbara, was with him. I was accompanied by another lawyer who was also working with me on Carl's case. The four of us made small talk and discussed details, such as Carl's wishes concerning the disposal of his remains. In short, I forgot about the IFP affidavit.

Finally, at 3 o'clock, while I was talking to Carl and his wife, a guard passed along a message that had been left by the clerk at the Supreme Court asking where the IFP affidavit was. I asked prison officials to send a notary to witness Carl's signature. Forty-six minutes later, a notary arrived. Regulations require death row inmates to have their hands shackled behind them when removed from the cages they sit in during visits, but Carl needed to sign an affidavit, so the prison guard, exercising her discretion, ignored the regulation and agreed to permit Carl's hands to be cuffed in front. He signed the affidavit, and a guard slid it to me through a slot in the wall. I drove back into town to fax it to the Supreme Court. But coming over the fax machine when I arrived at my hotel was the state of Texas's response to the papers I had filed in the Supreme Court the previous day. The hotel could not send my fax until it had finished receiving the other one from the state, and when I arrived at the hotel, page 2 of a thirty-page document was being received. I called the clerk at the Court, explained my dilemma, and promised that the IFP affidavit would arrive soon. Finally I called the person who was sending me the state's response and asked that the transmission be halted. We were thus able to fax the IFP affidavit to the Supreme Court at 5 o'clock. I called the clerk to make sure it had arrived, and she told me that it had and that the Court had denied Carl's appeal by a vote of seven to two, with Justices Stevens and Ginsburg voting to grant the stay. Four votes are required to grant certiorari, but five are needed for a stay. We had not come close.[38]

> When a life is at stake, the fact that one or a few claims may "fall through the cracks" and reach the merits is a small price to pay for utter and scrupulous fairness to an accused under sentence of death.[39]

Carl Johnson committed a horrible act; there is no question about it. But after he did so, the state's ignominy began. First it provided Johnson with a somnambulant lawyer, and then both the state and the federal court decided that the merits of Johnson's constitutional claims could not be reached because his sleeping lawyer had not raised them earlier. So if a death penalty advocate were to argue that Johnson was treated much better by the state than he had treated his victim, Ed Thompson, that person might be right,[40] but that hardly means that Johnson was treated all that well.

There is little left to say about the morality of capital punishment. The deterrence data remain indecisive;[41] the arguments flowing from retribution have not changed in millennia; and it is irrefutable that a capital punishment regime will on occasion execute an innocent man. Different people reach different conclusions about these facts. Still, three points bear emphasizing, for they have been largely obscured in the passion of recent death penalty debates.

The first is that the observation that the state treats the murderer better than the murderer treated his victim is, even if true, of no ethical moment. Who among us would accept the moral notion—or even the constitutional notion—that the state's action is morally and legally acceptable as long as the degree of pain it inflicts on the criminal is somewhat below the degree that the criminal inflicted on his victim? The simple fact is that whether the state ought to kill is a logically distinct moral question. This question has nothing to do with the pain inflicted by a particular murderer.

Second, the federal courts in the domain of death penalty appeals have become an abomination because they have ceased caring about the law. The courts of appeals hide their shameful opinions by not publishing them,[42] and the Supreme Court has never announced why it declines to review cases. Once upon a time Supreme Court justices endeavored to separate their political inclinations from their analysis of Eighth Amendment doctrinal claims. Justice Powell, for example, often voted for the state in death penalty cases even though he averred that he would vote against a death penalty were he a member of a state legislature. Likewise, before he reached the conclusion that the infliction of the death penalty was unavoidably arbitrary, and therefore unconstitutional,[43] Justice Blackmun often voted in favor of the state notwithstanding his personal opposition to the death penalty.[44]

Regrettably, the discipline that it takes to reach sound doctrinal conclusions without having one's analysis distorted by political passion has evaporated. Judges and justices routinely express impatience, anger, and frustration with lawyers representing condemned inmates. During the oral argument of a recent Texas death penalty case, for instance, Justice Scalia chastised the petitioner's lawyer for waiting until five days before the execution before seeking a stay. The lawyer answered that she had sought the stay the day after the state proceedings concluded—in other words, as soon as she was legally entitled to. Justice Scalia snapped: "Don't waste any more of your time.... I just want you to know that I'm not happy with the performance of [your organization]."[45]

When judges themselves start to opine (much less believe) that the law—that is, the Constitution of the United States—is defective if it thwarts the intense desires of the states to execute convicted criminals, then the rule of law has become subordinate to crass, often base, political impulses. Judges ought not need to be reminded what a constitution is.

All death penalty cases proceed through the same three stages that I discussed earlier—trial, direct appeal, and habeas corpus proceedings.[46] The purpose of the habeas corpus proceedings is to permit a new lawyer to review the entire case. Perhaps the single most important thing the habeas corpus lawyer does is to examine whether the previous lawyer was competent. And even though the habeas corpus proceeding has two distinct phases— one in state court and the other in federal court—the second stage is not redundant, because until the case arrives in federal court, the only people who have reviewed the issues are elected state judges—in other words, judges who are subject to political pressures. Federal judges are appointed for life, and therefore, at least in theory, are immune to political influence—an important immunity when called upon to protect the rights of those who have been convicted of murder.

If Carl Johnson's case were to recur today, the first stage, the trial, would be much the same as it was more than a decade ago: He might still receive an incompetent trial lawyer. That lawyer, even if superbly talented, would still be paid such inadequate wages that he or she would be forced to conduct a perfunctory investigation and would probably not locate much useful or relevant evidence. Johnson would probably receive the death sentence if the state sought it, because the state prevails almost all of the time, and if he did receive the death sentence, that sentence would almost certainly be upheld on direct appeal because the CCA reverses death penalty cases less than 1 percent of the time.

His state and federal habeas corpus proceedings would probably also be the same in outcome, but that outcome would occur much more swiftly. Since the time Johnson was executed, every state with someone on death row has enacted a law requiring that death row inmates be represented by appointed counsel in their state habeas proceedings if they cannot afford to hire their own. Most of these states, however, have also implemented timetables for filing the state habeas appeal. In Texas, the habeas appeal must be filed within six months. Similarly, the Antiterrorism and Effective Death Penalty Act of 1996 (AEDPA) requires that the federal habeas petition be filed within one year (and these clocks run simultaneously). Johnson's case remained in habeas corpus proceedings for seven years. If his case were to arise today, it would remain in habeas proceedings perhaps for half as long.

From the time I began to represent Johnson, his case, like most death penalty cases, had an air of inevitability about it. He was going to be executed. Rights may have been violated, but it was too late to do anything about that. I told him that more than once. Part of the job of a death penalty lawyer is to let the client know that he probably isn't going to win. Like all death penalty lawyers, I hoped that if I kept throwing serious legal issues at the courthouse walls, one would finally stick; and also like all death penalty lawyers, I knew that the ideal outcome was probably a fantasy and the more attainable goal would be to keep my client alive for a while longer while I kept throwing those issues.

Calvin Burdine is a former Texas death row inmate who was represented by the same lawyer who represented Johnson. That lawyer slept during Burdine's trial, just as he had during Johnson's. Half a decade after Johnson's execution, a federal court ordered that because of the sleeping lawyer, Burdine was entitled to a new trial. The state of Texas argued that Burdine should not receive a new trial because he could not prove that it would have mattered had his lawyer stayed awake. The federal court concluded that the lawyer had been asleep for lengthy portions of the trial and that it was reasonable to conclude that the result might have been different had the lawyer been conscious. Burdine's death sentence was reversed, and Burdine was moved off death row.

There are many differences between Burdine's case and Johnson's. What they have in common, however, is a sleeping lawyer. Burdine's case came out the right way because Burdine was lucky. Johnson was struck by lightning. All those sent to death row, in Texas and elsewhere, have some aspects in common—bad lawyers, impatient appellate judges, poverty. In that respect Johnson's case is typical. Yet his crime was no worse than the fifteen or twenty thousand other homicides committed in the year that he shot and killed Ed Thompson. In that sense, it is fair to say, Carl Johnson was struck by lightning.

When the clerk of the Court told me that Johnson's stay application had been denied, I called Carl to tell him that we had lost. He asked how it had happened so fast. I explained that the Court did not actually need the IFP affidavit to decide the case; they just needed it before they would tell us what they had decided.

He asked what the vote had been and I told him. "So we got two votes," he said. "That's pretty good. It's a lot better than being shut out." Then he thanked me.

Ordinarily, the inmate, on his last day, visits with friends and family until 5 o'clock.[47] Then guards take him from the Ellis I Unit, where death row was located, to the institution known locally as the Walls Unit, where the execution occurs. At 4 o'clock, prison officials told Carl's wife, Barbara, that Carl would be taken to the Walls at 4:15 instead of 5. They did not tell her why. She decided not to watch the execution.

Carl wanted to be cremated. Barbara carried out his wishes. But first she arranged for a funeral home to recover the body so that there could be a viewing for Carl's family the day following the execution. I asked Barbara why she insisted on having a viewing in a city where she and Carl had no friends or family. She had met Carl after he had been convicted and sentenced to death. Therefore, because death row inmates have no contact visits, she had never touched her husband, never kissed him or held his hand. The reason for the viewing, she told me, was to have the opportunity to feel his skin. "I know I never got to touch him while he was still alive," she told me, "but I just wanted to touch him once, just this one time, even though he's dead."

CHAPTER TWO

CESAR FIERRO'S COERCED CONFESSION

Everyone agrees that this case presents a due process violation,
the knowing use of perjured testimony.

JUDGE CHARLES BAIRD

At 3 in the morning in August 1979, police in Juarez, Mexico, rapped on the door of the house where the mother and stepfather of Cesar Fierro were sleeping. The two were rousted from their beds and driven to police headquarters. Fierro's mother was beaten; his stepfather was shown a *chacharra*, a device resembling an electric cattle prod, and told it would be used on his genitals. Neither was ever charged with a crime. At 7 that evening, the two were released and sent home.

Americans tend to believe that torture does not occur and that anyone who confesses to a crime must have committed it. Both beliefs are mistaken. The frequency of torture is difficult to document, but as the human rights violations at Abu Ghraib in May 2004 shockingly illustrated, its existence is certain. The incidence of false confessions is in fact subject to some quantification. More than one hundred and forty men have been released from prison on the basis of DNA evidence. In other words, DNA evidence has made it clear beyond argument that these men were innocent of the crime for which they were convicted. Of these exonerees, more than 20 percent signed confessions. This is an astonishing statistic that merits a pause: In nearly one-quarter of the cases where we can be scientifically certain that an innocent man was convicted, the wrongfully convicted inmate has confessed to the crime.

Several groups of people, including lawyers, law enforcement officers, and social scientists, understand why men confess to a crime they did not commit. These men are subjected to brutal interrogations and told that they will be convicted regardless of whether they confess. They are told that they can make things easier for themselves and their families if they admit to the crime. They are fed details of the crime by interrogators to make their eventual confessions believable. Interrogations are not videotaped or even tape-recorded in most jurisdictions, so when the inmate later attempts to disavow the confession, insisting that it was coerced, he can point to no hard evidence that would confirm his assertion.

If you are informed that you *will* be convicted of a murder, and if you have no reason, based on your own life experience, to doubt the police officer's certainty, and if you are also told that if you confess you might not get the death penalty, but that if you continue to deny the crime you certainly will, then—if you are a rational realist—it makes good sense to admit to doing something you did not do. People tend to believe confessions because they cannot imagine that they themselves would ever confess to something they did not do.

In February 1979, six months before Fierro's parents were hauled off to the Juarez police station, authorities in Texas found the body of Nicholas Castanon, a taxicab driver from El Paso, dumped in a city park. Castanon had been shot in the back of the head. Mexican police found his cab across the border in Juarez. The El Paso police soon arrested two men whom they suspected of murdering Castanon. Eyewitnesses had seen these men abandoning Castanon's blood-stained taxi on the same day that the police had found Castanon's body. For whatever reason, these two men were later released, and the investigation lay dormant for several months.

In late July, after the El Paso police had stopped aggressively working the case, a young man by the name of Geraldo Olague came into contact with Juarez police, either because the police suspected him of committing a series of robberies or because he approached them voluntarily. No one knows for sure. To this date, the circumstances of Olague's contact with Juarez police remain a mystery, for neither Olague nor the authorities will shed any illumination. What is clear is this: Olague told the Juarez police that he knew who killed Castanon.

According to Olague, he and Cesar Fierro, a Mexican national, had hatched a plan to rob Castanon. Olague said that he and Fierro had committed a string of robberies, and this would be another. He said that after taking Castanon's money, Fierro suddenly shot and killed him. According to Olague, Fierro's action took him entirely by surprise. They had planned a robbery, not a murder, and suddenly in July, months after the murder, for no apparent reason, Olague said he felt a sudden need to come clean.

Juarez, Mexico, and El Paso, Texas, seem at times like one big city separated by nothing but a narrow strip of the Rio Grande. Drivers on Main Street in El Paso can look to the south and see into the homes built into the hillside in Juarez. Juarez is poorer, but the cities share a common culture. Although Mexico has no death penalty, and its government considers the sanction barbaric, the Juarez police are notorious along the border for flouting the rights of its citizens in a way El Paso authorities could never get away with. The two police forces are constrained by different sets of laws and mores, and so they sometimes succeed in avoiding these constraints altogether by dividing the labor. The two forces work hand in glove with one another. So when Juarez authorities called the El Paso police and told them of Olague's statement, the El Paso police immediately traveled to Juarez to arrest Fierro.

That August, once in the custody of the El Paso police, Fierro immediately proclaimed his innocence. He admitted knowing Olague, admitted to participating in various robbery sprees with him, but steadfastly denied having murdered Castanon. Nevertheless, during a lengthy interrogation, Fierro eventually signed a confession that he and Olague had robbed Castanon and that he (Fierro) had then shot him.

Authorities charged Fierro with capital murder. Fierro, too poor to retain his own lawyer, had an El Paso criminal defense lawyer appointed to represent him. From the first meeting with his court-appointed lawyer, Fierro insisted that he had not killed Castanon. The confession, Fierro said, was untrue. The only reason he signed it, Fierro told his lawyer, was that while he was being interrogated in El Paso, the detective conducting the interrogation had put him on the phone with authorities in Juarez. Over the phone, the Juarez police told Fierro, he claimed, that his mother and stepfather, who lived in Juarez, were in police custody.

Fierro had lived most of his life in Juarez. He knew the methods of the Juarez police. He knew what a *chacharra* is. He therefore understood what this implied threat meant: Either Fierro would confess to the murder of Castanon, or the Juarez police would torture his parents. It was an easy choice. He confessed. His mother and stepfather were sent home.

During the initial meeting with his lawyer, Fierro claimed that the El Paso detective who had interrogated him, a man by the name of Medrano, knew that the Juarez police had taken Fierro's family into custody. Fierro said that Medrano had spoken to the Juarez police on the phone before handing the receiver to Fierro. On the basis of this story, Fierro's lawyer sought to suppress the confession. If the confession was coerced, then the judge could preclude the state from relying on it at trial. If the state could not rely on the confession, then it would almost certainly not be able to obtain a conviction, for there was no evidence, other than Olague's statement, linking Fierro to the crime. There was no physical evidence, no other eyewitnesses who could place Fierro in Castanon's cab.

At the suppression hearing, however, Detective Medrano denied Fierro's story. He said he had never spoken to Juarez authorities about whether they had Fierro's family in custody, and so he could never have used this fact—even if it was true—to threaten Fierro. The trial judge believed Medrano and ruled that Fierro's confession was admissible.

Fierro was convicted and sentenced to death. Because no physical evidence connected Fierro to the crime, his conviction and sentence rested entirely on two pieces of evidence: first, the testimony of Olague, and second, the confession. The confession included details provided by Detective Medrano, like the location and date of the crime, the disposal of the body, and the route Fierro had supposedly taken back to El Paso. Oddly, it also included a statement that his mother and stepfather had nothing to do with the crime.

Olague's testimony was needed to confirm the veracity of the confession, to preclude Fierro from disavowing it. His testimony was essential and, in a word, incredible. For example, neither at the trial nor since the trial has Olague ever explained why he waited nearly half a year before implicating Fierro. He originally told authorities he had known Fierro for only a couple of weeks before the murder of Castanon but later testified that he and Fierro had been committing robberies together for six or seven months. He said Fierro had taken a silver watch from Castanon;

the watch was never found. He said he and Fierro had sold the murder weapon to a rancher south of Juarez, but neither the rancher nor the gun was ever located. He said the cab had skidded out of control when Castanon was shot, jumping the curb and landing in someone's front yard, but no one in the neighborhood heard a gunshot or saw or heard the cab go out of control. During one bizarre moment, while Olague was testifying, he accused a member of the jury of having purchased a stolen CB radio from him. He said that he had committed more than forty burglaries and that the police were aware of them, but that he had been charged with only one offense.

Olague is, to put it bluntly, grossly unreliable, erratic, and apparently mentally unstable. Even Fierro's prosecutor has acknowledged that if all he had to go on was Olague's testimony, he would not have prosecuted the case.

Texas law, like the law of many states, renders it impossible to convict someone of a crime solely on the basis of the testimony of a co-conspirator. This sound rule recognizes the inherent unreliability of testimony from co-conspirators: There is always an incentive for one criminal to shift responsibility for the crime onto his partner. For nonsensical reasons, the Texas Court of Criminal Appeals (the highest criminal court in the state) did not treat Olague as Fierro's co-conspirator. It realized that to do so would undermine Fierro's conviction, and so the court stubbornly refused to use the word "co-conspirator" to characterize Olague. That stubborn refusal, however, does not change the fact that Olague's testimony is unreliable for precisely the same reasons that co-conspirator testimony is. We have no reason to believe him and many reasons not to.

The defense did what it could. It pointed out that Fierro had signed the confession—the details of which were provided by the detective conducting the interrogation—only because he knew what would happen to his mother and stepfather if he did not confess. It called his parents, who testified to the brutal treatment to which they were subjected. It called Fierro's landlord, who swore Fierro was at home on the night of the killing. The defense did what it could, but it could not overcome a confession that the prosecution insisted was voluntary. The "confession" was undoubtedly a crucial piece of evidence at his trial, perhaps *the* crucial piece of evidence. Without it, it is plausible that Fierro would not even have been convicted, and it is almost impossible to believe that he would have been sentenced to death.

Fierro ended up on death row for one reason only: Shortly after his arrest, a state court trial judge believed that Fierro had given his confession freely. Had that judge believed Fierro, who insisted the confession was extracted from him by threats to harm his parents, had the judge concluded that the detective who conducted the interrogation had been lying or not telling the whole truth, then the state of Texas would have been unable to use the confession against him. It would have had nothing more than the testimony of a deeply disturbed and incredible witness. The state probably would not have prosecuted Fierro at all.

Yet the judge did not believe Fierro; he believed the detective, and the reason is pedestrian. In almost all cases where a criminal defendant says one thing and a police officer says another, the judge accepts the police officer's version. In other words, unless the defendant's lawyers can locate hard evidence that contradicts the police officer's version of the truth, that version will become the accepted one. Fierro's lawyers did not have any hard evidence that would belie the police detective's insistence that Fierro's confession had been voluntary. The reason, however, is not that no such evidence existed; the reason is that the evidence was unknown to them.

A single piece of evidence of immense significance was not presented at the suppression hearing (at which Fierro's lawyer attempted to persuade the court not to admit Fierro's confession). The evidence consisted of a document written by Detective

Medrano while Fierro was in custody. The document indicated that Medrano knew that Fierro's family was in the custody of the Juarez police. This report should have been provided to Fierro's defense team in 1979, but it appears not to have been;[1] the document was not discovered by lawyers representing Fierro until 1994. After locating the report, Fierro's lawyers needed to determine which story was true: the one Medrano had testified to at the suppression hearing or the version reflected in what he had written in the newly located police report.

When Fierro's lawyers caught up with the detective, Medrano was close to death from cirrhosis of the liver. He signed what might be regarded as a deathbed confession: an affidavit swearing that what he had written in the police report was true. Medrano swore, in other words, that he had known that Fierro's parents were in the custody of Juarez police and that he had communicated this fact to Fierro. Medrano finally admitted that he had lied under oath at Fierro's suppression hearing. In other words, he admitted that Fierro's confession was coerced.

Fierro's lawyers then approached the district attorney who prosecuted Fierro. That lawyer signed an affidavit saying that he would not have used the confession had he known it was coerced. He also subsequently expressed the view that Olague was not a credible witness, and that without the confession he would have been unwilling to rest a case solely on Olague's testimony. Fierro's lawyers took these two pieces of evidence—the evidence establishing that Medrano had lied and the evidence that the prosecution would not have used Fierro's confession—to the Texas Court of Criminal Appeals. That court ordered that an evidentiary hearing be held before a judge to determine how Fierro's case should be resolved.

Fierro's lawyers went to El Paso and, over a period of several days, presented the evidence they had acquired. They demonstrated that Fierro's confession was indeed coerced, that the district attorney would not have prosecuted Fierro had he known of the coercion, and that there was insufficient evidence of Fierro's guilt to convict him, much less sentence him to death. The judge who conducted the evidentiary hearing concluded that Fierro should receive a new trial, and he recommended to the Court of Criminal Appeals (CCA) that it order a new trial.

Under state law, the decision of the judge who conducted the hearing operated as a recommendation to the CCA, rather than as a legal order. Fierro's lawyers therefore had to persuade the CCA to adopt the lower court judge's recommendation. At the oral argument before that court, lawyers from the El Paso district attorney's office took the position that the trial judge had erred in his conclusion that the confession was coerced, but that even if his conclusion was correct, Fierro should remain on death row because there was no reason to disbelieve Olague.

In a five-to-four decision, the CCA overruled the conclusion of the lower court judge. All nine members of the court agreed that Medrano had lied at the original suppression hearing in 1979. They agreed, in other words, that Fierro's constitutional rights had been violated and that his confession was therefore involuntary. Yet five members of that court also concluded that Fierro would probably have been convicted anyway and that the error pertaining to the coerced confession and Detective Medrano's perjury was therefore all "harmless." The Supreme Court of the United States declined to hear Fierro's appeal.

To understand fully why Fierro remains on death row, we must examine two radical legal developments, one of which arose early in Fierro's legal ordeal, and the other later.

It begins with a crime hundreds of miles away from El Paso, Texas. In September 1982, in Mesa, Arizona, an eleven-year-old girl named Jeneane Michelle Hunt was murdered. When police found her, she had a ligature around her neck and had been shot twice in the head with a large-caliber weapon. Police could not determine whether she had been sexually abused because her body was too decomposed. Suspicion turned to her stepfather, Oreste Fulminante, who had called the police two days earlier to report that Jeneane was missing. Yet despite inconsistencies in Fulminante's story, police in Arizona did not believe they had sufficient evidence against him, and Arizona did not immediately indict Fulminante for Jeneane's murder.

Fulminante left Arizona and traveled to New Jersey, where he was convicted of felonious possession of a weapon. He wound up at a prison in New York, where he began spending several hours a day with another inmate, Anthony Sarivola, a former police officer who had been convicted and sentenced to prison for extortion. While in prison, Sarivola became an informant for the FBI. He heard rumors that Fulminante had been suspected of the murder of Jeneane Hunt in Arizona, and he asked Fulminante about these rumors a number of times. Fulminante at first denied any knowledge or involvement, but his denials were vague and inconsistent, and they did not quiet Sarivola's suspicions. In the meantime, other inmates had also heard the rumors and were threatening to harm Fulminante—child murderers are not any more popular inside of prison than they are outside. Sarivola told Fulminante that he could protect him from the other inmates, but only if he knew exactly what had happened to young Jeneane. Fulminante confessed to Sarivola. He told him that he had driven Jeneane out into the desert on his motorcycle, strangled her, and sexually assaulted her. He made her beg for her life, then shot her twice in the head. Fulminante was returned to Arizona. On the basis of the statement he gave to Sarivola, as well as a second statement he gave to Sarivola's wife, Fulminante was convicted and sentenced to death.

It is hard to have much sympathy for Fulminante, but in America we do have rules. One rule is the Fifth Amendment to the Constitution, which among other things prohibits the police from coercing a confession. In appealing his conviction, Fulminante argued that his confession had been coerced, and that the state should therefore not have been permitted to use it against him. In 1991 the case of *Arizona v. Fulminante*[2] reached the Supreme Court. The first question for the Court was whether the confession had in fact been coerced or whether Fulminante had spoken freely and of his own volition. Only if the Court concluded that Fulminante's statement had indeed been coerced would it be required to address the second question, which involved the legal consequences of using a coerced confession.

Turning to the first issue, the Court held that the confession was coerced. Fulminante's slight stature meant that he was unable to defend himself in prison; consequently, the Court believed that his size made him especially vulnerable to threats from other inmates. The Court also observed that Fulminante had been in prison before, which meant that he had firsthand knowledge of the type of violence to which he might be subject. The Court took notice of the highly coercive environment in which Fulminante resided, and it further insisted that Fulminante's low intelligence level rendered him still more susceptible to threats. In view of all these factors, the Court concluded that when Sarivola had offered to protect Fulminante in exchange for Fulminante's sharing of the details of Jeneane Hunt's murder, Sarivola had coerced him into confessing. Fulminante spoke to Sarivola not because he chose to do so freely, but because he was scared.

Having thus answered the coercion question, the Court turned to the second issue. Contrary to popular myth, the mere fact that a constitutional violation has occurred at a trial does not necessarily mean that the prison inmate will have his conviction reversed. The Supreme Court has divided the universe of errors into two categories: structural errors and trial errors. A structural error is thought to undermine the fundamental idea that the trial must be fair. Consequently, if a structural error occurs, the defendant automatically receives a new trial. The universe of structural errors, however, is exceedingly small. Indeed, only two kinds of errors are regarded as structural. First, if the state deprives a defendant of a lawyer—that is, if the state physically prevents the defendant's lawyer from attending the trial—then a structural error has occurred, and the defendant is entitled to a new trial. Second, if the judge presiding over the trial is biased, then another structural error has occurred. But aside from these, all errors are said to be trial errors.

The characterization of almost all errors as trial errors has great practical significance; whereas the occurrence of a fundamental error means that the defendant will automatically get a new trial, the occurrence of a trial error does not necessarily lead to a new trial. Instead, when confronted with a trial error, an appellate court performs what is known as harm analysis; the court asks whether the error was harmful, and it answers this question by speculating on whether the jury would have reached the same verdict had the error not occurred.[3]

At the time that Fulminante's case reached the Supreme Court, most courts and commentators—and four justices of the Supreme Court—believed that a coerced confession, like the physical denial of counsel or a biased judge, represented a structural error, meaning that if in fact the police had coerced a confession, the defendant would automatically receive a new trial, at which the coerced confession could not be used as evidence. In the *Fulminante* decision, however, the Supreme Court ruled to the contrary. By a vote of five to four, in a decision authored by Chief Justice Rehnquist, the Court concluded that even coerced confessions fall into the category of trial errors. A defendant who is convicted on the basis of a coerced confession no longer automatically receives a new trial. Rather, when faced with a coerced confession, the role of the appellate court is to review all the other evidence and determine whether the other evidence is sufficient to support the jury's verdict. As Chief Justice Rehnquist concluded, even a defendant who is convicted on the basis of a coerced confession is not entitled to a new trial if the coerced confession was "harmless," where "harmless" means that the appellate court reviewing the case believes that "the evidence other than the involuntary confession was sufficient to sustain the verdict."[4]

Death penalty cases, like life itself, owe much to the sheer luck of timing. If Fierro's case had arisen ten years earlier, prior to the Supreme Court's decision in *Fulminante*, Fierro would have been entitled to a new trial once he established that his confession had been coerced. As it happened, however, Fierro did not reach the federal courts until after the Supreme Court had decided *Fulminante*. As a result, although he could prove that his confession had been coerced, this, by itself, did not entitle him to a new trial. He also had to prove that without the confession, the state had not presented sufficient evidence to establish his guilt beyond a reasonable doubt. Four judges on the Texas Court of Criminal Appeals thought he had sustained that burden, but five believed that the evidence of Olague was enough to sustain Fierro's conviction and sentence. Not a single significant claim in Olague's testimony could be corroborated, but the highest state court nonetheless regarded that testimony as sufficient to lead to an execution. But the state courts do not have the final say; the federal courts do. This is where a second radical legal development becomes central to understanding Fierro's case.

Fierro's case is not the only one that has been affected by this legal development. It is fair to say that virtually every death penalty case in America has felt it. As I have pointed out, between 1976, when the death penalty was reinstated, and 1995, federal courts reversed either a conviction or a sentence in nearly one out of every two death penalty cases.[5] This is obviously a stunning statistic. It means that a constitutional error that could not be characterized as harmless has occurred in nearly half of all death penalty cases.

There has long been a basic conflict in federal habeas corpus review. On one hand, the federal courts have a powerful interest in vindicating federal constitutional protections. On the other hand, states have an interest in what is known as finality. Defenders of the value of finality claim that there comes a point at which a convicted defendant should no longer be permitted to compel the state to expend resources in defending the legality of his conviction or sentence. Out of obeisance to the value of finality, the Supreme Court, beginning in the early 1980s, began to restrict the cluster of claims that could be raised in habeas corpus proceedings. The Court placed substantive limits on the types of claims that could be raised by inmates (for example, claims that evidence was obtained without a proper warrant cannot be brought in federal habeas corpus proceedings), as well as procedural restrictions on how and when certain claims must be raised. Finally, during the Clinton administration, Congress moved to codify these restrictions.

In 1996 Congress enacted the ominously and appropriately entitled Antiterrorism and Effective Death Penalty Act of 1996 (AEDPA). For purposes of federal habeas corpus—appeals brought by death row inmates who were convicted in state court (as opposed to federal death row inmates, like Timothy Mc-Veigh)—the statute contains two critical provisions, both of which have played central roles in Fierro's ordeal. (The sections are included in their entirety in the notes.)

One section of AEDPA, called section 2244,[6] deals with what are known as second or successive habeas petitions—that is, a habeas petition that an inmate files after already having filed one. Under this provision, the federal court must dismiss all successive petitions without addressing the issues they raise unless one of two criteria is satisfied. These criteria are known as gateways because they act as a conduit that permits a death row inmate who has already been to federal court once to return to federal court. Unless the prisoner can satisfy these gatekeeping provisions, he cannot get into federal court; anything he files will be dismissed, and the federal courts will not address the merits of his case.

The first exception that allows a death row inmate to file a successive habeas petition arises when the Supreme Court articulates what is known as a new rule and also holds that this new rule is retroactive to cases that had already been decided at the time the rule was articulated. Owing principally to the value that the federal courts place on finality, most rules are not retroactive. Consequently, timing plays an important role in many cases. If a principle is not articulated until after an inmate is convicted and sentenced to death, then, in most cases, it is too late for that inmate to take advantage of it. In general, only "watershed" rules are retroactive; the epitome of a watershed rule is the Supreme Court's 1963 decision in *Gideon v. Wainwright*,[7] which held that indigent criminal defendants are entitled to counsel. Because this rule was retroactive, it meant that even an inmate who had already filed a habeas petition at the time *Gideon* was decided could file a second petition, seeking relief on the basis of *Gideon*. But there are very few retroactive new rules. For example, in 1989 the Supreme Court decided the case of *Penry v. Lynaugh*.[8] The Court ruled that Texas law did not give juries in death penalty cases the necessary leeway to decide whether someone who is retarded should be spared from death. At the same time, the Court declined to characterize its decision as a new rule. Consequently, the many death row inmates whose trials had been affected by the same error that plagued Penry's were not entitled to relief. Penry himself got a new trial; others in his same position whose cases had arisen several years earlier were executed.

Because the Court articulates very few retroactively applicable new rules, the second criterion is the more pertinent one for most inmates who wish to file a second habeas petition. The second gateway provision requires that a death row inmate who desires to file a second habeas petition establish three conditions: (i) that a constitutional violation has occurred; (ii) that the violation could not have been discovered previously; and (iii) that had the violation not occurred, no reasonable juror would have voted to convict the inmate (or sentence him to death).

This second gateway provision was Fierro's best hope for relief. He had established a violation—namely, a coerced confession. He had shown why it could not have been discovered earlier. And he insisted that no reasonable juror would have voted to convict him solely on the basis of Olague's testimony.

But Fierro still had his work cut out for him. Under a different provision of AEDPA (28 U.S.C. section 2254),[9] a federal court must show great deference to the conclusions of state court tribunals. Section 2254(d) prevents a federal court from granting relief to a death row inmate who has been denied relief by the state court unless the state court's decision (i) "was contrary to, or involved an unreasonable application of, clearly established Federal law," or (ii) "was based on an unreasonable determination of the facts in light of the evidence presented in the State court proceeding." The word "unreasonable" does all the work in these two provisions. In interpreting AEDPA, the Supreme Court has held that a state court decision can be wrong, yet it can still not be unreasonable. In other words, it is not enough for a death row inmate to persuade a federal court that the state court got the wrong answer; the inmate must also prove that the state court's answer was not even close to correct—that it was so far wrong as to be deemed unreasonable. If a state court concludes that two plus two equals five, the state court got the wrong answer, but not by a large enough margin to warrant intervention by a federal court. For Fierro's purposes, there could be no escape from death row simply by proving that no reasonable juror could have found him guilty solely on the basis of Olague's testimony. He also had to prove that the state court's conclusion to the contrary was unreasonable; he had to show that when the state court added two plus two, it came up with ten—with an answer that was not even close to correct.

Fierro had a second problem as well. Prior to the enactment of AEDPA, there was no statute of limitations in federal habeas corpus proceedings. An inmate could bring his claim at any time. To serve the value of finality, however, Congress included a one-year statute of limitations in AEDPA. The statute begins to run from a variety of dates, depending on which is applicable in a particular case.[10] In Fierro's case, the statute began running from "the date on which the factual predicate of the claim or claims presented could have been discovered through the exercise of due diligence." However, Fierro's case was in the midst of litigation at the very moment that AEDPA was being enacted, so it was far from clear how the statute would affect his particular case. As we will see, it did affect it directly.

Whether Fierro is innocent is something we do not and cannot know. What we do know is that police used a form of torture to extract a confession from him and then lied about it under oath. We know that the police detective who lied later admitted he had lied. We know that the district attorney who prosecuted Fierro said he would not have used Fierro's confession had he known all the facts. We know that the only evidence against Fierro came from a witness whom even the prosecutor did not believe and whose testimony could not be corroborated in even a single salient respect. And finally we know that the courts, in spite of all this, declined to disturb Fierro's conviction or sentence. One question, obviously, is whether Fierro is innocent of murder; but there is a second, less obvious yet equally compelling matter, which is how our justice system could have produced this result.

The answer to this question has two components. The first deals with the proceedings in the state courts. The second has to do with the increasing unwillingness and inability of the federal courts to disturb the conclusions reached by state tribunals.

In about forty states, including Texas, judges are elected (either when they first become judges or subsequently, in so-called retention elections). All nine members of the Texas Court of Criminal Appeals are elected officials. Not only must they run for office, but they even run in partisan elections. One consequence of electing judges is that they lose their independence and become beholden to interest groups, in the same way that politicians are. In California in the mid-1980s, the state supreme court's chief justice was voted out of office after her court ruled in almost every death penalty case it confronted that the execution could not be carried out because there had been constitutional violations.[11] Similarly, in Texas in the early 1990s, a trial judge made a ruling that resulted in the release of a man who had murdered a police officer, and although the legal soundness of the judge's ruling was never really in question, the judge's decision so outraged the police and the district attorney's office—not to mention the voters—that a candidate was recruited to run against the judge and the judge was overwhelmingly defeated in the subsequent election.[12]

Support for the death penalty ebbs and flows. For an entire generation, however, support for capital punishment has not fallen below 60 percent and has occasionally approached 90 percent.[13] When so much of the population supports the death penalty, judges will care more about making sure death penalties are implemented than about safeguarding a criminal's constitutional rights. Moreover, even in a system where judges are appointed, the person who appoints them must be wary: A governor or a president who appoints judges or justices who are viewed as soft on criminals will almost certainly not be in a position to appoint many more.

All nine judges on the CCA who heard Fierro's appeal agreed that the police had lied and that the consequence of the lie was that Fierro's confession had been coerced. Had Fierro's appeal reached the CCA prior to the Supreme Court's decision in the *Fulminante* case, then the mere fact that his confession was manifestly coerced would have resulted in a new trial. Yet *Fulminante* was already the law of the land, meaning that Fierro had to prove that the coerced confession had not been harmless, that it had been essential to the state's ability to procure a conviction. Five of the state court judges concluded that he did not meet his burden, that Olague's testimony was enough. Of the four judges who concluded that Fierro was entitled to a new trial, three had already determined that they would not run for reelection when their current terms expired. All five judges who voted against Fierro ran for reelection in the election cycle following their decision in his case, and all were handily reelected.

Part of the answer to the question of how the Fierro case could have happened, therefore, is that state court judges are elected, and elected officials—unless they are on their way out of office (as Governor Ryan was, for example)—can issue rulings that are favorable to condemned killers only at the risk of their political futures. But there is a second part of the answer to the question, and it has to do with the demise of the federal courts as the protectors of federal constitutional values.

As I have mentioned, prior to the enactment of AEDPA, federal courts concluded in nearly half of all death penalty cases that the defendant was entitled to a new trial or to be removed from death row. Nearly half of all capital murder trials involved constitutional violations that were deemed not to be harmless. Death row inmates typically prevailed in federal court, rather than state court, for the mirror-image reason that state court judges are loath to rule in favor of death row inmates. Unlike their state-court counterparts, federal judges are appointed for life. They cannot be removed from office by an electorate angry because they are issuing rulings that benefit convicted murderers. Unlike state-court judges, who must run for election or retention, federal judges do not feel political pressure. They are free to be faithful to the rule of law, and for a generation, they were.

But two events happened. The federal courts, including the Supreme Court, grew exasperated by death penalty appeals. (Examples of this exasperation are discussed in chapter 7.) The Supreme Court gradually but steadily shrank the category of claims that death row inmates could raise in federal court, and first the Supreme Court and then Congress implemented procedural rules that made it extremely difficult for death row inmates to obtain judicial relief even when they could identify a constitutional violation. Since the enactment of AEDPA, there has been no systematic analysis of how many death row inmates prevail in the federal appeals and either win a new trial or are released from death row. The anecdotal evidence, however, suggests that the number is no more than 1 in 10, and perhaps as low as 5 or 6 in 100. There are two explanations for this plummeting success rate, and neither has anything to do with the magical transformation of death penalty trials. They are still characterized by the same sorts of constitutional problems—including coerced confessions—that were common before 1995. What has changed is the enactment of AEDPA and the characterization of nearly all constitutional errors as subject to harm analysis. It is no longer enough to prove a constitutional violation. It is no longer enough to prove that the state court got the wrong answer or that the death row inmate was harmed by the constitutional violation. To obtain relief, the death row inmate must show that there was a mistake, that the mistake was harmful, and that the state court's conclusion to the contrary was not only wrong but objectively unreasonable. Few death row inmates prevail in their appeals, not because their trials were fair or free from constitutional infirmity, but because proving that an error was harmful is difficult or impossible.

Criminal trials are not laboratory experiments where it can

easily be shown that altering a single fact will change the outcome. Consequently, requiring death row inmates to show that the error they are complaining about *caused* the conviction imposes a legal standard that is higher than any other standard—and is perhaps impossibly high. Thus, in one extraordinary case in 1996, the Supreme Court held that the state can lie to the defendant about the nature of the evidence it intends to introduce at the punishment phase of the defendant's trial as long as the defendant cannot prove he did not commit the crime (the case was *Gray v. Netherland*).[14] And in a perhaps even more extraordinary case, in 1993 the Supreme Court held that the question of whether a death row inmate is innocent is simply not of constitutional magnitude *(Herrera v. Collins).*[15] Put differently, and without exaggeration, even if a death row inmate can conclusively and unmistakably prove that he did not commit the crime for which he was convicted and sentenced to death, this, standing alone, will not matter. Being innocent, in short, is not enough to get a convicted murderer off death row.

Before Fierro's lawyers located the evidence that proved that Detective Medrano had been lying, Fierro had already filed a habeas petition. By the time he was able to file a new petition, AEDPA had been enacted. The Supreme Court then ruled that AEDPA applies to petitions that are filed after the statute became effective, even if the death row inmate's conviction occurred prior to the statute's enactment.[16] Fierro therefore had to pass through the gateway in section 2244, which identifies the narrow category of claims that can be raised in a second habeas petition, and he also had to comply with AEDPA's statute of limitations provision. Shortly after the Texas Court of Criminal Appeals, by a vote of five to four, ruled that Fierro had not proved that the coerced confession had caused him any harm, the state of Texas set an execution date. Prior to the enactment of AEDPA, lawyers for a death row inmate who wanted to obtain a stay of execution would ask the federal district court to issue a stay. Following the enactment of AEDPA, however, the district courts are required to dismiss any action brought by a death row inmate who has already had a federal habeas petition. Consequently, Fierro's lawyers asked the United States Court of Appeals for the Fifth Circuit—the court that hears appeals from the federal courts in Texas, Louisiana, and Mississippi—to authorize him to file an additional habeas petition. Fierro's lawyers filed this so-called motion for authorization in the Court of Appeals on October 20, 1997. The motion laid out the argument that the El Paso police had coerced Fierro's confession by having him talk to the Juarez police, who threatened to harm Fierro's parents unless he confessed, and the motion concluded that without the coerced confession, Fierro would not have been convicted, and indeed would not even have been prosecuted. The Court of Appeals granted the motion on November 11, 1997.

When a court of appeals grants a motion for authorization under AEDPA, a death row inmate has received permission to file a new habeas petition raising the issues that were addressed in the motion for authorization. Fierro's motion, of course, dealt entirely with the legal issues associated with the coerced confession and the fact that the El Paso police had lied at the suppression hearing in 1989 when they denied any knowledge of coercion. Having obtained permission from the court of appeals to file a new habeas petition, the case returned to the federal district court in El Paso, where the petition would be filed and ruled upon. The federal district judge entered what is known as a scheduling order, which directs when various motions and responses and replies must be filed. Neither Fierro nor the state of Texas objected to the scheduling order put in place by the federal judge. Then, as required by that order, Fierro filed his habeas petition in federal court on February 27, 1998—some three months after the court of appeals had authorized his new petition.

The state of Texas then took the position that Fierro had

waited too long and that the federal district court therefore had to dismiss the petition without addressing its merits. The state argued that the one-year statute of limitations had started running on November 28, 1996, the date on which the state court (the CCA) had ruled against Fierro. Fierro made three arguments in response. First, the clock did not start running until some time later. Second, even if it had started running on November 28, his motion for authorization, which fully delineated the nature of his claims, had been filed in October 1997, well within the one-year statutory period. Finally, the state had waived the statute of limitations by agreeing to the scheduling order that the federal judge had entered; if the state was going to invoke a statute of limitations, it should have done so as soon as the trial judge directed that Fierro's petition be filed in February.

Fierro lost. The federal district court—the same court that had entered a scheduling order telling Fierro when to file the habeas petition—ruled that the statute of limitations began to run on November 28, 1996, that the filing of a motion for authorization did not count for purposes of satisfying the statute, and that Fierro had therefore waited three months too long. The court did not address the merits of the petition. Instead, it simply dismissed the petition as untimely. The Court of Appeals agreed. It ruled that Fierro had waited too long, and that none of the reasons he proffered for having waited warranted extending the one-year statute. The same Court of Appeals that had authorized Fierro to file an additional habeas petition in view of his powerful evidence of innocence and the uncontested fact of a coerced confession ultimately disposed of the case on procedural grounds. The Supreme Court then declined to review the case.

Fierro may never be executed. The International Court of Justice (ICJ) in The Hague has heard an appeal from Mexico involving scores of Mexican nationals on death row in the United States. In violation of a treaty to which the United States is a signatory, many of these Mexican citizens, including Fierro, were not permitted to speak to consular officials immediately after their arrest. The ICJ ruled that many of these Mexican citizens, including Cesar Fierro, are entitled to new trials. There is a great deal of uncertainty as to how this judgment will be implemented in the United States, but it is quite possible that if Fierro avoids lethal injection, it will be because an international tribunal has intervened, and not because an American court has enforced federal law.

I began representing Fierro in 1989. Soon after the federal court appointed me to his case, the judge presiding over the first habeas appeal convened a hearing in El Paso. At that hearing, I met Fierro's family: his daughter and former wife, his mother and his niece. Several of them spoke very little English and had no idea what the lawyers and the judge were talking about during the hearing. After the hearing I explained to them how I thought the case would proceed. I told them that I thought it would be over in two or three years. I did not tell them that I thought Fierro would be my first client to get off death row, and indeed to walk out of prison altogether, because I did not want to inflate their hopes. But I did think that would happen, and that is what I told the other lawyers working with me on the case. I was obviously wrong.

Years later, Fierro was still in prison, and he began to develop illusions. He started returning my letters unopened, and when I would go to the prison to see him, he would refuse to see me. Soon he stopped communicating with any of his other lawyers as well. He accused us of working with the state to try to have him executed. He was going insane.

By 2004, it was imperative that one of his lawyers tell him what had happened in the ICJ litigation. In addition, I had heard rumors from several inmates about Fierro's condition. They told me that he would spread feces on himself and the walls of his cell, that he would refuse to shower for six months or longer, that his hair had grown long and wild, that he mumbled to himself while pacing in his cell at all hours of the night, that he would scream gibberish and beat his head against the walls, and that the guards would have to gas him and forcibly extract him from his cell whenever they wanted to search it. The reports I received made it clear, in short, that Fierro was mad. The Constitution prevents the states from executing the insane,[17] and I had to see Fierro to see if he was in fact insane.

I went to the prison with a lawyer, who is also a social worker from Mexico and speaks perfect Spanish (my own is far from perfect). I had been in contact with lawyers for the prison, because if Fierro was not going to come out to see me, I was going to have to go to his cell to see him. The prison lawyers assured me that he would come out, and I suspect that he did so because they did not tell him the truth about who wanted to talk to him.

Fierro entered the visiting cage and squinted at me without blinking for close to a minute. In Spanish he asked who I was, and I told him my name. He repeated the question. I told him that I was his lawyer. He screamed that he did not have a lawyer and repeated the question again. I told him that I was a professor. He repeated the question, and I did not know what to say. We were talking in Spanish, and I thought that perhaps I had missed some nuance in his question. I looked at the lawyer I was with. She shrugged. The problem was not linguistic, then. Fierro looked at her as well and asked her the same question. None of her answers satisfied him. He was becoming visibly upset. He started to scream and then banged the phone against the Plexiglas separating him from us. Suddenly he became quiet and started to grin. He said he was on a hunger strike and he patted his stomach. When I had last seen him ten years earlier, he had been fleshy and soft and weighed close to 200 pounds. Now he weighed perhaps 120. He repeated that he was on a hunger strike and then asked us to get him food. The lawyer who was with me went to the vending machines to buy him a soda and sunflower seeds. While she was gone, he asked me again, in Spanish, who I was. I told him I wanted to tell him about what was happening to his case. He repeated the question. I said nothing. Fierro shifted to English and asked me who sent me. I told him in English what I had already told him in Spanish. He again grew agitated, screaming that he had no lawyer, that he needed no lawyer. He asked me if I knew his wife. When I said yes, he asked me how much she weighed. I thought I had perhaps misunderstood him—Fierro had not seen his former wife for twenty years and probably had no idea how much she weighed—and during the pause Fierro assumed that I did not understand his question. He asked derisively whether I wanted to switch to French. I do not speak French. Neither does he. The guard tried to pass the food we had bought for him through the slot in the door, but when Fierro started to snatch it violently, the guard recoiled, dropped the food, and slammed shut the slot. Fierro banged on the door, dropped the phone, and turned sideways in the cage. He was finished talking to us. He found a piece of paper, about the size of a pea, and started to bounce it off the wall, over and over again, refusing to look at us anymore. He would occasionally bang on the door or scream something I could not make out. I told the guard that we were through with him, but I sat in front of him until they took him back to his cell. When the guards came to get him, they were laughing.

I used to think Fierro would walk out of prison because I thought it was quite likely that he is innocent. Now I hope he is not. I hope I was wrong and that he committed the murder, because the alternative is that he has spent the last twenty-five years of his life going insane in a sixty-square-foot cell for a crime he had nothing to do with. His mother has died. His daughter no longer visits. He thinks his lawyers are trying to injure him. He is incapable of having friends and carrying on a conversation. The guards taunt him and laugh at him. Yet if Fierro dies in prison, it will not be because Texas proved that he killed Nicolas Catanon. It will be because Fierro did not convince the state court that he did not, and because no federal court will even let him try. If Fierro is executed, it will be because a technicality allowed the authorities to coerce a confession from him and then get away with it.

CHAPTER THREE

JOHNNY JOE MARTINEZ'S FATAL FIVE MINUTES

*The line separating good and evil passes not through states
nor between political parties either, but straight through
the human heart.*

ALEXANDER SOLZHENITSYN

At 3:25 a.m. on July 15, 1993, nineteen-year-old Johnny Joe Martinez killed Clay Peterson, a clerk at a convenience store in Corpus Christi, Texas. After committing the crime, Martinez walked to a nearby beach, fell to his knees, and began crying. He then walked to a seaside motel, called 911 from a phone in the lobby, and told the operator that he had stabbed the clerk at a 7-Eleven. He sat outside and waited for the police to arrive.

Officers responded quickly. Upon their arrival, Martinez surrendered immediately and offered no resistance. Without success, he tried to help the police find the knife he had used to commit the crime. On the drive to the police station, he inquired about the condition of the man he had stabbed. As it happened, Peterson had just died.

Once at the police station, Martinez asked to talk to the police immediately. He did not want a lawyer. For just over an hour and a half, beginning at 5 a.m., he worked on a statement and confessed to killing Clay Peterson. The officer who interviewed Martinez described his behavior as "upset and remorseful." Martinez, who had been drinking for more than seven hours at the time of the crime, was also described as inebriated, but he never used his drunkenness as an excuse for what he had done.

When he was killed by Martinez, Clay Peterson was twenty years old. He was working as a clerk at the convenience store while studying. He hoped to enter the ministry. Peterson was stabbed eight times. When Martinez fled, Peterson was still alive. He called 911 from the telephone in the store and gave a brief description of the attacker. Before an ambulance could arrive, Peterson had died from massive blood loss caused by one of the stab wounds.

There were no warning signs that Martinez would commit this murder. He had never been convicted of or even arrested for any crime. He had never acted violently, not even when, as a young man, he was taunted for his effeminate characteristics. But on one night, drunk and in the company of another man to whom he was sexually drawn, he took a life. I repeatedly asked Martinez to explain that night to me, and he tried, but in truth he did not understand himself what he had done. He could describe what happened, but he could not explain why.

Murders range from despicable and wrong to unspeakably detestable and vile. There are no common murders. There are no ordinary homicides. Every murderer has wrongfully taken a human life. And yet the Supreme Court has ruled that a state cannot impose the death penalty on someone merely because that person commits homicide.[1] The death penalty must be reserved for a narrower category of killings. The Eighth Amendment requires that the sentencing jury, in arriving at the appropriate sentence, make an "individualized determination on the basis of the character of the individual and the circumstances of the crime."[2] For this very reason, when the Supreme Court reinstated the death penalty in 1976 by upholding the newly written death penalty statutes in Texas, Georgia, and Florida, it struck down laws from North Carolina and Louisiana because those two states had wanted automatically to sentence to death anyone convicted of murder. As the Court put it in the Louisiana case, providing for the mandatory execution of someone who commits murder violates the Constitution because it does not permit the jury a "meaningful opportunity" to consider the "circumstances of the particular crime" and the specific "attributes of the individual offender."[3] The Supreme Court ruled in 1976 that states can have the death penalty, but they must allow the jury to consider every aspect of the crime and every dimension of the criminal's character in deciding whether that murderer should be put to death. This became known as the principle of "individualized consideration."

And so, although it is true that there are no minor murders, it also remains true that the death penalty is not designed for men like Martinez. Yes, he committed an abominable act, but the state of Texas was not free to execute him merely by proving what he did not contest: that he wrongfully murdered Clay Peterson. The state had to prove more: that the crime was unusually horrific or that the murderer would probably kill again. But in Martinez's cases, the state could not prove either. The state did show a videotape to the jury, and that tape vividly captured Martinez repeatedly stabbing Peterson, but even in those horrific images Martinez seems more scared than insane. And we know that as soon as he left the camera's view, he walked outside, started to cry, and dialed 911. In death penalty cases, the state wins when it succeeds in making the murderer seem more like a savage animal than a sentient human being, but Martinez's biography suggested that the state would not easily be able to hide his humanity. So how exactly did he end up on death row?

The simple answer is that his lawyers made two costly mistakes. The first one could have been fixed, but the second one was catastrophic.

To satisfy the "individualized consideration" principle, every state with the death penalty has implemented a bifurcated process in capital cases. A death penalty trial is actually two different trials. At the first, the state must establish that the defendant has committed the act for which he is being charged. If the jury finds the defendant guilty, then, at the second stage, the state puts on evidence that the defendant should be executed. The very purpose of the second trial is to permit the jury—to compel the jury —to examine the defendant's individual characteristics. Is the defendant unusually young? retarded? truly remorseful? Has he committed other acts of violence? What good deeds has the defendant performed? Could he be expected to live a violence-free life in prison? Might he warn other inmates in prison away from a life of crime?

The defense lawyer's task at the punishment phase is to persuade the jury that the defendant is worth saving, that he has redeeming qualities. The point of individualized consideration is not that murders can be overlooked or excused, but that some murders warrant a life sentence rather than the death penalty. The defense lawyer's job is to persuade the jury to spare the client's life. It is as simple as that and just as daunting: Few tasks in trial law are more challenging than the punishment phase of a death penalty case. The lawyer must persuade a jury to spare the life of someone whom the jury has already convicted of a gruesome crime. At the typical death penalty trial, the defendant does not testify. So the jury does not even hear the voice of the man whose fate they hold in their collective hands. Yet the jury certainly has heard about the victim, a human being, who was robbed of life. It has probably seen grisly photographs of the crime scene. It has heard about the violent act of murder itself over a period of several days, if not weeks.

Then the punishment phase begins. This is when the state paints a picture of the defendant as a savage animal. The state tells the jury about other crimes he has committed, often calling as witnesses the victims of those other crimes. The state even tells the jury about other crimes that the defendant is suspected of committing, even if the defendant has not been charged with or convicted of those other crimes. (These crimes are known as un-adjudicated offenses—the word *unadjudicated* signaling that the defendant has not been convicted of committing them. But the courts have upheld the state's reliance on these other crimes at death penalty sentencing trials.)[4] Before the defense lawyer ever puts on a witness, the jury can find many reasons to fear and loathe the defendant. To apprehend the enormity of the defense lawyer's burden, imagine having to persuade the jury that con-victed Timothy McVeigh in the Oklahoma City bombing case to spare his life. That is what the trial lawyer representing a capital defendant has to do.

Martinez's trial differed from the norm in several notable re-spects. Most significantly, the state did not introduce any punish-ment-phase evidence at all, for there was nothing to introduce. Martinez did not have a checkered past. He was not a career crim-inal. There were no victims of other crimes. There were no other crimes at all. Martinez was not a defendant whom the jurors could easily regard as a savage animal rather than a human being. He was a soft-spoken, effeminate, boyish-looking young man. Yet he did commit murder, and the state did request the death penalty. That meant Martinez's lawyer had to do something.

Martinez's lawyer did not. He barely put on a case at all. He did slightly more than nothing, but not nearly enough. At the punishment phase of the trial, the most critical stage of most death penalty trials and certainly the most important stage of Martinez's trial, Martinez's lawyer simply went through the motions. He made no investigation to speak of and called only five witnesses. His defense case takes up fewer than forty pages of a trial record that is more than a thousand pages long. There were half a dozen potential defense witnesses whom the defense lawyer did not even know about, not because they were hiding, but because he did not bother to look for them. There were people who could have told the jury why Martinez's life should be spared, but the jury did not hear from them because Martinez's lawyer did not find them. The only witnesses he called were witnesses who had found him. This, in short, is not how defense lawyers are supposed to operate.

In Texas, when a jury sentences a defendant to death, the case goes immediately to Texas's highest criminal court (the supreme court for criminal cases, as it were), which is called the Texas Court of Criminal Appeals (CCA). This first appeal is known as the direct appeal. Defendants have a constitutional right to a lawyer for the direct appeal, just as they have a constitutional right to be represented by counsel at trial. Historically, the CCA upholds death sentences more often than any other state's highest court (with the Virginia Supreme Court coming in a close second). The CCA upholds death penalty cases about 98 percent of the time, usually by a vote of 9 to 0. If a defendant gets 2 or 3 votes from the CCA, the case is unusual.

On his direct appeal, Martinez received 4 votes. The CCA upheld his conviction and death sentence by the narrowest possible margin, 5 to 4. The four judges who voted to set his death sentence aside reached their conclusion by focusing on the evidence before the jury during the sentencing phase of the trial. In most death penalty states, the jury gives individualized consideration to the defendant by considering a list of criteria that the state has deemed relevant, such as whether the murder was especially heinous, the number of victims, their ages, and the like. In Texas, the jury typically answers two questions. The first is whether the defendant may be dangerous in the future. If the answer is in the affirmative, then it decides whether the defendant has introduced sufficient mitigating evidence to warrant a life sentence, rather than a death sentence. If it answers the mitigation question with a "no" after answering the future dangerousness question with a "yes," the defendant automatically receives the death penalty.

The four judges on the CCA who believed that Martinez should not be executed concluded that there simply was no evidence of future danger, that the jury made a mistake when it answered that question in the affirmative. The state, after all, had not even put on any evidence at the punishment phase. When the Supreme Court struck down the death penalty in 1972, Justice Stewart wrote that the death penalty was arbitrary in the same way that being struck by lightning is arbitrary: There is no rhyme or reason as to why juries sentence some defendants to life and others to death. Some defendants who commit especially horrific murders get leniency; others who commit more ordinary murders receive death. To address Justice Stewart's concerns, state courts, when reviewing death sentences during the direct appeal stage, conduct what is known as a proportionality analysis: They compare the death sentence in the case before them to other cases from the state to ensure that defendants who have committed similarly heinous crimes are punished in equivalent fashion.

In performing this analysis in Martinez's case, the dissenting CCA judges emphasized that Martinez did not have a violent past, that he had turned himself in, and that he had been remorseful from the moment he had committed the crime. The dissenting judges pointed to previous cases in which the court had found insufficient evidence to support the death penalty, cases substantially more aggravated than Martinez's. For instance, the CCA had previously set aside a finding of future dangerousness in a case where the defendant had sexually assaulted and stabbed a bound victim fourteen times, once through the heart; the CCA had also set aside the death sentence in a case where a defendant who shot a convenience store clerk had a reputation for not being a peaceful and law-abiding citizen, had previous convictions, and was on probation at the time of the offense; in yet another case, the CCA set aside a finding of future dangerousness where the defendant strangled the victim to death after robbing her. In all of these cases, the defendants had been neither remorseful nor cooperative, yet the CCA had spared their lives. To the dissenting judges, this pattern made no sense. Martinez's death penalty was like being struck by lightning.

The direct appeal in Martinez's case made it clear that the evidence to justify the death sentence against Martinez was minuscule. Of course, Martinez had committed a serious crime, and he certainly deserved punishment for it. But the evidence in Martinez's case was so thin that his death sentence survived by *only one vote*. Even the smallest change in the evidence presented to the jury might have persuaded the jurors to sentence Martinez to life in prison instead of death. And, in fact, such evidence existed. Evidence that might have persuaded at least a single juror to spare Martinez's life was there at the time of the trial, but the jury never heard or saw it. That was the fault of Martinez's trial lawyer. No federal court considered the evidence, either—the result of the development of a legal system that has come to favor speed and finality over fairness and principle.

Martinez's first attorney, his trial lawyer, made the mistake of not telling the jury the story of Martinez's life, which would probably have led the jury to spare him. That mistake could have been corrected, and it almost was, had the CCA granted relief. But Martinez's later lawyer, the lawyer who handled his state habeas corpus appeal, made a second mistake, and his mistake was unfixable. His mistake led directly to Martinez's execution.

*   *   *

A death penalty case has, as I have indicated, several distinct stages: the trial, the direct appeal, the state habeas corpus proceeding, and the federal habeas corpus proceeding. To understand how the death penalty system works in America, it is important to remember three facts about these various stages of a case. First, for all intents and purposes, the only opportunity that a death row inmate will have for a federal judge to consider whether his trial was fair will be during the federal habeas review. Second, between 1976 and 1995, nearly half of all death row inmates prevailed during their federal habeas appeals, thereby receiving new trials or moving off death row (and into the general prison population). Third, the Antiterrorism and Effective Death Penalty Act of 1996, or AEDPA for short, significantly limited the ability of federal courts to grant relief to death row inmates. Indeed, in the years leading up to AEDPA, the Supreme Court had created numerous limitations on federal habeas corpus review. For example, the Court had ruled that a death row inmate could not assert in federal habeas corpus proceedings that the police had seized evidence illegally. Further, the Court enacted various procedural restrictions as well. The most significant of these is the so-called independent and adequate state ground doctrine. Under this doctrine, a federal court generally cannot address an issue that the inmate did not properly present to the state courts and was therefore waived under state law. For example, suppose that a death row inmate argues that his trial lawyer was ineffective. If state law requires that the inmate raising this claim file his appeal of an adverse decision within thirty days, and if the inmate files it on the thirty-first day—one day late—and if the state court therefore dismisses the appeal (without addressing the question of whether the trial lawyer was in fact ineffective), then a federal court will lack the power to address the merits of the issue. The failure to adhere strictly to state procedural rules, in other words, can (and often does) preclude a federal court's review of the legality of the death sentence. As a practical matter, these doctrines mean that the third stage of a death penalty case—the state habeas stage—is critically important, not because very many inmates win during state habeas, but because a misstep during that stage will prevent the inmate from winning later.

The purpose of state habeas corpus appeals is to permit a new lawyer, not associated with the previous proceedings, thoroughly to examine the trial for fairness. Thus, once Martinez lost his direct appeal, and the case entered state habeas proceedings, the job of his state habeas lawyer was to start at the beginning. Unlike direct-appeal proceedings, state habeas proceedings permit attorneys to look outside the formal record of the case in order to test the fairness of the proceedings against the defendant. The basic idea is for the habeas lawyer to see what the trial lawyer could have done differently. Habeas lawyers ask questions such as: What evidence is there that the trial lawyer did not find? Why didn't the trial lawyer locate it? How might the evidence have made a difference? Answering these questions requires that the habeas lawyer engage in substantial investigation. The lawyer must do more than simply read the trial transcript (this is the job of the direct appeal lawyer). The habeas lawyer must reinterview witnesses, determine whether there are other potential witnesses who were not interviewed, and if there are, then find and talk to them. Often, the state habeas lawyer will need to consult with experts, including ballistics and DNA specialists. Finally, and perhaps most important of all, the habeas lawyer must not only have the skills and inclination to conduct a thorough factual investigation, but also keep abreast of a rapidly changing and exceedingly arcane branch of law.

Despite the fact that, as a historical matter, death row inmates routinely prevailed in their federal habeas corpus appeals, and despite the great complexity of the area, the Supreme Court has ruled that death row inmates do not have a constitutional right to counsel during habeas corpus proceedings. As a result, a death row inmate cannot complain if his lawyer's performance is abysmal. If there is no right to counsel at all, then even a terrible lawyer is more than the inmate can demand.[5]

Yet although the Supreme Court has declined to hold that the Constitution demands that death row inmates receive habeas lawyers, the legislatures have reacted differently. Congress has provided a statute whereby a death row inmate is entitled to counsel during federal habeas proceedings. Furthermore, recognizing that the state habeas stage of the case is crucial as well as complex, most states provide statutes whereby death row inmates have a lawyer to represent them during state habeas proceedings.[6] The Texas statute, for example, which governed Martinez's appeal, provided that Martinez would receive "competent counsel."[7] The statute also placed a burden on the lawyer, by requiring that the state habeas lawyer "investigate expeditiously . . . the factual and legal grounds for the filing of an application for a writ of habeas corpus."[8] And of course, the lawyer, as is true of all lawyers in all types of legal proceedings, was under an obligation to confer with his client and keep his client apprised of ongoing proceedings.

As it turned out, the state's promise to Martinez that he would receive a competent habeas lawyer was empty, and the empty promise had dire consequences.

As provided by state law, a court appointed a lawyer to represent Martinez in state habeas proceedings. In time, that lawyer filed a document that he entitled "Writ of Habeas Corpus." But just because you call a pig an eagle doesn't mean the pig can fly. This so-called writ bore no resemblance to what even the most modestly qualified lawyer would have filed. Moreover, Martinez's lawyer filed this application without ever visiting his client on death row, talking to him on the phone, or writing him a letter except to inform Martinez that he had been appointed to the case. Once Martinez learned of the appointment, he tried to call the lawyer, but death row inmates must place their long-distance calls collect, and Martinez's lawyer refused to accept any of the telephone calls. The lawyer did not conduct any investigation at all, much less an exhaustive one, and he did not hire any expert witnesses or investigators, even though the law provided money for him to do so.

The appeal that the lawyer filed presented four claims. The first two claims simply repeated arguments that had already been rejected on direct appeal. The state habeas attorney acknowledged that one of these claims had already been rejected by both the United States Supreme Court and the CCA, but invited the habeas trial court to "revisit this proposition for the plain and clear reason that it is wrong." That argument doesn't usually persuade an appellate court, especially when the appellate court is the same one that issued the opinion now being characterized as "plainly and clearly" wrong. State habeas petitions filed by competent lawyers routinely reach one hundred pages. Many are two or three times that length. The entire state habeas petition filed by Martinez's lawyer was less than six pages long. The lawyer sent his client a copy of this application months later, *after it had already been denied by the trial court.*

Any experienced trial lawyer could look at the document Martinez's lawyer filed and immediately see that the lawyer had no idea what he was doing. Yet in a boilerplate order, the CCA denied relief. One judge, however, refused to go along. He wrote a stinging dissent, pointing out that the

> Applicant is represented by counsel appointed by this Court. The instant application is five and one half pages long and raises four challenges to the conviction. The trial record is never quoted. Only three cases are cited in the entire application, and no cases are cited for the remaining two claims for relief. Those claims comprise only 17 lines with three inches of margin.

Count 17 lines on this page. That is how much effort the lawyer who was appointed to try to save Martinez's life made. The dissenting judge noted that Martinez's lawyer had not sought reimbursement for travel or investigatory expenses; nor had he requested any expert assistance in preparing the application. Indeed, the habeas lawyer's records indicated that the lawyer had spent less than fifty hours on the case. The judge recommended that "the merits of the application should not be reached. Instead, this matter should be remanded to the habeas court to determine whether applicant has received effective assistance of counsel."

Following the decision of the CCA, the lawyer that the court had appointed to represent Martinez filed a document he called "Motion for Reconsideration." As it happens, Texas law prohibits motions for reconsideration in habeas corpus proceedings—yet a final aspect of state habeas corpus law of which Martinez's lawyer was unaware. The substance of the motion reads in full as follows:

[Martinez's attorney has] handled many direct appeals *but has never handled a post-conviction writ of a death penalty case and therefore must humbly agree with the dissenting opinion in this case (without joining in its reasoning) that merits of this application should not be reached.* Also Petitioners [*sic*] attorney requests that he be allowed to withdraw from the case and another lawyer be appointed to represent Petitioner in this cause.

The lawyer did have the courtesy to send a copy of this motion to Martinez. Martinez was shocked by its contents. He had not even known that the CCA had denied his petition in the first place. In fact, Martinez had not known that the petition had ever been filed. Martinez suddenly realized that his entire state habeas proceedings had gone by without his ever once talking to his lawyer or seeing the documents that were filed on his behalf.

Martinez knew that his lawyer's performance could create serious problems for him. Like many death row inmates (and prison inmates generally), he had learned a bit about habeas corpus law. He understood it well enough to grasp the interplay between the doctrine of procedural default and the requirement of exhaustion. Under the exhaustion requirement, a federal court is generally not permitted to address any issue that has not been first presented to the state courts. Under the doctrine of procedural default, a federal court generally lacks the power to address any issue that was not properly preserved in state court. The fact that Martinez's lawyer had not presented a number of viable legal issues to the state courts meant that the federal court would lack the power to address these very issues. Martinez had lost his direct appeal by a vote of five to four in the CCA—the same court that had addressed his habeas petition. He therefore knew that his only chance to get off death row would be to prevail in federal court. Yet he could not prevail in federal court unless he at least gave the state court an opportunity to address his claims. So he wrote the CCA a series of letters, begging that court to help him find a fair solution.

Martinez's first letter to the judges on the CCA was dated May 8, 1998 (the letters are reprinted without any corrections). He wrote:

> I'm writing you this letter concerning my State Habeas Corpus proceedings. My lawyer . . . filed my State Habeas Corpus Writ . . . knowing that he had no clue of how to prepare a proper one. . . . He admits to the courts he has handled many Direct Appeals but never has handled a State Habeas Corpus Writ of a death penalty case.

> I have tried many times to contact [state habeas counsel] with no responds. The only time he contacted me was when he told me he was appointed to my case. He wouldn't except my phone calls or answer my letters.

> I'm asking to have my State Habeas Corpus proceeding reconsidered. I need to refile it because my lawyer was incom-

petent to do so. I'm asking to have a competent lawyer appointed to me to refile a legitimate application for me and a few months to do it in....

The brief was not even in a brief format, it morally looked like this inexperience lawyer just wrote down sentences of his thought and didn't raise any issues from the record or elsewhere that I sent him and told him I wanted raised and preserved....

I need a competent lawyer and a few months to give this new lawyer a chance to refile my State Habeas Corpus Writ. Can I please have this letter granted and a few months with a new lawyer that can refile my State Habeas Corpus Writ for me?

In the Motion to Reconsider that [the lawyer] filed to the Criminal Courts of Appeal on May 5, 1998, he practically admits that he didn't know what he was doing in handling a State Habeas Corpus Writ. He is also requesting to be allowed to withdraw from my case without even consulting me at all. [He] does not know what he is doing. There fore I pray that you will appoint me a competent attorney. An attorney that knows how a State Habeas Corpus Writ proceedings process works and a few months to give him to file my State Habeas Corpus Writ.

To this letter, which was addressed to the state court judges, Martinez attached a representative letter he had written to his lawyer. That letter, dated February 28, 1998, began:

I wrote you a letter on the 9th of this month and I still have not heard from you. Sir I need to hear from you since you have not come up here and spoken to me. Sir I have written you numerous times and I have not heard from you. Sir this is my life we are dealing with here....

I want you to get in touch with my family so they can help you look into some very important things that will benefit and help me in my case. Have you hired the investigator I told you too so he can talk to numerous helpful witnesses. Theirs one particular witness I want you to talk to and his name is Santos Leal. . . . I know if you file a motion for investigator funds to the C.C.A. they will grant it and supply $2,500 for us to hire one. These things I'm telling you are very important issues I want you to raise. Their are numerous witnesses that I believe will help me on my State Habeas Corpus Writ we just need to get a hold of them. . . . Sir I beg you to answer this letter. It's urgent that I hear or see you so I can speak with you on these very important issues. Thank you for your time and concern in this matter. Please, keep in touch. Take care and God bless.

Martinez's efforts to get his lawyer to do something were far from desultory; they were constant. Thus, in the February 28 letter Martinez sent to his lawyer, a copy of which he sent to the CCA, Martinez referred to a letter he had previously sent on February 9, 1998. That letter reads as follows:

I am writing to you concerning my Writ of Habeas Corpus Proceedings. . . . I would like to know the status of my appeal. When I referred back to the last letter I received from you which is dated June 9, 1997, you mentioned that you would advise me of any further developments in my appeal, so I am wondering if there has been any new developments on my appeal or has anything helpful surfaced. You also mentioned in your letter that you would try to come up here sometime soon and talk with me about my appeal, I am wondering how soon that this could be possible for I would like to speak with you about a few things. I am wondering about the due date on my appeal, when is the due date, for have we had an opportunity to hire an investigator to search issues or run down leads to save my life?[9]

Sir these are just a few things that have been on my mind lately. I am in the dark here and I really need to know what is going on? I have not heard from you in a long time and this makes me wonder if this is a bad sign, is there something wrong? Please get back with me as soon as possible and let me know what is going on with my Habeas Corpus appeal, please keep me informed of any and all things dealing with my appeal proceedings, O.K.

Sir what is going on. I mean what have you done on my habeas proceedings thus far? Please get back with me and let me know!

Sir please don't get me wrong, I am not trying to sound pushy or anything like that, it's just that I'm in the dark here and my life is on your hand, I am putting all my faith and hope in you, so please keep me informed and lets stay in touch O.K.!?...

Sir I do not want to die and you are the only one that can help me and prevent this, please do your best, please keep in contact with me and my family so that we can help you with any and all things you do or may need help with O.k!?

Sir I'm going to close this letter for now to get it to you as soon as possible please get back with me at your earliest convenience on everything in this letter here above. Thank you for your time and concern in this matter, please keep in touch, my life is in your hands and I'm putting all my trust in you. I'm closing for now. Take care o.k. and God Bless!

Martinez's lawyer never replied, not to the letter sent on February 9, or to the subsequent letter sent on February 28.

On May 11, 1998, three days after writing the CCA and asking them to remove his lawyer from the case, Martinez wrote to his lawyer once again:

Sir, I'm writing you this short letter to ask and tell you a few things. I received the Motion for Reconsideration you filed, but their was no enclose letter from you explaining what happen or is going to happen next. I understand that my State Habeas Corpus Writ has been affirmed.

I was reading the motion and I read a part where you stated in the motion where you humbly agreed with a "dissending opinion." What was the "dissending opinion" the judge(s) sent you on this case? I would please like for you to send me a copy of whatever that "dissending opinion" was or any responds the Criminal Courts of Appeals sent you about the State Habeas Corpus Writ you filed for I could read it and have a copy for my files.

Sir before the C.C.A. releases you, will you **PLEASE** file one more motion for me because I need to exhaust all my state remedies. I need you to please file a Stay of Execution pending filing of my Federal Writ 2254.

Sir, in the motion you filed you said that this was your first time you ever filed a State Habeas Corpus Writ, so understandably did not know exactly how to prepare the brief. Sir *there was many things not presented in the brief that I really wanted to be raise so it could also be preserved for my Federal Writ*. But sir don't get me wrong in what I'm about to ask you, I am trying to get the court to let me refile my State Habeas Corpus Writ to *raise some more issues*. [Asks state habeas counsel to execute affidavit acknowledging his lack of experience and ineffective preparation of the writ.] I really need your help in order for me to be able to *refile my Writ*. Will you please help me here

69

and send me a sign[ed] and notarize[d] affidavit stating such. It's the only way I can think of to *get another chance at my State Habeas Corpus Writ proceedings*. Will you write back soon and let me know your thoughts on this, Thank You!

Again Martinez's lawyer never replied. On May 20, 1998, CCA denied the motion for reconsideration without explanation. Martinez's state appeals were at an end.

Martinez wrote to his lawyers at least half a dozen unanswered letters, and these letters sound increasingly desperate because he *was* increasingly desperate. Martinez was trying repeatedly and frantically to get his court-appointed state habeas lawyer to investigate his case because he knew it was his only opportunity. Sensing that chance slipping away, he begged the CCA to appoint him a new lawyer who would properly investigate his case. Why was Martinez so concerned? For one simple reason: Not only will a federal court not consider any issue that is not raised first in state court, but the death row inmate will not be able to raise it in state court unless he raises it in his first state habeas petition. Martinez understood that. Martinez's future—his life—depended on that first state habeas petition, and Martinez sensed that the lawyer appointed to represent him lacked either the desire or the ability, or both, to do his job.

The exhaustion requirement—the doctrine that Martinez had good reason to fear—is not entirely lacking in rationale. The federal court system requires state prison inmates to present all of their federal constitutional claims and evidence to the state courts before presenting them to the federal court in order to reduce friction between the federal and state courts. It can cause tension when a federal court—sometimes one federal judge—reverses a conviction or sentence. States want to lock prisoners up and execute some convicted murderers, and federal courts interfere with that desire when they grant habeas corpus relief. To reduce friction, the federal courts require state inmates to present all their claims in state court. Thus, the state courts have a full and fair chance to correct any violations of the federal Constitution before the federal court intervenes in the case. The state courts will not be "surprised" by an inmate who wins a reversal of his conviction based on a new legal theory he has never presented to them. Finally, to force inmates to present their claims to the state courts, the federal court punishes them severely if they do not exhaust their claims. With few exceptions, if an inmate does not exhaust his claims, the federal court will find them "procedurally defaulted," which means that it will *refuse to decide them*. By not presenting viable legal claims on Martinez's behalf to the state courts, Martinez's lawyer ensured that the federal courts would not be able to consider those issues either.

Nor was it possible for Martinez to try to get a better lawyer and return to state court later. Like most states as well as the federal government, Texas wanted to get away from piecemeal litigation of death penalty cases. It did not want a death row inmate to raise a racist jury claim in one habeas petition and then raise an ineffective assistance of counsel claim in another. It wanted everything raised together, and at once. Thus, at the same time that the state enacted a law guaranteeing that death row inmates get a lawyer to represent them in their state habeas appeals, it also provided that, with very few exceptions, they would get one and only one trip through the state habeas system. One of the sponsors of the new Texas law, State Representative Pete Gallegos, explained the point of the new law:

> And we tell individuals that, everything that you can possibly raise the first time, we expect you to raise it initially, one bite of the apple, one shot.... [Answering questions] I think we'll have less filed, because what we're attempting to do here is to say, raise everything at one time. You get one bite of the apple. If you have to stick the kitchen sink in there, put it all in there.

And, we will go through those claims, one at a time, and make a decision, but none of this, one—one—every week you file a new petition which is currently basically what happens.[10]

Everything including the kitchen sink: that's what a state habeas petition should resemble. The seventeen lines of petition filed on behalf of Martinez could not be supplemented in a later petition because Texas law forbids death row inmates from filing a second state habeas application if the legal claims in the second application *could have been presented in the first application*.[11] Any claim that "could have been" presented in Martinez's first state habeas application, but was not, could not thereafter be considered by the Texas courts. And any claim that was not considered by the state courts could not thereafter be considered by the federal courts.

After his state habeas corpus petition was denied, Martinez entered federal court. The federal court allowed the lawyer who had been appointed by the state to withdraw from the case, and the federal judge appointed new lawyers to represent Martinez. Martinez's new legal counsel immediately recognized that the court-appointed state habeas lawyer had performed incompetently. The new lawyers determined that the state habeas lawyer had performed no investigation, and that they would therefore have to investigate and research the case anew. Because Martinez had always been indigent, his counsel asked the federal court for assistance to help him evaluate his case. The federal district judge held a hearing at Martinez's request. During that hearing, the procedural difficulties that Martinez would later confront became apparent. The state took the position that the judge should not allocate any resources for an investigation because the federal court would not address the merits of any of the issues Martinez sought to present, since they had not been presented in state court. Martinez's lawyers explained that Martinez had effectively not received representation in state court, and they described in some detail the mistakes the state habeas lawyer had made. The federal judge made no effort to hide his astonishment at the level of representation Martinez had received in state court. The judge then probed the state's position that Martinez's claims had all been waived:

[STATE ATTORNEY]: You're not going to have a review by the state courts because the claim's procedurally barred....

THE COURT: Why is the case procedurally barred?

[STATE ATTORNEY]: Because the claims were not presented in the first [state] habeas application.

THE COURT: Okay. Now, the reason it's not presented in the first habeas application is because Petitioner says, well, I had inadequate counsel...they gave me a lawyer, he wouldn't do what I said, he was not attentive to his work, nobody would have done it like this. And your answer is, well, he's not entitled to a good lawyer anyway.

[STATE ATTORNEY]: The precedent [to that effect] is long standing....

THE COURT: Well, I'm going to tell you something. I don't like what we're doing. I am going to—We are going to examine the effectiveness of state habeas counsel. We're going to make the record for the Circuit. And however I decide it there'll at least be a record and they can find out what occurred. Because I believe that until the Supreme Court decides you're not entitled to effective habeas counsel at the trial level [of a state postconviction proceeding] that that issue is still open.

[STATE ATTORNEY]: They've decided that, Your Honor....

THE COURT: Well, maybe they'll want to look at it again after the AEDPA has been passed. Maybe they'll try to say, well, maybe now that the burden's a little bit shifted and now that the state courts are more in the play, now that they control more of what happens, then they bear more of the responsibility to provide competent counsel.[12]

As the conversation between the federal judge and the assistant attorney general illuminates, the state of Texas took the position in federal court that it was not required to ensure that Martinez's lawyer performed competently, despite the fact that state law guaranteed him "competent" counsel. The state's position may suffer from moral vulnerability, but unfortunately for Martinez—and many others—it was, and still is, legally sound.

The Sixth Amendment guarantees indigent defendants the right to be represented by effective counsel. For purposes of the Sixth Amendment, a lawyer's effectiveness is measured by what that lawyer did (and did not do) and by the effects of those actions on the result of the trial.[13] When a death row inmate argues that his trial lawyer was ineffective, the reviewing court asks two questions to rule on the claim: Did the lawyer's performance fall below an objective standard of reasonableness, and did the performance cause prejudice to the defendant (in other words, would the result have been different but for the lawyer's deficient performance)?

Although criminal defendants rarely prevail when they bring claims based on ineffective performance, the resolution of these claims does focus precisely on what the trial lawyer did (and did not do).

Death row inmates hoped, and expected, that the Texas law guaranteeing "competent" counsel would be interpreted in accordance with the federal guarantee of "effective" counsel. In Martinez's case, if one were to ask whether Martinez had received competent legal assistance while his case was still in state habeas review, the answer would obviously have been that he did not. But the question that is germane for purposes of the U.S. Constitution was deemed to be irrelevant for purposes of state law. In the case of *Ex parte Graves*,[14] the Texas Court of Criminal Appeals interpreted the Texas statute that guarantees death row inmates the assistance of competent counsel during their state habeas proceedings. The CCA ruled that "competency" means that the lawyer who is appointed to represent the inmate must be qualified at the time of the appointment to handle the case; the CCA expressly held that competency is *not* measured by examining "the final product of representation."[15] According to the three dissenting judges, the standard of competency adopted by the CCA in the *Graves* case meant that any lawyer whose license had not been suspended and who was alive at the time of the appointment was competent within the meaning of the statute, and there is great force to the logic of the dissenting judges, but they were precisely that: dissenting judges. The majority of the court ruled that the Texas statute does *not* mean that the lawyer "must render constitutionally effective assistance."[16] The court's interpretation in the *Graves* case stripped the adjective "competent" of any meaning, and the result was that when Texas argued that Martinez was not entitled to a lawyer who actually performed competently, the state's argument was correct. The federal judge, despite his evident unhappiness with the state's position, realized that his hands were tied. The court refused to act on Martinez's repeated requests for investigative and expert assistance.

In the case of *Williams v. Taylor*, the Supreme Court ruled that a lawyer who represents a client facing the death penalty must always "conduct a thorough investigation of the defendant's background."[17] The reason is that the jury must make an individualized determination of whether the state should execute the defendant, and it cannot make that determination without learning the salient details of the defendant's life. Hence, even though the federal court would not give Martinez's habeas lawyers the resources to conduct an investigation, those lawyers elected to pursue the investigation themselves, at their own expense, to determine whether Martinez's trial lawyer had done his job. They learned that he had not.

To prepare for the punishment phase of Martinez's death penalty trial—probably the most critical stage, particularly since Martinez did not contest whether he was guilty—Martinez's trial lawyer met on a single occasion with a group of Martinez's family members including Martinez's mother, sister, and brother. He did not even bother to meet with them individually. The lawyer never asked any of them important questions concerning Martinez's background, such as whether Martinez had ever been exposed to any emotional or physical abuse or misconduct in the home. The lawyer asked a few questions about how Martinez had done in school, and then he left and never questioned Martinez's family members again. He did not even see them again until they showed up to testify at Martinez's trial.

In-depth interviews conducted by Martinez's federal habeas counsel revealed a much richer tapestry of Martinez's background—a tapestry that by no means excuses the murder that Martinez committed but would undoubtedly have helped to humanize him to the jury. Martinez's father abandoned the family when Martinez was very young. His mother worked in bars, drank heavily, and rarely saw Martinez, his older brother, David, or his younger sister. Martinez's stepfather routinely beat his mother in front of the children. On one occasion, the stepfather beat Martinez's mother so severely that she suffered a miscarriage. This stepfather was soon murdered outside a tavern.

Following his stepfather's murder, Martinez's mother started living with a heroin dealer. The dealer got Martinez's mother addicted, and she began to sell heroin herself. She traded food stamps for drugs, would steal her children's possessions, and sell them to support her habit. At that time, Martinez was ten years old. During this period, Martinez was sexually abused by a neighbor. This older man sodomized Martinez repeatedly. He first warned Martinez not to talk about it to anybody and later paid him to remain silent. Martinez remained deeply ashamed of this abuse, thinking he might somehow have led the older man on.

Martinez was an effeminate man. The boys in his neighborhood taunted him and called him a faggot. Yet Martinez never responded aggressively to insults or beatings, preferring just to walk away. Martinez finally left home when he was fourteen, living with friends when he could and on the street when he could not.

Martinez's federal habeas counsel learned these details of his life simply by performing a routine factual investigation, by doing the things that all habeas lawyers are supposed to do. The information came from Martinez himself, from his family members, and from people in the community who knew him. His mother, who had since given up drugs, admitted the details of her past and said she would have testified about these details at Martinez's trial if she had been asked.[18] Instead, the jury heard none of this evidence, from either Martinez or his family members. Would it have mattered? That is a hard question to answer with certainty. But we do know that juries tend not to sentence defendants to death if they view the defendants as human beings, or if they believe they understand how the defendant could have come to commit such a horrible crime. If the trial lawyer had gathered this available evidence and placed it before the jury, he would have been able to demonstrate mitigating factors that might have persuaded the jury to spare Martinez's life. In addition, he would have been able to emphasize the fact that Martinez had never engaged in any violence before the murder, even though he had been repeatedly and severely provoked. Martinez was not a Ted Bundy, a Charles Manson, or a Timothy McVeigh; he was not a defendant who would have been nearly impossible to humanize. On the contrary, he was remorseful from the moment of his crime and had suffered an abusive upbringing; a compassionate jury might well have voted to spare him. The trial lawyer's failure to locate this evidence did not result from the elusiveness of the evidence itself; it resulted from the trial lawyer's failure to look.

Martinez alleged that he had received ineffective assistance of counsel from his trial attorney. He requested a live hearing in federal court so that he could put on his witnesses. One of those witnesses would be the trial attorney himself, who could defend his actions. After hearing all the evidence, the federal judge could determine whether Martinez's rights had been violated.

Martinez was never granted that hearing. On August 25, 1999, the federal district judge denied Martinez all relief. He did not decide that Martinez's claims lacked merit. Rather, he concluded that he could not actually decide Martinez's claim. The law, he declared, was clear:

> Martinez's court-appointed state habeas attorney had not presented this claim during state habeas corpus proceedings.

> Because Martinez had not presented this claim in a proper, timely manner in state habeas corpus, it was unexhausted and "procedurally defaulted"; therefore, the federal court *must simply ignore it* and *cannot decide it.*

In other words, Martinez was victimized twice by bad lawyers. First, his trial lawyer neglected to put important evidence before the jury. Second, his state habeas lawyer made exactly the same mistake by also failing to collect the evidence. Neither lawyer did his job. The inept performance of the first lawyer meant that the jury did not hear critical evidence; the inept performance of the state habeas lawyer meant that the federal court could not hear the evidence. By the time Martinez's case reached federal court, there was no longer a question of whether he would be executed; there was only the question of when. He did make a powerful argument in his behalf—that the state had promised him a competent habeas lawyer but had then provided him with a lawyer who, by his own admission, did not know what he was doing—but strong moral claims often do not translate into successful legal ones. Indeed, the federal district judge expressed moral outrage at Martinez's predicament, yet also felt that his hands were tied.

The predicament Martinez faced resulted from a confluence of three developments. First, AEDPA provides that the incompetence of state habeas counsel does not constitute a basis for legal relief under federal law, so Martinez could not prevail in federal court simply by showing that his state habeas lawyer had thrown away viable claims.[19] Second, the Texas Court of Criminal Appeals ruled that the incompetence of state habeas counsel also does not provide a basis for legal relief under state law. Finally, the Supreme Court ruled in *Coleman v. Thompson* that incompetent performance by a court-appointed state habeas lawyer is not an excuse for procedural default.[20] *Coleman* is a complicated case that addresses a complicated legal issue, but it is worth lingering over because it affects dozens if not scores of death row inmates. One cannot finally understand what happened to Martinez without understanding what happened to Roger Coleman eight years earlier.

Coleman was executed in Virginia for the murder of Wanda McCoy, a crime he may not have committed. His case received significant national attention because of his compelling claim of innocence, but its significance to Martinez lay in its more arcane procedural aspects.

Like Martinez, Coleman had been represented at his trial by a lawyer whose competence was open to serious question. Unlike Martinez, however, Coleman had superb state habeas lawyers who presented evidence in state court that Coleman's right under the Sixth Amendment to be represented by competent counsel had been violated. Nevertheless, the state court judge ruled against them, signing the order denying relief on September 4,

1986. On that day, the judge who had presided over the evidentiary hearing was out of the county where the trial had been conducted (and where the habeas hearing had been held), but Virginia law required that the order be filed in the county where the trial had taken place. The judge therefore mailed the order to the appropriate county clerk, who entered the order on September 9. The clerk's office mailed certified copies of the order to the lawyers, and the date on both the clerk's transmittal letter and the certified order was September 9. These seemingly unimportant dates are crucial, so bear with me.

Under Virginia law, a notice of appeal must be filed no more than thirty days after entry of the judgment from which appeal is to be taken. Lawyers from the law firm in Washington, D.C., who were representing Coleman in state habeas proceedings prepared the notice and sent it to a lawyer in Virginia, who was serving as their local counsel. That local lawyer in turn mailed the notice to the county clerk on October 6. Under Virginia law, because the notice was sent by ordinary mail (as opposed to certified or registered mail), it was effective when *received* by the clerk. (Had it been sent by certified or registered mail, it would have been effective on dispatch.) The clerk received the notice on October 7.

We are almost finished with a detailed recital of dates. The reason the recitation is needed is that eventually, the attorney general's office decided that it would contest Coleman's appeal on procedural grounds, by arguing that his notice of appeal had not been filed on time. The attorney general took the position that the relevant date for purposes of calculating the time for filing the notice was the date on which the judge had *signed* the order, not the date on which it was filed. In other words, the attorney general maintained that the thirty-day period began to run from September 4, not September 9. If the attorney general was correct, then Coleman had until October 4 to file his notice of appeal. But October 4 was a Saturday, and under Virginia law, if the thirtieth day to file a notice fell on either a Saturday or a Sunday, the party filing the notice of appeal had until the following Monday. According to the Virginia attorney general, in other words, Coleman was required to file his notice of appeal by Monday, October 6. And in fact, Coleman's lawyer *had* mailed the notice on the 6th; it was not received until the 7th, however, and because the notice was sent by regular mail, it was not effective, under state law, until it was received. Coleman's notice of appeal, under this theory, was one day late. For want of the price of a registered letter, the state was able to take the position that Coleman's appeal should not be heard.

Coleman's lawyers filed their appeal with the Virginia Supreme Court in December 1986. Less than a week later, the state moved to dismiss the appeal on the sole ground that the notice of appeal had not been filed in time. The Virginia Supreme Court, however, ordered the state to brief the merits of the issues raised in Coleman's petition. But the following April, it issued an order granting the state's motion to dismiss. The Virginia Supreme Court did not address the merits of Coleman's arguments because it apparently concluded that his notice of appeal had been filed a day too late.

Recall that under the independent and adequate state ground doctrine, a federal court cannot address the merits of a death row inmate's legal claims if the state court has disposed of those claims on procedural grounds. However, the independent and adequate state ground doctrine has long contained an important exception. If a death row inmate can show "cause" for failing to adhere to the state law procedure, and can also show a violation of federal law that resulted in prejudice (meaning that he was either wrongfully convicted or wrongfully sentenced to death as a result of the violation of federal law), then the independent and adequate state ground doctrine will not preclude the federal court from addressing the merits of the inmate's claims.

The actual prejudice prong of this exception is exceedingly difficult to meet; it requires that a death row inmate prove that the result of his trial or sentence would probably have been different had the error not occurred. Few inmates can satisfy this onerous standard, and there is no particularly good reason to think that Roger Coleman could have satisfied it either. But Coleman never got the chance to try to prove that he had been prejudiced by his trial lawyer's ineffectiveness, because the Supreme Court ruled that he could not clear the first hurdle of showing "cause" for having failed to adhere to the state's procedural rules. Coleman had made two arguments. First he said that the lawyer's failure to meet the deadline was itself cause. The Supreme Court rejected that argument, reasoning that the lawyer was acting as the death row inmate's agent. Second, Coleman responded that in that case, the lawyer was ineffective, and his ineffectiveness should constitute cause. The Supreme Court rejected that argument as well, reasoning that death row inmates are not entitled to counsel during habeas corpus proceedings, and so they are also not entitled to effective counsel. (If you are not entitled to any lawyer at all, you are certainly not entitled to an effective lawyer.)

Roger Coleman was executed on May 20, 1992 without having any federal court review whether his trial lawyer had been ineffective, and whether he would have been found not guilty had he received the benefit of competent trial counsel. His case came to stand for a proposition that proved fatal to Martinez: If a death row inmate is represented during state habeas proceedings by a lawyer who does something to cause all the inmate's legal claims to be waived, the inmate cannot overcome that waiver—and thereby empower the federal court to consider the issues—merely by establishing that his state habeas corpus lawyer was incompetent.

In assessing the significance of what the Martinez case teaches us, an important question is whether it is unique. Unfortunately, it is not, in Texas or in any other state. For example, a study released in North Carolina in 2002 found that approximately 20 percent of the state's death row inmates were represented by lawyers who had been sanctioned by the state bar.[21] In Texas, nearly one in four death row inmates was represented by a lawyer who had been reprimanded, placed on probation, suspended, or banned from practicing law by the state bar of Texas.[22] Moreover, capital defendants who were represented by lawyers appointed by the state are 28 percent more likely to be convicted and 44 percent more likely to be sentenced to death than capital murder defendants who have the resources to retain their own lawyers. One-third of the death row inmates executed during George Bush's tenure as governor were represented by lawyers who were later disciplined by the state bar.[23] A detailed study of 251 state habeas corpus petitions filed on behalf of Texas death row inmates between 1995 and 2002 found that nearly one-fourth of these petitions were fifteen pages long or less.[24] Nearly three-fourths of these petitions raised no claims at all that were based on additional investigation. Martinez did not receive an unusually bad lawyer; he got what most death row inmates get.

In Tennessee, at least thirty-nine lawyers who have been disciplined by the state bar have represented defendants in capital cases. Tennessee currently maintains a list of lawyers who are approved to represent indigent capital defendants, and that list includes a lawyer convicted of bank fraud, another convicted of perjury, and a third whose failure to order a blood test let an innocent man languish in jail for four years on a rape charge. Eleven such lawyers remain on the Supreme Court's list for future appointments in capital cases.[25] In Virginia, lawyers who represent indigent capital defendants are six times more likely to be subject to disciplinary proceedings than other lawyers, and 10 percent of death row inmates were represented by a lawyer who later lost his license to practice.[26] In Kentucky, nearly a quarter of the state's death row inmates were represented at trial by lawyers who were subsequently disbarred or had their license suspended.[27]

This phenomenon is not limited to the Old South.[28] In Washington State, fewer than 1 percent of all attorneys are ever disbarred. Yet a study conducted by the *Seattle Post-Intelligencer* found that one-fifth of the eighty-four people who have faced execution in the last twenty years were represented by lawyers who had been, or were later, disbarred, suspended, or arrested. The state has had three executions: one man was defended by a lawyer who was later disbarred, one was prosecuted by a lawyer who was later disbarred, and the third man represented himself. [29] In Illinois, at least thirty-three death row inmates were represented by a lawyer who, at some point, engaged in such egregious conduct that he was either suspended from the practice of law or disbarred.[30] In Pennsylvania, more than twenty death row inmates were represented by lawyers who were later disbarred, suspended, removed from capital cases because of incompetence, or committed suicide when faced with criminal prosecution.[31]

State legislatures are aware of the abysmal lawyering that occurs at many capital trials, which is why they enacted laws to ensure that death row inmates receive competent habeas lawyers, who might help them argue that their trial representation has been constitutionally ineffective. But as Martinez's case illustrates, writing a law is one thing, and enforcing it is quite another. Texas, for example, like every other death penalty state, has a statute guaranteeing death row inmates a right to counsel during habeas review, and that statute assures inmates that their lawyers will be competent. But all that *competent* means is "a pulse and a bar card."[32]

Whereas the Martinez case shows how the lives of death row inmates rest in the hands of incompetent lawyers, the case of Gregory Demery shows that the courts are indifferent to this phenomenon even when they know it is occurring and have the power to correct it. In Demery's case, the Texas courts appointed a lawyer to handle the state habeas proceedings, and soon after he received the appointment, that very lawyer went to work as an assistant district attorney. Needless to say, aside from inspiring very little confidence, the lawyer's decision was unethical. Soon, however, the lawyer left the district attorney's office—not because he became aware of the ethical complexity of representing Demery while serving as a prosecutor, but because the State Bar Association suspended him. The bar discovered that the lawyer had (among other things) forged a legal document by making it appear that it had been filed by a certain date when in fact it had not.

The Texas courts knew all of these facts—including that the lawyer was suspended from practicing law in the state—but they took no steps to replace him. He was "competent" at the time he was appointed—the test the Texas courts adopted in the *Graves* case—and that was the end of the matter. Like Martinez's counsel, Demery's lawyer never wrote or visited his client. He did not even bother to read the letters his client sent to him. (They were returned to Demery unopened.)

Demery died on death row of complications stemming from AIDS. Had he not, he would have died from a lethal injection, not because his trial was free of constitutional errors, but because the suspended lawyer that the state appointed to represent him caused all of his legal claims to be waived. The Martinez case is not unique in the slightest. It is how the system works.

After losing in federal court, Martinez had two cards left to play. By the time the federal court ruled that it could not reach the merits of his case, there were dozens of death row inmates in Texas alone, and dozens more in other states, whose rights had been similarly affected by incompetent state habeas lawyers. First, Martinez and two other death row inmates whose execution dates had been scheduled filed a civil rights lawsuit in federal court. (The other inmates were Gary Etheridge and Napoleon Beazley, both of whom have since been executed.) They argued that by promising them competent state habeas lawyers and then giving them lawyers who did not know what they were doing and

who caused their legal arguments to be waived, Texas had ultimately denied them the opportunity to have a federal court address the merits of their cases. Because federal law provides that
federal courts cannot address issues that are not properly presented to the state courts, the state is in a position to nullify judicial review by providing lawyers to death row inmates who do not
properly present the claims in state court. The federal court of appeals ultimately ruled against Martinez, Etheridge, and Beazley,
and by extension the many other inmates who were similarly affected. But again the court did so without even addressing the
merits of the argument. Instead, the court of appeals concluded
that because these inmates were on death row, the only legal device they could use to obtain judicial review was the writ of habeas
corpus, and their writ of habeas corpus had already been denied
on the authority of the Supreme Court's decision in *Coleman*.

Martinez was down to his last hope: the clemency process.
But *hope* is too strong a word to describe the clemency process in
Texas. Death row inmates do not receive clemency in Texas. Not
counting the three or four cases of mentally retarded death row
inmates who have been moved off death row once their mental retardation was established,[33] only in three cases out of well over
three hundred executions has the clemency board recommended
that a death row inmate be moved off death row and given a
life sentence instead. Each of these cases is aberrational. Death
penalty lawyers file clemency petitions on behalf of their clients
because when someone's life is at stake, lawyers tend to leave
nothing on the cutting room floor, but when they are writing the
petitions, they know it is a mere formality.

Shortly after I had filed the clemency petition, I visited Martinez on death row to discuss our remaining options. The civil
rights action we had filed had not yet been denied, and I was
describing the theory of the case, as well as our options for appeal. When I finished outlining the options, Martinez asked me
whether I ever sleep.

I suppose that like many death penalty lawyers, I have often wondered the same thing about my clients. Do they sleep all the time or never? If you knew the day you were going to die, would you try to remain unconscious until that day arrived, or would you try never to sleep between now and then? I did not answer him. Instead I asked him how he was sleeping. "I used to sleep ten or twelve hours a day," he told me, "but lately I've only been able to sleep about six." He paused and then told me that two things were on his mind. First, he was terrified of being buried beneath a generic tombstone in a pauper's grave in a corner of the prison yard. He did not find Jesus or Allah on death row, as many inmates do. He was already religious when he arrived in prison. He wanted to know whether I could help him raise $5,000 for a Catholic burial.

Second, he asked whether I thought it was a good idea for him to have a face-to-face meeting with the mother of the young man he had stabbed and killed in a drunken stupor eight years earlier.

Martinez told me he had raised a little money for the burial, but I already knew that a woman who wanted to remain anonymous had arranged for the burial, so I told Martinez that he need not worry, that I would take care of it. The other issue was up to him. He fidgeted nervously. It wasn't because the calendar was marking his last days, but because the mother of the man he had stabbed, to whom he had written one sorrowful letter seven years earlier, wished to see him. Martinez wanted to let her see him, and he also wanted to see her, but he was scared. He told me the chaplain had urged him to meet with her. But Martinez didn't trust the chaplain. He trusted me, and he wanted to know whether I thought he should do it.

Several years earlier, the Texas Department of Criminal Justice had implemented a victim mediation program. Victims of violent crimes such as rape could, if they and their abuser wanted to, undergo a process whereby they would meet face-to-face. The victim would have the opportunity to ask why, and the criminal could repent and ask for forgiveness. The system appeared to be rather successful, but it had been used only once before in a death penalty case. On that occasion, the murderer and a family member of his victim had conversed across a wire-laced, bulletproof, Plexiglas screen. The people who run the program were planning to have Martinez meet with the mother of his victim face-to-face. The program had received permission from the warden to have the meeting take place in a prison chapel.

I told Martinez that he could meet with the young man's mother if he wanted to. It would not affect our case either way. In my heart I knew that neither the civil rights action that was still pending nor any other eleventh-hour tactic I could think of would make any difference. Death penalty lawyers delude themselves into thinking that this time it will be different, that this time a court will realize that the inmate's rights were violated and that he should not have been sentenced to death. Without this delusion, death penalty lawyers could not be death penalty lawyers. But when we are honest, when we are not in the middle of representing a client, we know that it is a delusion, and we will tell you so. For the three years I had been representing Martinez, I implored the state and federal courts, using a series of innovative yet ultimately futile arguments, to address the merits of his case. All the courts turned us down, claiming that various procedural rules meant that we could not have the merits addressed. Nobody listened.

I told Martinez to either meet with the mother of his victim or refuse. It was completely up to him. I wanted him to understand, however, that whatever he decided, the case would not be affected. "You may as well do what you think is right, because either way, we aren't going to prevail." That was exactly how I put it. I did not predict that we were going to lose or that he was going to be executed. I told him, sterilely, that we wouldn't prevail. Martinez dropped his head and said, so softly I could barely hear him, "I killed her only son. The least I can do is meet with her."

On Friday, May 3, less than three weeks before Martinez's scheduled execution, I arrived at the prison for the 8 o'clock mediation. Martinez came in with his hands cuffed together and then to a waistband. He sat shackled at a table. The rest of us in the room made small talk and discussed the procedure for the mediation. The chaplain told me that the victim's mother would be given a chance to make an opening statement. Then Martinez could speak. Then they would go back and forth, responding to questions posed by the mediator.

A crisis arose. The assistant warden decided that the meeting would have to occur in a different room, and I would not be permitted to remain in that wing of the prison. When I told Martinez about this development, he became nervous. He said that if I could not be near him, he would not go through with it. The program operators scrambled to reach the warden, who was traveling. More than an hour later, he authorized the session to go forward in the room where we had assembled. Moments later, Lana Norris, Clay Peterson's mother, walked into the room.

During the half hour or so in which the mediation personnel were trying to reach the warden, I was alone with Martinez. He was shivering with fear, the chain around his waist tinkling like ice cubes in a glass. "There's nothing I can do to bring him back," he said. "I made five minutes of mistakes in my life, and they are mistakes I can't fix. She is going to hate me. I would hate me, too. I do hate me."

His prediction was as wrong as a prediction can be. Norris took her place at the table. "Excuse me," she said, interrupting the chaplain. "The first thing we need to do here is pray." She reached across the table, clasped Martinez's manacled hands, bowed her head, and asked for wisdom and understanding. Then she let him loose, looked him straight in the eye, and told him she had forgiven him years ago. The tension melted out of Martinez, and his shoulders collapsed with relief. Norris turned to the chaplain and asked whether he wanted to say something; he told her to just go ahead. So she did. As Martinez softly cried, she asked him the questions she had always wanted answered: Why her son? Why that store? Why stab him more than once? Why had he drunk so much? Who was the man he was with? Whose idea was the robbery? Why, why, why? Martinez answered them all. Two hours later the chaplain asked if anyone needed to use the toilet, but Martinez and the woman ignored him and talked for two hours more.

The murder had been captured on a security videotape in the convenience store. Martinez testified at his trial, and when confronted with the video, he kept repeating that he could not believe his eyes. He told Norris the same thing. She told him that when she watched the tape, she did not understand why he was doing it, and he told her that he didn't either. She asked how his mother was holding up. She knew what it was like to lose a son. At one point Norris said to him, "I do not want to see you dead"; Martinez blurted out, "Will you write a letter to the parole board for me?" She said she would think about it.

Over the course of representing many death row inmates, I have met several family members of murder victims. Only a handful have said anything to me. After the four-hour meeting between Norris and Martinez (which was interrupted by some legal wrangling over the use of the video that was being made of the session), she and I walked out of the prison together. Out of sensitivity to her, I did not want to follow up on Martinez's request; out of loyalty to my client, I felt that I had to.

I did not ask her. I had taken to the prison a copy of the clemency petition I had filed. I planned to give it to Martinez, but after the session, I told Martinez I would get him another copy, that I wanted to give the one I had to Norris. As she and I walked out, I told her that if she had any questions after she had read it, —assuming she even wanted to read it—to please get in touch with me. I left town for the weekend. When I got back on Sunday afternoon, there was a message from Norris at my office. She wanted to write a letter on Martinez's behalf.

As expected, Martinez lost all his legal appeals. We also lost in our request that the clemency board commute his sentence to life in prison. The vote was 9 to 8. I would have preferred to have a vote of 17 to nothing. It would have meant that there was nothing more I could do. A vote of 9 to 8 meant that maybe I should have spent one more hour, two more hours, another day, on the clemency petition. Maybe that was all I needed to do to change one more mind and save a life. For Martinez, though, the vote was good. It meant that people besides his family and his lawyer and the mother of his victim knew he ought to live.

On the day of the execution, scheduled for 6 p.m., the Supreme Court turned down our final appeal a little after 4. I informed Martinez's family and friends, who had gathered outside the prison, and watched people who knew better lose the sliver of hope they had held on to. Two weeks earlier, when I had visited Martinez on death row to tell him that we were out of legal options, he had asked whether I would witness his execution. I would have liked to have had an excuse to say no.

An hour before his scheduled execution, I met with Martinez in the holding cell outside the death chamber. He had read an article I had written for a popular magazine where I pointed out that he was being executed not for his own mistake but for the mistakes of his lawyers. He asked me if he could say in his final statement what I had written in my article. I told him of course he could. It was his final statement; he could say whatever he wanted.

One news report characterized his final statement as bitter. That report illustrates the hazard of using adjectives to describe people we do not know. Someone who didn't know Martinez might have thought that he was blaming others—the courts, for instance, or his previous lawyer. He was actually thanking me.

We had tried nine times to have a court address the merits of the case. We did not have nine appeals, because an appeal means that someone addresses your arguments. Someone listens to you. We had nine failed efforts of having someone pay attention. I was bitter. Martinez was resigned.

Martinez had been a model prisoner. Nonviolent and compliant, he did not view the guards as his enemy. They were doing a job. That is why his final hours took prison officials by surprise. In our final meeting Martinez told me that the prison spokesman had come to visit him to ask why he had forced the guards to "gear up." That was an expression I had not heard in fifteen years of representing death row inmates. Four guards were outside the holding cell, standing off to the side, trying to respect our privacy. Then I noticed something on a bench adjacent to where they were standing: riot helmets with face masks. The gear. Martinez had told the guards that he was not going to fight (not going "to buck" was the expression he used), but neither was he going to walk the fifteen feet to the gurney. They were going to have to carry him. Because of Sister Helen Prejean's book and the eponymous movie, everyone knows the expression "dead man walking." Isn't it odd that prisoners walk to their deaths? Even after they have been sentenced to die, a judge instructs them to rise, and they do. Why is that? They shuffle to the gurney, holding still to make it easier for their executioners to strap them down and insert intravenous needles that will inject the poison that will kill them. Why? Is it because they know that resistance would be futile, or because they want to help their killers pretend that they are not human? Martinez would not be complicit. That morning, when they told him to change his clothes, he refused. They had to change him. When they told him to stand up, he didn't. They had to lift him. When they told him to get in the van, he didn't. They had to hoist him.

Martinez told me about this non-violent resistance when I visited him two hours before he died because he wanted to remind me that he believed that killing was wrong, whether he was the killer or the victim. He believed that it is harder to be good than to be bad, but the advantage of goodness is that people aspire to it. They want to be good. His purpose in his final hours was to show them how they could be good. "I won't walk," he said to me. "I will not walk." He was not mad or bitter. Those are the wrong adjectives. He was telling me that he had not forgotten, even now, that he was a human being with will, not a cow at the slaughterhouse.

He nodded toward a closed metal door and asked me whether that was the room where they did it. "I think so," I said. "What, you've never been in here before?" I told him I hadn't. "You've never witnessed one of your clients get executed?" I told him he was only the second one who had asked. He wanted to know why I hadn't witnessed the other guy's. I told him it was because I had been filing an appeal until moments before the injection. He started to suggest another appeal I could file for him. He stopped in midsentence and shook his head, realizing the futility of it. He cried softly for a moment. I told him I was sorry. He put his fingers to his lips. "Shhh. I know you did everything. You've done everything for me, man," he said. "I wish I could pay you." He asked me to tell his mother, who was not going to witness the execution, that he loved her and that he was sorry. He told me to leave, that he would be okay. And so I left.

Martinez told the prison spokesman they wouldn't need to gas him. He was not going to buck, wasn't going to try to hurt anyone. They would, however, need to carry him. If regulations required them to gear up for that, they should get the gear. His point would not be lost on them.

Death row inmates have no contact visits, with their families or anyone else. So the last person to touch Martinez's skin, other than the geared-up employees of the Texas Department of Criminal Justice, was Lana Norris, the mother of Clay Peterson, the young man Martinez had killed. During their meeting, when she clasped his hands in prayer, when she told him that she had forgiven him, I saw Martinez cry for the first time.

In his final statement, Martinez smiled as he thanked a long list of friends and supporters—a list that the warden must have thought would never end, because he gently squeezed Martinez's shoulder, letting him know that he should wrap it up. He thanked me and told me to be sure to tell everybody what had happened: that people can do wrong without meaning to and without knowing it, and we have a duty to tell them.

Not counting Martinez, the last person who smiled before the execution was me. We witnesses had been sitting outside the execution chamber for about ten minutes longer than the intricately choreographed procedure requires. I hoped that the governor was thinking about granting a commutation, but the realist in me knew that that far-fetched possibility was not the reason for the delay. What was taking a long time was that Martinez was limp, forcing the guards to carry him, reminding the people who were doing this that they had the power not to.

Martinez knew he could not escape. He also knew that by not walking, his executioners could not escape either. Forcing those who take a human life to confront what they are doing is probably a small victory, but it was the only victory he had.

CHAPTER FOUR

SOME ARE RELEASED, OTHERS ARE EXECUTED

Yes, we do make mistakes. In fact, we make many. Since Gary Gilmore was executed by a firing squad in Utah in 1977, beginning the modern death-penalty era, nearly 13 people have been released from death row in America for every 100 killed.[1] Eighty-seven percent would be a terrific free-throw-shooting percentage in the National Basketball Association, but it is intolerable as a death penalty statistic. It means that historically, we seem to be getting it wrong more than 10 percent of the time.

Most death penalty prosecutions are not DNA cases. Convictions rest on circumstantial evidence, on confessions, on eyewitness identifications, and on forensic testimony (such as ballistics evidence). In a rape case, if DNA testing establishes that the man convicted of perpetrating a rape could not have been the attacker, we can say with confidence and certainty that we made a mistake and sent an innocent man to prison. But what is the equivalent for a death penalty case that involves no DNA? If a man is convicted on the basis of testimony from a single witness, and that witness is later found to be a pathological liar, can we say that an innocent person is on death row? What if a man is convicted on the basis of testimony from a single witness who later recants and says that she was mistaken?

Because most death penalty cases do not involve DNA, they are neither black nor white; they are gray with ambiguity. And yet, despite the fact that DNA is not an issue in most death penalty cases, you would have to be the most ingenuous person ever to have lived to believe that no innocent person has ever been executed in America. (And I am not talking just about lynchings; I am talking about executions that have taken place since the death penalty was reinstated.) To believe that no innocent person has ever been executed, you would have to trust either that the death penalty system is free of mistakes or that we catch all of the mistakes in the nick of time. The first belief has long since been revealed as a fantasy; some death penalty cases do involve DNA, and so we can be as close to certain as is humanly possible in some cases that innocent men have been sentenced to death.

A conservative estimate of criminal trials in general is that the wrong person is convicted between 3 and 5 percent of the time.[2] Some scholars believe that the error rate in death penalty cases may be even higher.[3] But even if it is the same as the error rate generally, we can predict that somewhere between 100 and 250 people on death row should not be there.[4] Moreover, even if we had no evidence, the belief that we catch every mistake would be unwarranted for the simple reason that it is incompatible with what we know about human nature and institutions. Mail gets delivered to the wrong houses. Computers crash. Space shuttles explode and disintegrate. Police, prosecutors, judges, and jurors err.

As I have already suggested, and as I expressly argue later, focusing on the execution of innocent people is a distraction in the contemporary death penalty debate. Nevertheless, some people continue to believe in capital punishment but also think that the death penalty must be abandoned if innocent people are executed.

If that represents your viewpoint, then you should seriously re-think your commitment to the death penalty, because innocent people have been executed and will continue to be executed in the future. We are imperfect human beings; it is in our nature to err.

This chapter and the next focus principally on three typical death penalty cases. All three turned on a combination of unreliable circumstantial evidence and unreliable eyewitness testimony. Two involved witnesses who recanted, and two involved witnesses who were not heard from. DNA played a role in none of them.

Although DNA had nothing to do with the convictions I discuss in this and the following chapters, cases involving DNA can teach us an important lesson about the evidence that did figure in the convictions. Since 1989, approximately 150 people have been exonerated on the basis of DNA evidence.[5] Nearly all of these cases involved convictions for rape or sexual assault. What it means to say that these men have been "exonerated" is that DNA proved that they did not commit the crime for which they were convicted and sentenced to prison. It does not mean simply that we can no longer have confidence in the evidence supporting the conviction; it does not mean simply that the guilty verdict must be set aside for legal reasons. It means we can be certain that we made a mistake; we can be certain we sent an innocent man to prison. And this substantial body of cases where we know we made a mistake permits us to analyze how it is possible to make such grave errors. What went wrong in these cases?

These cases have several common features. Astonishingly, in approximately 25 percent of them, the innocent man confessed to the crime.[6] Contemplate that statistic for just a moment: In one out of four cases where we *know* we got it wrong and convicted an innocent man, that man confessed. One might think that no one would confess to a crime he did not commit, but the DNA cases prove that this phenomenon occurs consistently. Far from being foolproof evidence of guilt, confessions are common even in cases where the suspect is unquestionably innocent. Erroneous confessions occur for a variety of reasons: Police overwhelm the will of the suspect with lengthy and abusive interrogations, they threaten or coerce the suspects, or they lie and tell the suspects they will be better off if they confess. For someone who has not faced a persistent interrogator, understanding how some people —many people—confess to crimes they did not commit is unfathomable. But facts are facts; it happens regularly.

Even more unreliable than confessions is the testimony of eyewitnesses. For essentially the same reason, we have a difficult time understanding how eyewitnesses can be so often wrong yet so certain at the same time. Because we trust our eyes, we are confident that if we saw something or someone, we could identify the person. Because of our confidence in our own ability, we tend to trust others when they tell us what they believe they witnessed. And yet we know with scientific certainty that eyewitness identifications are spectacularly unsound. In more than two-thirds of the DNA exonerations, the state introduced eyewitness identification against the defendant. In other words, in 70 percent of the cases where the DNA permits us to *know* that we sent an innocent person to prison, eyewitnesses pointed to the defendant at the trial and swore that they were certain that he was the wrongdoer.

When we approach death penalty cases, therefore, we should remember the lessons that the DNA cases teach us: Even in the face of a confession, we should not be quick to assume that the death row inmate is guilty, and that when a death penalty case rests on an eyewitness identification, it rests on one of the least reliable forms of evidence that are ever introduced in a criminal trial.

Randall Dale Adams got off of death row because of a movie. He spent twelve years awaiting execution after being convicted of the murder of Robert Wood, a Dallas police officer who was shot five times and bled to death on the side of the road on Saturday,

November 29, 1976, two days after Thanksgiving. Adams would have become a statistic—for he almost certainly would have been executed—had Errol Morris, a documentary filmmaker, not become interested in his case. And had Adams been executed, it would have been impossible to prove that we had executed an innocent man, but that is exactly what we would have done.

Adams was not a career criminal. At the time he was tried for the murder of Officer Wood, he had never been convicted of, or even charged with, any crime. There was not a jot of physical evidence to connect him to the murder. There was not the faintest hint of a motive. Indeed, the evidence against Adams was remarkably thin: testimony from a reward-seeking, attention-hungry, unemployed mother; and testimony from sixteen-year-old David Harris, a career criminal, who claimed he was with Adams at the time of the murder. In exchange for providing this damning testimony, Harris, who was ineligible for the death penalty due to his age, was not charged with anything—and charges pending against him in another state were mysteriously dropped.

Harris's good fortune ran out, however, when he was later convicted of another murder and received the death penalty. The state of Texas executed him on June 30, 2004.

However, long before he was executed, Harris recanted in the Adams case. During an interview, he said that contrary to the testimony he had given, he knew for a fact that Adams was innocent. Harris implied that the reason he was so sure was that he had been the shooter. He added that if Adams had not had bad luck, he (Adams) would not have had any luck at all. But that cliché was not exactly right, because Adams did have one piece of colossally good luck: Errol Morris became interested in his case.

From the moment of his arrest, Adams denied any involvement in the crime, and his story remained consistent and constant in every detail. He said that he had recently moved to Dallas to look for work and had managed to find it. One night, on Thanksgiving weekend, he had run out of gas on the highway and pulled over to the side of the road. Harris, whom Adams had never met before, stopped his car and picked Adams up. Harris told Adams that he was out of work and was passing through town. Adams, grateful for the assistance, told Harris that he should stay in Dallas and look for work at the place where Adams worked as a laborer. The two men bought something to eat and went to a drive-in movie; Adams was not interested in it and asked Harris to drive him back to his hotel, where he was staying with his brother. Before he went inside, Adams said good-bye to Harris. According to Adams, he was back at his hotel before ten o'clock and was asleep before eleven. Harris would later imply that he was upset that Adams had not offered to let him stay at his hotel. Adams was unaware of this as Harris drove off.

Shortly after midnight, Officer Wood and his partner noticed a car without its headlights on. Wood turned on his patrol car's flashing lights and signaled the other car to pull over. Police protocol calls for one officer to approach the driver's window while the other stands outside the patrol vehicle. It is not clear, however, whether, as Wood approached the driver's window, his partner remained in the patrol car or stood outside it. This detail, to which Morris's film calls great attention, is important not simply for what it indicates about the officer's commitment to following procedure but primarily for what it indicates about her ability to accurately describe the driver of the car. In any case, it is clear that immediately after Wood was shot, Wood's partner emptied her revolver at the fleeing car. She told investigators that the car was a blue Chevy Vega; in fact, she was mistaken. The car proved to be a Mercury Comet, a detail ascertained when Wood's partner underwent hypnosis. Wood, shot five times, bled to death on the side of the road.

To homicide investigators and district attorneys, nothing is more brutal than the murder of a cop. When a police officer is shot and killed on the job in Texas—or in any other state—no expense is spared in pursuing the killer. Morris's film emphasizes this salient fact. Investigatory zeal is not necessarily a bad thing, but it can become so when it outpaces judgment. Fifty investigators began an intensive search for Wood's killer. Unfortunately, several weeks and hundreds of man-hours were squandered because of the erroneous belief that the killer had been driving a Vega. Police and other law enforcement officials tracked down virtually every blue Vega in Texas looking for a bullet-riddled vehicle. This investigative feat was impressive, but it only hindered the investigation, because it meant that officers were not pursuing leads that had a chance of proving relevant.

Aside from her mistaken description of the vehicle, Wood's partner told investigators that the car that she and Wood had pulled over had a single occupant. She also said that the car's occupant was wearing a jacket with a fur collar. Only later did she say that there may have been two occupants. That night David Harris happened to be wearing a parka with a fur collar. Adams remembered this detail, and Harris's parka was later recovered. Adams's only jacket, the one he wore that evening, was made of blue denim.

In December, with Officer Wood's murder still unsolved, Harris was arrested for stealing a car in Vidor, Texas, an East Texas town with a substantial Ku Klux Klan population. Vidor had its own fifteen minutes of ignominy when three white males chained James Byrd, a young black man, to the back of a pickup truck and dragged him for miles down a country road, killing him. Two of the three are on death row. They became—in 1999— the first white men sent to death row in Texas for killing a black victim. (Make of that statistic what you will.)

Harris was well known to local law enforcement authorities in Vidor, and in the preceding weeks, he had been boasting to local residents about having shot a policeman in Dallas. Following his arrest for automobile theft, however, Harris said that he hadn't killed the Dallas officer after all but knew who had. In part his story dovetailed with that of Adams. Harris said he had picked up Adams from the side of the highway and that Adams told him he had run out of gas. Harris testified that the two had dinner, drank beer, and went to a drive-in movie. Harris knew the hotel where Adams was staying. But on the crucial detail, of course, Harris's story diverged; he said that Adams had shot Officer Wood as Wood approached their car. At the time, Harris was ineligible for the death penalty because he was only sixteen; Adams was twenty-eight. Morris's film implies that authorities were pleased to have a suspect they could lawfully execute. Adams was arrested on December 21.

From the outset, Adams admitted having spent several hours with Harris but steadfastly denied involvement in any murder. Adams did not own a gun, but he said he knew that Harris had a gun in the car because he had brandished it before Adams. Adams could not recall how much time the police spent interrogating him, but it was long enough for him to smoke two packs of cigarettes. Adams said that the police obliquely threatened to injure him, maybe even kill him, if he did not sign a confession, but Adams would not. He eventually signed a statement, which Adams said he understood to be nothing more than an acknowledgment that he knew Harris and had spent several hours with him after running out of gas. In their press release announcing Adams's indictment, however, the police called it a confession.

In many respects Adams's case is unremarkable, but in one important regard it was quite unusual for an indigent defendant in Texas in the 1970s: Adams had highly competent trial counsel. His lawyers believed in him and fought aggressively on his behalf. They were confident they would secure an acquittal. They nevertheless made three mistakes. First, they overestimated the importance of a lack of evidence in a case in which a police officer has been killed; second, they underestimated David Harris's magnetic charm; and third, they did not take into account the jury's willingness to rely on sorcery dressed up as science.

Harris testified that he had picked up Adams in a car that he

(Harris) had stolen; Harris added that later that evening, for no apparent reason, Adams, who had never been arrested, shot Officer Wood as he was approaching the vehicle that Harris had stolen. The story made no sense, but it was partly supported by the testimony of Emily Miller, a white woman who had been recently fired from her job as a gas station cashier for stealing. Miller testified that she had seen a bushy-haired man shoot Officer Wood as she sat in the passenger seat of a car that her husband was driving. Miller's husband was black. Unlike his wife, he did not testify that he had seen anything. Although Miller's husband could not verify the story, Miller had an explanation for that. "Black people," she said, "they don't like getting involved." Miller herself had come to the attention of the Dallas police after she was arrested for disorderly conduct and taken to the police station for booking. While there she volunteered that she knew something about the Wood murder. The disorderly conduct charge was dismissed, as were pending robbery charges against Miller's daughter.

In Texas and elsewhere, as we have seen, capital trials proceed in two phases.[7] In the first, the jury determines whether the accused is guilty of the offense, in Adams's case, the intentional murder of a police officer. The jury found Adams guilty on May 4. The second stage is the punishment phase. At the time of Adams's trial, sentencing juries in Texas had to answer two questions: whether the defendant had acted deliberately and whether there was a reasonable probability of his being dangerous in the future. (Following the Supreme Court's decision in *Penry v. Lynaugh*,[8] the Texas legislature added a new question: If the jury answers the future dangerousness question in the affirmative, it must then consider whether, in view of all the mitigating evidence proffered by the defendant, he should be sentenced to life rather than death.)[9]

The first question was nearly always answered in the affirmative under the former Texas sentencing law because the jury had, in effect, already answered it at the guilt-innocence phase of the trial by concluding that the defendant acted intentionally. In modern death penalty litigation, the critical question is probably the mitigation question, but at the time of Adams's trial, the critical question was the second. If the defendant could show that he would not be dangerous in the future, then the jury would answer the second question in the negative, and the sentence would be life rather than death.

To persuade a jury to return a "yes" answer to the future dangerousness question, Texas prosecutors (as prosecutors elsewhere) introduce so-called expert psychiatric testimony. In Adams's case, devastating testimony came from a Dr. James Grigson, a man who, it is fair to say, is a discredited charlatan. (Grigson died in June 2004.) His behavior in the Adams case was typical of his modus operandi: He spent fifteen or twenty minutes interviewing Adams, a man to whom he had never spoken before. Never mind that Adams was gainfully employed at the time that Officer Woods was murdered and had no prior criminal record and no history of violence. None of those details gave Grigson any pause. Grigson's testimony, which lasted for more than two and one-half hours, was both certain and persuasive. He asserted that Adams was a psychopath and would undoubtedly kill again.

Here is an interesting, albeit unsurprising, detail about Grigson: What he said in the Adams trial is what he routinely said in capital murder trials. As the Texas Court of Criminal Appeals noted, Grigson was always 100 percent certain of his opinion that the defendant against whom he was testifying would kill again.[10] On the basis of Grigson's testimony, the jury sentenced Adams to death.

Here it is worth noting that Adams was not only not guilty, but also not dangerous. Having long since been released from prison (in 1989), Adams has neither killed nor injured anyone. He has committed no crimes at all. But if he had been executed, there would have been no way to prove that Grigson was wrong.

Indeed, one of the difficulties with disproving Grigson's preposterous claims is that he was so effective a witness. Juries believed
him and therefore sentenced to death nearly everyone against
whom he testified, making it difficult to establish that had the
accused *not* been sentenced to death, no violent behavior would
have ensued.

Unfortunately for Grigson's credibility, when the Supreme
Court set aside the Texas death penalty in 1972,[11] many people
against whom Grigson testified had their death sentences commuted to life sentences, and many of those inmates were subsequently paroled. The Supreme Court's decision therefore had the
unanticipated consequence of providing some data against which
the reliability of Grigson's predictions could be assessed. In the
late 1980s, a Dallas-area assistant district attorney instructed an
investigator to track down a number of the paroled murderers
against whom Grigson had testified to see what had become of
them. The DA expected them all to be in prison, probably for
homicide, and anticipated using these data to buttress Grigson's
air of authority when he would call upon Grigson to testify in future death penalty cases. The DA's plans went awry. Of the dozen
paroled murderers his investigator was able to locate, not a single
one had committed another violent crime, and only one had committed any crime at all (a robbery). The murderers who had never
been paroled were uniformly living nonviolent and compliant
lives in prison. In short, the investigator was unable to identify a
single instance in which Grigson's predictions had come true; instead, the investigator stumbled upon many men who proved that
Grigson's predictions were false.[12]

This empirical evidence of Grigson's ineptitude came to light
far too late to do Randall Adams any good. Grigson's avuncular
demeanor and rapport with the jury were more powerful factors
for the jury than Adams's nonviolent and noncriminal past. The
jury accepted Grigson's assessment that Adams was a dangerous
psychopath. Adams was sent off to death row. The Court of Crim-

inal Appeals, the highest court in the state for criminal matters, affirmed Adams's conviction and sentence by a vote of nine to nothing.[13]

As I have suggested, Adams won release from death row because of a movie, but the movie would not have been made—there wouldn't have been time—had Adams not had very fine legal counsel. His lawyers took advantage of an Eighth Amendment principle that precludes the state from stacking the jury in a death penalty case. In *Witherspoon v. Illinois*,[14] the Supreme Court held that a state could not remove a potential juror from a jury panel just because that potential juror expresses moral qualms about the death penalty. Even such a juror, the Court held, must be permitted to serve on the jury if he or she can swear an ability to obey the oath that jurors take to uphold and enforce the law, as instructed by the trial judge. Any other rule, the Court reasoned, would create a death-qualified jury—that is, one predisposed toward death.

A decade after *Witherspoon*, Texas prosecutors were still violating the principle it established. In Adams's case, prosecutors, in accordance with a then-extant statute, excluded jurors who were unable to swear that a potential death sentence would not "affect" their deliberations.[15] Of course, in a death penalty case, we should perhaps want *only* those jurors who will be "affected" by the seriousness of what they are doing. Texas prosecutors, however, wanted a very different profile; they preferred jurors who could sentence a man to death as easily as they could swat a mosquito. So, despite the Supreme Court's pronouncement in *Witherspoon*, Texas prosecutors would eliminate potential jurors who simply took their responsibility seriously and regarded death penalty cases as grave matters. Adams was sentenced to death by twelve men and women who were not even "affected" by the magnitude of what they were doing. Consequently, following his defeat in the Court of Criminal Appeals, Adams, through his lawyers, appealed to the Supreme Court of the United States, arguing principally that this Texas practice violated the rule of *Witherspoon* by creating a jury predisposed toward death. The Supreme Court, by a vote of eight to one, with only Justice Rehnquist dissenting, agreed.[16] After twelve years on death row, Adams received a piece of good news: his death sentence was unconstitutional.

Following the Supreme Court's decision, Adams's lawyers went back to the state courts to try to win his release. However, in the interim, Governor Bill Clements had commuted Adams's death sentence into a life sentence, so the Court of Criminal Appeals determined that Adams should not be released from prison, because the only thing the Supreme Court had held was that the death sentence itself was unlawful; it had not set aside Adams's conviction.[17] Adams had won in the Supreme Court, but the state of Texas still refused to allow him to go free.

In the meantime—and unsurprisingly—David Harris had not reformed. Having served time in a military stockade, as well as in correctional facilities in Texas and California, he acquired a lengthy criminal record that included violent assault and armed robbery. In the end he broke into a couple's home and attempted to abduct the girlfriend of Mark Mays. When Mays retrieved his own gun to protect himself and his girlfriend, Harris shot him to death. Harris was arrested, convicted of capital murder, and sentenced to death. He was executed in 2004.

Errol Morris did not begin filming *The Thin Blue Line* until Harris was on death row. In the final interview with Harris, Harris is asked, "What do you think about whether or not [Adams] is innocent?" "I'm sure he is," Harris answers. "How can you be sure?" asks the interviewer, and Harris replies, "'Cause I'm the one that knows."

In the late 1980s, following the release of *The Thin Blue Line*, Adams's lawyers commenced state habeas corpus proceedings. The Court of Criminal Appeals eventually ordered a new trial.[18] Adams was ordered released from prison. Immediately following the Supreme Court's decision in Adams's case, Henry Wade, the Dallas district attorney, vowed a retrial. Adams's lawyers were anxious to have one and invited the DA to push forward. The state's bluff had been called, yet neither Wade nor any of his successors ever pursued another trial. Adams was at last a free man.

On a moonless night in May 1981, a young black man walked up behind Bobby Lambert in the parking lot of a grocery store in Houston. The man shot Lambert and fled, leaving Lambert with $6,000 in cash in his pocket.

Lambert was murdered by a gunman with a .22-caliber pistol. Police arrested Gary Graham two weeks after the shooting. When the state executed him on June 22, 2000, Graham became the 222nd person to be put to death in Texas since the state resumed executions.

The differences between the Randall Adams case and the Gary Graham case are as follows: (1) Adams is white, and Graham was black; (2) Adams's challenge to his death sentence occurred before the enactment of AEDPA, before Congress and the federal courts, including the Supreme Court, made it not only possible, but common, for major constitutional violations in death penalty cases to go uncorrected (Graham's challenge came after AEDPA); (3) Adams was released from prison, and Graham was executed.

In most other salient respects, their cases are the same. Like Adams, Graham was convicted despite a lack of physical evidence. Also like Adams, he was convicted on the basis of eyewitness testimony. Yet two of the three witnesses who testified against Graham at his trial could *not* identify him as the murderer. Two other witnesses from whom the jury did not hear swore that Graham was *not* the shooter. Two of the jurors who sentenced Graham to death swore they would have held out against the death penalty had they heard the testimony of these two witnesses.

Why didn't the jurors hear from the two witnesses who saw

the shooting and were certain that Graham was not the shooter? Because Gary Graham was represented by one of the state's most notoriously inept death penalty lawyers. That lawyer conducted no investigation at all. That lawyer therefore did not locate evidence that, at a minimum, creates reasonable doubt as to Graham's guilt and, at a maximum, stands as convincing proof that Graham was not the shooter. Whereas Johnny Martinez paid with his life for the mistakes of his appellate lawyer, Graham was executed because of his trial lawyer's incompetence. Even though Graham's habeas lawyers were superb, by the time they got involved in the case there was nothing they could do.[19]

Police originally arrested Graham on charges of robbery and assault. The robberies had occurred across town from where Lambert was murdered. When Graham was arrested, he had in his possession a .22-caliber handgun, the same caliber used in the Lambert murder. At Graham's trial, the jury learned of this detail. It also heard from Bernadine Skillern, who was in the grocery store parking lot when the murder occurred. She witnessed the killing at a distance of thirty to forty feet through the windshield of her car in the dimly lit lot. Skillern testified that she had a glimpse of the front of the shooter's face twice—once for a "split second" and then again for two or three seconds.

Aside from the gun evidence and Skillern's testimony, there was no evidence to connect Graham to the crime. He did not appear to know Lambert. There was no DNA linking him to the crime. And he did not appear to have taken any of Lambert's money. He was, however, a seasoned criminal. He had committed many robberies, some of them violent. Perhaps it was easy for the jury to overlook the weakness of the case against him for killing Bobby Lambert when the evidence that he had committed other crimes was so strong.

More than a decade after he was convicted and sentenced to death, Graham finally obtained the assistance of lawyers who actually investigated the case. What they learned caused the state's case against Graham completely to unravel. For example, the gun Graham had in his possession at the time he was arrested was indeed a .22, the same caliber used in the murder, but the jury had not been told that the Houston Police Department's own ballistics expert had concluded that Graham's gun could not have been the weapon used to kill Bobby Lambert. Same caliber, wrong weapon, but Graham's trial lawyer had not bothered to learn that crucial detail, so the jury did not learn it either.

Perhaps more important, the jury did not hear from all of the eyewitnesses. When police investigated the Lambert murder, they identified four eyewitnesses in addition to Skillern (for a total of five). Three, including Skillern, testified at the trial. Of these three, only Skillern testified that Graham was the shooter. The other two witnesses described the shooter only in general terms and could not say that Graham had committed the crime. But with one woman saying that Graham was the shooter, and two others saying that they could not be certain, the jury did not hear from anyone who would swear that Graham was innocent.

Two people, however, would have told the jury precisely that, yet the jury had no knowledge of them. The problem was not that they were in seclusion or difficult to find. Indeed, when police investigated the murder, they interviewed these two witnesses. The witness statements were included in the investigation file that the prosecutors handed over to the defense. Graham's trial lawyers either failed to read the file or failed to appreciate the significance of its contents, or they simply didn't care. Whatever the explanation, Graham's lawyers did not call these people as witnesses or even interview them prior to the trial.

Had these two witnesses testified, it seems safe to predict that the jury would have acquitted Graham, not simply because there were two of them (as opposed to one witness who said that Graham was the shooter), but also because their testimony was significantly more reliable than that of Skillern. Whereas Skillern saw the shooter from a distance of 30 or 40 feet in poor lighting, the witnesses who said that Graham was not the shooter had been less than 10 feet away from him and had seen him in bright light. The jury that sentenced Gary Graham to death did not choose to believe Skillern over these other two witnesses; it chose to believe Skillern because she was the only person they heard.

As we have seen in the Fierro and Martinez cases (discussed in chapters 2 and 3), the fact that federal law guarantees a lawyer for death row inmates matters very little, because various procedural hurdles make it impossible for even the most tenacious lawyers to prevail. The case of Randall Adams proved that an innocent man can be convicted even if his trial lawyer is good. That of Gary Graham showed that even an innocent man can be convicted if his trial lawyer is incompetent. And in this regard, Graham's tale is hardly unique. One death row inmate in Texas was recently moved off death row because his trial lawyer had slept through portions of this trial. That inmate was lucky. Another half dozen inmates who were represented by the same sleeping lawyer have already been put to death. In a different case, the Fifth Circuit court of appeals ordered that a death row inmate receive a new trial because his appointed lawyer had, at the time of the trial, been involved in a personal relationship with the state's key witness.

In the year and a half preceding the Graham execution, one lawyer appointed by a trial court to represent two indigent capital defendants was reprimanded not once but twice by the Texas Bar Association for official misconduct. Another was cited by the state bar for interfering with an official investigation by producing false documents. A third, who represented two defendants, was suspended from the practice of law for ethical violations. One of my clients was represented during state habeas proceedings by a lawyer who was suspended from the practice of law while those proceedings were still pending (yet the lawyer continued to file dismally poor pleadings on behalf of this inmate anyway).

Was the evidence against Gary Graham strong enough to support a conviction, much less the death penalty? Virtually any reasonable observer would say no. Graham's problem, however, was that federal law prevented the courts from being a reasonable observer. Once his trial lawyer failed to do his job, the courts quit paying attention to the question of whether an innocent man was sentenced to die.

Under federal law, when a death row inmate can show that his trial lawyer did not discover evidence of the inmate's innocence that he could have discovered, that inmate can attempt to establish in habeas corpus proceedings that his trial lawyer had been ineffective.[20] However, in Graham's first habeas corpus proceeding, in state court and subsequently in federal court, his habeas lawyer did not assert that Graham's trial lawyer had been ineffective for failing to locate evidence of Graham's innocence. Why? Because that lawyer, in a surreal episode of déjà vu, replicated the mistake of Graham's trial lawyer and conducted no investigation. He repeated every major mistake that Graham's trial lawyer had made: He did not locate and interview eyewitnesses, even though their names were in the police reports of the crime; he did not understand that the ballistics report had established that Graham's gun was not the murder weapon. Just as the jury that sentenced Graham to death had not heard from the witnesses who would have sworn that Graham was not the shooter, the court that denied Graham relief in his habeas appeals also never learned that these witnesses existed, and this time the responsibility lay with Graham's inept appellate lawyers. The state of Texas had given Graham several sets of lawyers, and none had done what he or she was supposed to do. Graham may as well have been representing himself.

At last Graham got new lawyers, who conducted an investigation. They read and understood the ballistics report, realizing that it meant that Graham's gun was not the murder weapon. They located and interviewed the other witnesses. They appreciated that these witnesses had taken a longer and better look at the murderers, that they would have testified that Graham was not the shooter, and that their testimony would almost certainly have changed the outcome of the trial. In the summer of 1993, they filed a second habeas corpus petition. The law, however, then and now, is hostile to claims that are raised in a second (or later) habeas petition. Consequently, under the law that existed at the time Graham's lawyers filed a second petition on his behalf, the federal court would not consider the merits of the argument they were raising unless Graham's lawyers could point to a good excuse (known as "cause") for not having raised the argument sooner,[21] and unless they could also show that Graham had been harmed (or "prejudiced") by the mistake they were complaining about. At the time Graham's lawyers filed the second habeas petition on his behalf, they could avoid having to establish "cause" if they could point to an extraordinarily high degree of prejudice—in other words, if they could demonstrate he was convicted even though he was "probably actually innocent."[22]

The reason that the evidence of Graham's innocence was not located sooner and put before a judge or jury was that his previous lawyers had not done their job. Unfortunately for Graham, under federal law, the fact that a previous habeas lawyer fails to do something cannot establish "cause."[23] Because Graham would not be able to establish "cause" for not having raised the argument sooner, his only hope was to show an extraordinary degree of prejudice: to show that he was actually innocent.

Another requirement of federal law is that death row inmates proceed to state court before federal court. This is known as the "exhaustion" requirement. One must exhaust the opportunities for relief in state court before asking a federal court to intervene.

The idea that underlies the exhaustion requirement is that it is insulting to state courts when federal courts reverse murder convictions or death sentences on the grounds that state authorities violated the defendant's constitutional rights, so the state courts are given the first opportunity to correct the error. Graham's lawyers therefore asked the state court to address the evidence showing that Graham was innocent. When the state courts denied Graham any relief, he was finally permitted to proceed to federal court.

But Graham fared no better in federal court. Federal law requires that federal courts show great deference to the conclusions of the state courts, and the federal district court believed that this obligation of deference demanded that it rule against Graham's claims.[24] Graham appealed the district court's decision to the court of appeals, and for the first time it appeared that Graham would get an opportunity to prove his innocence. The court of appeals sent the case back to the trial court, because it realized that not a single court, neither state nor federal, had ever examined what the court of appeals characterized as "a large body of relevant evidence":[25] evidence that seemed to establish that Graham was innocent but that neither judge nor jury had ever considered.

Graham therefore returned yet again to state court so that the state court could examine the relevant evidence that it had so far ignored. But when Graham requested a hearing, the Court of Criminal Appeals ruled that he was not entitled to it under state law. The state court did not say why; it simply issued the boilerplate order that it routinely issues when deciding that a death row inmate will not be given another chance to have a hearing in state court.[26] The court did not evaluate the new evidence; it did not seek to determine whether Graham was innocent. Instead it invoked procedural barriers to prevent Graham from having the evidence of his innocence evaluated and weighed.

Once again Graham turned to federal court. But during the

years between the federal court of appeals' noticing that his case presented significant evidence that no court had addressed and the time he made it back to federal court, Congress had enacted the Antiterrorism and Effective Death Penalty Act of 1996 (AEDPA). Prior to AEDPA, as I indicated earlier, Graham could avoid having to establish "cause" if he could show great "prejudice." AEDPA changed that. Following its enactment, a death row inmate seeking to have a federal court address the merits of a claim that had not been raised sooner had to show cause *even if* the inmate could show that he was actually innocent. But AEDPA did not tinker with the definition of "cause." Consequently, just as Graham could not establish cause when he first went to court to establish his innocence in 1993, he also could not show cause when he returned to federal court in 1998. To show cause, Graham had to show that the new evidence that proved he was innocent could not have been discovered previously through the exercise of due diligence. But of course he could not show that because the evidence was there all along; it certainly *could* have been discovered through the exercise of due diligence. Graham's problem was precisely that his previous lawyers had not been diligent. Now that fact meant that the federal court would not grant him relief. The courts decided that they could not address the merits of Graham's claims because it would have been possible for those claims to have been raised sooner.[27] No court would look at the evidence because the evidence had been there all along. By a vote of five to four, the Supreme Court also refused to intervene. On June 22, 2000, guards forcibly dragged a resisting Graham from the holding cell to the execution chamber. Graham began his final statement: "I would like to say that I did not kill Bobby Lambert." His final words were: "They are murdering me tonight."

CHAPTER FIVE

INNOCENCE IS NOT ENOUGH

In the typical murder case, where there are no co-conspirators and no DNA, one person whom we can name truly knows whether he is guilty: the accused. But law is not metaphysics. We talk as if we know, when in fact ultimately we do not. We believe that Graham was innocent or that he was not, but the evidence, in all honesty, underdetermines either conclusion. And yet the language that courts and lawyers use, and that all of us perforce use, is the language of guilt and innocence. And so we should therefore pause here to ask what might appear to be an absurd question: Is it constitutional to execute someone who is innocent? If Gary Graham was innocent, was it unconstitutional to execute him? That question is more complicated than one might expect, and the answer is less clear than one might hope. And sadly, the answer given by the state of Texas does not indicate that the government is especially worried about it.

The origin of the need to ask this extraordinary question goes back to February 19, 1992, when the state of Texas was preparing to execute Leonel Herrera. Before 1995, executions in Texas took place shortly after midnight. The execution warrant directed the warden to carry out the execution "before sunrise" on a certain date. That meant that executions occurred between midnight and dawn. (Executions now take place "after 6 p.m." on a given date, meaning that they occur between 6 o'clock and midnight.) Herrera was set to die on February 19. Shortly before that date, his lawyers located evidence that they believed established that Herrera was not the killer. Because AEDPA had not yet been enacted, Herrera's lawyers, like Graham's lawyers several years later, believed that they could persuade a federal court to entertain his claim if they could establish that Herrera had suffered great prejudice—that he was probably innocent. They filed their habeas petition in federal court, and, after losing in the lower courts, they reached the Supreme Court on the day before the scheduled execution, February 18.

Herrera sat in a holding cell adjacent to the execution chamber while the Supreme Court decided whether to hear his appeal. According to Supreme Court custom, the Court will agree to hear a case if four justices want to hear it (this policy is the so-called rule-of-four). However, by the time Herrera's case reached the Supreme Court on February 19, his execution was imminent, and five votes were required for him to gain a stay of execution. It is therefore possible in theory for a death row inmate facing execution to persuade the Court to hear his case, yet not persuade the Court to stop his execution. (I discuss this practice in greater detail in chapter 7.) The justices continued to ponder Herrera's case through the night. Dawn was approaching, and still the Court had not issued an order either halting the execution or directing that it could continue. At last, shortly before dawn broke over East Texas, at which time Herrera's death warrant would have expired, the Texas Court of Criminal Appeals stayed the execution to await a decision from the Supreme Court. That decision came later in the day, after Herrera had been returned to his cell on death row. Four justices had voted to hear Herrera's case. However, five justices had voted *not* to halt his execution. In other words, although the window for carrying out the execution on February 19 had already expired, the Supreme Court expressly indicated that even though it had agreed to hear Herrera's appeal, there was nothing preventing the state of Texas from proceeding with the execution in the interim.[1]

Remarkably, a Texas trial court took up the invitation to have Herrera executed before the Supreme Court could hear his case. That court set another execution date, April 15. If Herrera were to be executed, then the Supreme Court would never address the question he was raising, because, to put it clinically, his case would have been moot. The Supreme Court does not issue so-called advisory opinions—opinions that announce the law in the abstract without having application in a particular case—and if Herrera was already dead, the Court's opinion would not apply to his case. In a rare victory for the rule of law, however, the Texas Court of Criminal Appeals intervened. By a vote of five to three (with one judge not participating), the state's highest criminal court stayed the execution. Three judges would have permitted the execution to go forward, but a majority concluded that it would be "improper" to permit an execution to go forward in the case of an inmate whose appeal the Supreme Court of the United States had already agreed to decide.[2]

And so it happened that Herrera's case made it to the Supreme Court prior to his execution. The questions for the Court were whether the Eighth Amendment to the Constitution forbids the state from executing someone who is innocent, and whether a death row inmate can, through his habeas corpus appeals, attempt to prove that he is innocent. Herrera lost, and he was eventually executed, but that is not what makes his case memorable. His case is memorable because of the Supreme Court's intimation that the issue of his innocence might be irrelevant. The Court noted that, historically, naked claims of actual innocence do not provide a basis for a federal court to overturn a state court conviction.[3] In other words, it is not enough for a death row inmate to prove he is innocent; he must also show something else (like prosecutorial misconduct, or ineffective assistance of counsel, or *something* that represents a *traditional* constitutional violation). Herrera could not show anything else. Unlike Gary Graham, who insisted that his trial lawyer had been incompetent for not putting on evidence that he was innocent, Herrera could point to no failure of his trial lawyer, for the supposed evidence of his innocence did not come to light until many years later. Graham lost because his incompetent lawyer could have presented evidence of Graham's innocence but did not; Herrera lost because he had nothing other than evidence of innocence. According to Chief Justice Rehnquist, what Herrera had was not enough. He could not get off death row merely by showing that he was innocent; he was also required to "supplement" his claim with some other complaint. A "freestanding" claim of actual innocence did not authorize a federal court to grant Herrera relief.[4]

There is a disagreement among death penalty scholars as to whether *Herrera* is still good law. Some believe that a naked, stand-alone claim of actual innocence now does permit a federal court to grant relief.[5] But the Supreme Court has never said as much. And perhaps it is scandal enough that there is even a debate about this question. Dissenting in Herrera's case, Justice Blackmun put it starkly: "The execution of a person who ... is innocent comes perilously close to simple murder."[6] It does indeed, but the state of Texas is unconcerned. Thus, when Herrera's case was argued before the Court, Justice Kennedy asked the lawyer representing the state: "Suppose a prisoner sentenced to die [subsequently discovers] a videotape proving someone else committed the murder. Does it violate the Eighth Amendment to execute him?" The lawyer from the attorney general's office replied succinctly, "No."[7]

* * *

One major reason innocent people end up on death row is that prosecutors frequently seek a death sentence in cases where the only real evidence of guilt is circumstantial. (Circumstantial evidence is "evidence of a number of different circumstances which, taken in combination, point to the existence of a particular fact upon which the guilt of the accused persons depends because they would usually exist in combination only because a particular fact did exist.")[8] At times, an entire population can be convinced of guilt on the basis of circumstantial evidence, as was the case with the convictions of Timothy McVeigh and Terry Nichols. But few capital murder defendants have the quality of representation that McVeigh and Nichols had, which means that substantially weaker circumstantial cases routinely go unchallenged. Overall, around one-sixth of all death penalty convictions have been based on circumstantial evidence. Nearly 20 percent of Texas death penalty cases have relied significantly on accomplice testimony at the guilt-innocence stage of the trial, and accomplice testimony requires only minimal corroboration to result in a conviction under Texas law.[9] Further, in more than two dozen cases, the prosecution has relied heavily on the testimony of so-called jail snitches, that is, inmates who were jailed with the capital defendant prior to trial and who subsequently testified against the capital defendant at the trial in exchange for leniency.

Racism also plays a role in sending innocent men to death row. The most notorious example in Texas is probably the 1981 case of Clarence Lee Brandley, a black man who worked as a janitor at a high school in Conroe, Texas. One Saturday morning, while Brandley and four other janitors (all of whom were white) were working, the body of a female student was found at the high school. She had been raped and strangled. Brandley and one of the white janitors were immediately singled out as the primary suspects.

Brandley protested his innocence from the outset. When he asked a Conroe police officer to tell him why he was being arrested in spite of the absence of any evidence, the officer responded, "You're the nigger, you're elected." During the pendency of the prosecution, even Brandley's court-appointed trial lawyer routinely referred to Brandley as a nigger.

The case against Brandley was based entirely on circumstantial evidence, and the jury that heard the evidence was all white. Although pubic hairs with "negroid characteristics" were allegedly found on the body of the dead girl, the prosecution never offered expert testimony that the hairs belonged to Brandley. Indeed, the hairs subsequently disappeared from the prosecutor's exhibits and to date have not been found. Brandley's jury deadlocked in favor of conviction eleven to one, with a single juror holding out. The single juror was harassed and called a "nigger lover" by his fellow jurors. The judge declared a mistrial, and prosecutors tried Brandley again. Again an all-white jury heard the case. The jury found Brandley guilty and sentenced him to death.

During Brandley's habeas corpus appeals, lawyers determined that prosecutors and police had failed entirely to investigate the possibility that three of the white janitors were responsible for the murder. This failure was especially troubling in view of the fact that law enforcement officials had discovered pubic hairs on the victim's body that belonged not to the victim but to another Caucasian.[10] Not only did the state make no effort to determine to whom the hairs belonged, it also did not disclose to the defense the existence of these hairs. Like the supposedly Negroid hairs found on the victim, these Caucasian hairs have disappeared—as has a semen sample recovered from the crime scene, which was never even tested for blood type.

One of Brandley's coworkers, a white janitor, wanted to testify on Brandley's behalf, but state authorities pressured him to lie and then persuaded him not to testify at all. Another white janitor was subsequently captured on videotape by Brandley's habeas counsel engaging in a conversation with another man, which established that they, and not Brandley, had raped and murdered the victim. The Texas Court of Criminal Appeals held that the police and prosecution had blindly focused on Brandley without any evidentiary justification. The court also determined that the state authorities had suborned perjury and suppressed exculpatory evidence. The court ordered Brandley released, and the charges against him were subsequently dropped.[11]

Not all prosecutorial misconduct is racist, however, as the case of Kerry Max Cook exemplifies. Cook was tried and sentenced to death for the 1977 murder and sexual mutilation of a Texas college coed. At Cook's first trial, the prosecutor—who committed suicide a few months later—introduced three main pieces of evidence: testimony by a twenty-two-year-old snitch who claimed that Cook confessed to the sex murder while awaiting trial; a single fingerprint found on the *outside* of the patio door leading into the victim's apartment; and alleged eyewitness identification by the victim's roommate. The prosecution also introduced testimony from Cook's homosexual lover, who had nothing of relevance to say, but who did testify in graphic and extensive details about his and Cook's sexual habits. The trial prosecutor's theory of the case was that Cook was a psychotic homosexual misogynist who, after being unnaturally stimulated by the movie *The Sailor Who Fell from Grace with the Sea*, had murdered the victim and eaten her sexual organs.

Either at trial or shortly thereafter, each of the three main pieces of evidence was undermined. The eyewitness admitted that she originally described the man she saw as having short "silver" hair; Cook, at the time of his arrest shortly after the crime, had shoulder-length black hair. There was someone who matched the witness's description: On the very day of the murder, the victim had broken off an illicit affair with a married man who had short, silver hair and who, by all accounts, was deeply upset by the breakup. The snitch recanted after the trial, claiming that Cook had never admitted to the murder; he conceded that he had committed perjury at trial by claiming that the prosecution had not offered him a plea bargain in return for his testimony against Cook, when in fact the state had done so. Finally, in addition to the fact that Cook's fingerprints were not even found inside the victim's apartment, the prosecution's fingerprint expert was entirely discredited after the trial. After the case against him finally came apart, Cook was eventually released from death row.[12]

Whether innocent people are released or executed depends more on sheer luck than on actual evidence. Randall Adams, Clarence Brandley, and Kerry Cook were not released from death row because of DNA evidence. Gary Graham, whose evidence of innocence was stronger than that of any of the released men I have mentioned, was executed.

How many people on death row are innocent? How many innocent people have been executed? These questions are impossible to answer. What we can say with certainty is that people are convicted on the basis of fallible testimony. And people are sentenced to death on the basis of baseless predictions. Some endings are, if not happy, at least not tragic. Others are not. Many stories, like that of Anthony Graves below, are still in progress.

In the sleepy town of Somerville, Texas, in the middle of a hot and sticky August night in 1992, six people spanning three generations were beaten, shot, stabbed, and left to die in a burning house.[13] The dead included Bobbie Davis, her sixteen-year-old daughter, Nicole, and four of Bobbie's grandchildren, ages four through nine. Somerville firefighters found the six bodies when they responded to reports of the fire, at around 3 in the morning.

Two of the young victims were the children of Lisa Davis, another daughter of Bobbie who was at work at the time of the murders. The youngest victim, Jason, was the son of Lisa Davis and Robert Earl Carter. Several weeks before the murder, Lisa Davis had filed a paternity suit against Carter, seeking additional child support. Carter had been served with the suit four days before the mass murder.

Police had no early leads. Then Carter appeared at the victims' funeral with bandages on his face, ears, and hand, all concealing burns. Police called him in for questioning. Carter initially insisted that he was innocent and had no knowledge of the killings. But after police told him that he had failed a polygraph test, Carter admitted he was involved in the killings. (Carter conceded that he was present, but he did not admit to the killings.) Police, however, did not believe he could have carried out the murders alone. Some victims had been shot, and others had been stabbed and bludgeoned. And there were just too many of them for the police to conclude that Carter had acted on his own. They pressed him to name an accomplice. Carter refused. Police continued to tell Carter that they knew he did not commit the crime alone. Eventually, Carter said that a man had helped him, his wife's cousin, a man named Anthony Graves. Authorities indicted Carter, Graves, and Carter's wife, Theresa (known as "Cookie"). Carter was executed. The case against Cookie was never pursued. Graves remains on death row, protesting his innocence.

The case against Graves consisted of three categories of evidence: testimony concerning the knife used in the slayings, testimony from jailhouse informants, and the testimony of Carter himself.

Graves's former boss, Roy Allen Rueter, testified that he gave Graves a knife made from a mail-order kit. Rueter had kept an identical knife for himself, and his knife was entered into the evidence. The medical examiner testified that Rueter's knife matched the wounds suffered by the victims. A Texas ranger who had observed the autopsies testified that Rueter's knife fitted "like a glove" into the head wounds suffered by two of the victims.

Based on the testimony of the coroner and the law enforcement officer, one might think that Rueter had given Graves a hunting knife. In fact, according to Rueter, the knife was "nothing but a souvenir that would have broken apart before it could have been used to puncture skullcaps or inflict the many stab wounds suffered by the victims." Rueter said that when a police investigator first examined the weapon, he made a sarcastic remark about how "dangerous" it was and "chuckled about the rubber band that basically held it closed together." Later, the lead prosecutor, Charles Sebesta, as well as Assistant District Attorney Bill Torrey, told Rueter that the knife was the murder weapon. Incredulous, Rueter agreed to testify that he had given a similar knife to Graves. Rueter was right to be incredulous.

After Graves went to death row, an independent forensic anthropologist (Dr. Harrell Gill-King from the University of North Texas) examined the evidence at the request of Graves's appellate attorneys. He concluded that the methods used by the Texas Department of Public Safety (DPS) and the medical examiner to compare Rueter's knife with the victims' skullcaps were not only "unscientific" but also destroyed the original evidence., According to the chief medical examiner for Bexar County (Robert Bux), the wounds themselves could have been inflicted by any single-edged knife. Moreover, since Graves's trial in 1994, the competence of the medical examiner who testified against Graves has been called into serious question. In one high-profile case involving a murder conviction of an eleven-year-old girl, three independent forensic analysts disputed the critical testimony given by the medical examiner. In short, it would be wrong to characterize the knife Graves owned as a toy, but it would also be wrong to characterize it as a murder weapon, and the evidence linking it to the murders was utterly unreliable.

The second piece of evidence against Graves came from jailhouse informants and employees. Police had placed Graves alone in a cell across from Carter's. Ronnie Beal, a restaurant owner and former sheriff's department employee, testified that he overheard Graves say through the prison intercom system, "Keep your damn mouth shut. I done the job for you. Make them make their own damn case." He also said he heard Graves tell Carter that they needed to protect Carter's wife, Cookie. Jailer Shawn Eldridge testified that he overheard Graves tell Carter through the intercom, "I did it, keep your mouth shut." A local rancher, John Robertson, who assisted at the jail, testified that he heard Graves tell Carter over the intercom that "we fucked up big time" and that Carter would have to take the blame for the crime because he had been burned. Robertson also said he overheard Graves tell Carter that they had to protect Cookie, and that they had destroyed all the evidence. Finally, John L. Bullard, an inmate at the jail who was in a cell adjoining Graves's, said he heard Graves ask Carter whether Carter had told police "everything." Bullard heard Carter answer in the negative, and then the two men started using hand signals.

When police believe they have a suspect in a murder investigation but can locate not a whit of physical evidence against that person, it is certainly convenient to have a witness testify that he heard the suspect bragging about destroying all the evidence. But there is more than the usual suspiciousness about coincidences to undermine the credibility of the witnesses who supposedly overheard Graves talking to Carter. An investigation performed by Graves's appellate lawyers casts doubt on every aspect of the testimony from people who supposedly overheard Graves talking in jail. Most significantly, in a sworn affidavit, John Bullard stated that Sebesta gave him a sentence reduction in return for his testimony at Graves's trial. Bullard, who was taking psychotropic medication at the time, was clearly confused about his role as a prosecution witness. He told Graves's lawyers: "When I testified I thought I was *helping* Graves the whole time." He said that when Graves was first brought to the Burleson County Jail, Graves asked Carter: "Why did you put my name in something I didn't know about?" Bullard said he told a prison guard and the district attorney that he thought Graves was innocent. Nevertheless, the district attorney manipulated Bullard's testimony to make it sound incriminating in front of the jury, and Bullard did not apprehend the manipulation.

Graves was moved from his solitary cell at the Burleson County Jail to a cell he shared with Gregory "Scotty" Burns. Burns told Graves's lawyers in 2003 that the intercom in the cell he shared with Graves had been ripped out, leaving only a hole in the wall and a few detached wires. He stated that the intercom in Carter's cell may have worked, but that the jail was old and nothing could be heard over the intercom unless someone "screamed and hollered." However, conversations inside the jail could be easily overheard. Burns said he heard Carter apologize to Graves for lying. Sebesta wanted Burns to testify against Graves, Burns said, and told Burns that the state had forensic evidence linking Graves to the crime. But Burns refused to lie.

John Brymer, another inmate who was present in the Burleson County Jail with Graves and Carter, came forward in 2003. Brymer stated that only three cells in the jail had working intercoms, and he confirmed that the intercom in Graves's cell did not work. Brymer, who was a trustee at the jail and could move around and talk to other inmates, said Graves told him to tell Carter that Carter needed to tell law enforcement the truth about the murders. Brymer said Carter responded that he would tell the truth, and "the truth would set Anthony free." Brymer also stated that jail authorities told him that they would be "willing to help me if I had information to help them concerning the cases against Robert Carter and Anthony Graves." Brymer nevertheless refused to testify against Graves, and stated that he had "never heard Anthony Graves make any statement that made me think he was guilty." In fact, Brymer emphasized that Graves consistently maintained his innocence.

The final piece of evidence against Graves, and probably the most significant, came from Carter himself. Carter testified that he went to the Davis home that night with the intention of killing Lisa Davis because she had demanded more child support for their son, Jason. Carter said Graves participated in the murders because he was angry with Bobbie Davis after she received a promotion that Graves's mother, Doris Curry, wanted at the Brenham State School, where both women worked. Carter testified that Graves called Carter's residence at about 11:30 p.m., and that Cookie's daughter Tremetra Ray answered the telephone. Graves supposedly asked Carter whether they were "still on" for the murders. Carter said yes, and picked Graves up at his house at about 12:30 a.m. Carter testified that the two men went into the Davis house—Carter with a gun and a hammer and Graves with a knife. Carter said he shot Nicole while Graves killed the rest of the family. Carter testified that he poured gasoline on the bodies and was burned when he ran into Graves in the doorway and fell into the flames. The murder weapons were never recovered.

It seemed preposterous that Graves would kill a house full of people for the absurd reason that Carter said he had agreed to participate in the crime,[14] and it was. Almost immediately after Graves's conviction, Carter recanted his testimony. He insisted that he had committed the murders alone, and he said that Graves had not been there. Carter told the same story—that Graves had nothing to do with the murders—to more than half a dozen people, including four of his lawyers,[15] two residents of death row,[16] and a woman Carter characterized as his "second mother" (Marilyn Adkinson). On May 31, 2000, Carter became the 218th person executed in Texas since the death penalty resumed. In his short final statement, he recanted yet again: "It was me and me alone," said Carter. "Anthony Graves had nothing to do with it. I lied on him in court.... Anthony Graves don't even know anything about it."

Carter's dying words were not his first public recantation. He had been proclaiming Graves's innocence since before Graves's trial. The prosecutor later admitted he knew that Carter said

Graves was uninvolved, but he did not care. Carter testified at a grand jury hearing in 1992, several weeks after the murders occurred, that he had fabricated the story he gave to Texas Rangers (a statewide law enforcement agency) implicating Graves. He said he lied because the rangers had told him they would let him go if he named an accomplice. He also said that rangers told him that if he did not give them a name, "something bad" would happen to him while he was being transported back to the county jail. Many years later, in a sworn deposition that Carter provided to Graves's lawyers two weeks before his own execution, Carter said that the district attorney and police investigators knew that he was lying about Graves's involvement simply to protect his wife. Carter said that prior to testifying against Graves, he had told a Texas ranger investigating the case and the district attorney's investigator that Graves had no involvement. On the very eve of his testimony in Graves's trial, Carter said he told District Attorney Sebesta that Graves was innocent, but Sebesta had replied that "he didn't want to hear that." Carter's assertion that Sebesta had pressured him to testify against Graves notwithstanding, Carter's insistence that Graves was innocent was also a charge he had made before. For example, in a letter that he wrote to Marilyn Adkinson, Carter admitted that he "lied on an innocent man to keep my family safe. I even told the D.A. this before I testify [*sic*] against Graves, but he didn't want to hear it."[17]

Sebesta knew that Carter was reluctant to testify against Graves.[18] Sebesta therefore recruited Carter's brother, Hezekiah, to visit Carter in jail and urge him to testify in accordance with Sebesta's theory. Sebesta has also acknowledged that Carter proclaimed Graves's innocence,[19] but that did not stop him from leaning on Carter's brother to urge Carter to implicate Graves, and it also did not cause him to tell defense lawyers what Carter had told him. Hezekiah later said that his brother told him that he had serious reservations about what he was going to do and he "felt bad" about it.[20] Why would Carter lie? The most plausible explanation is that he did it to protect his wife, Cookie. According to Graves's former boss Roy Rueter, Sebesta's lead investigator told him that if Carter did not testify against Graves, as he had promised he would, the prosecution would go after Cookie as the second person at the murder scene.[21] Carter sent Graves to death row because otherwise his wife would be executed.

At his trial, Graves's lawyers pinned their hopes on an alibi witness, who testified that Graves was at home when the murders occurred. Unfortunately for Graves, the alibi was provided by his brother,[22] whom jurors could choose to disbelieve as biased. Graves's defense also attempted to undercut a critical aspect of Carter's story, by calling Cookie's daughter, Tremetra Ray, who testified that (contrary to Carter's claim) Graves never called the Carter residence on the night of the murders. Had the jury heard more exculpatory evidence, it almost certainly would have acquitted Graves (instead of sentencing him to die). And the jury could have heard more because there was more to hear. An investigation performed after Graves arrived at death row not only undermined every aspect of the prosecution's case, but also seems to have established that Graves is, as Carter insisted with his dying breath, innocent.

Stripped of any ornament, the state's theory was that Graves had a motive to commit the crime because his mother had been passed over for a promotion, and he had an opportunity to carry out the murders with a knife his boss had given him. No physical evidence of any type placed Graves at the scene: no hair, no blood, nothing. And no witnesses placed him there either, with one exception: Robert Carter, who testified reluctantly and later recanted.

We now know that the two pieces of evidence besides the Carter testimony were similarly unreliable. The knife evidence, as we have seen, was shamanism. Knife wounds that the prosecution claimed were inflicted by a knife like Graves's could have come from any single-edged knife. The only reason this fact cannot be illustrated visually is that when the state's forensics "expert" took a knife similar to the one Graves owned and inserted it into the victims' skullcap wounds, he destroyed the physical evidence, making it impossible for Graves to prove how unreliable the prosecution's theory was. The victims were stabbed, in the aggregate, sixty-one times, yet the state never bothered to perform a strength test on a knife similar to the one they said Graves had owned, perhaps because they knew exactly what the results of any such analysis would be.

The "motive" component of the state's case was as nonexistent as the "opportunity" component. The state claimed that Graves stabbed five people to avenge his mother's honor. Rick Carroll, who from 1982 to 1992 supervised both Bobbie Davis and Graves's mother, Doris Curry, at the Brenham State School, where Graves's mother worked, told Graves's lawyers that he promoted Bobbie Davis from shift supervisor to administrative assistant in 1991 or early 1992—at least six months before the murders.[23] Graves's mother had not even applied for the position. According to Carroll, Doris Curry was not upset about Bobbie Davis's promotion. "There were people jealous of Bobbie Davis, but Doris Curry was not one of them," Carroll said. Similarly, ex–Somerville Police Chief Joel Fisher stated that after investigating the promotion story, "law enforcement authorities decided that Bobbie Davis's promotion did not play a role in the case" and that Carter's promotion motive story was "not credible."[24] The prosecution never bothered to talk to Carroll. This is not really a surprise; the prosecution did nothing if the possible consequence would be to undermine the case against Graves.

No motive, no opportunity, and substantial evidence of Graves's innocence: At a grand jury hearing before Graves was indicted, his then-girlfriend, Yolanda Mathis, testified that Graves was at home with her (and Graves's brother) on the night of the murders. She was prepared to testify to this fact at Graves's trial, but District Attorney Sebesta announced that the state would prosecute her as an accomplice if she testified on Graves's behalf. Afraid and alone, Mathis fled the courtroom. The jury never heard from her. Long since separated from Graves, she has sworn that she was with Graves the entire night of the murders and regrets to this day that her fearful unwillingness to testify helped result in the conviction of an innocent man.[25]

The jury also did not hear from Dietrich Lewis, Graves's sister, who was also at the house with Graves, his brother, and Mathis on the evening of the murders. Lewis swears that the district attorney and another law enforcement officer asked her to testify that Graves was not at the house, and when she refused to lie, law enforcement officials told her that they would arrest her for outstanding traffic warrants if she testified as a witness for Graves. Finally, Albert "Squeaky" Wright has claimed that he stopped by Graves's apartment twice on the night of the murders, once to use the telephone and once to get some bread. He said he was at Graves's apartment from approximately midnight until 12:45 a.m. or later, and he saw Graves there with Mathis.[26]

Anthony Graves is in prison for stabbing and bludgeoning five people to death with a mail-order knife and a hammer. He did not have a weapon capable of inflicting the lethal wounds. He did not have any reason to kill anyone in the house, much less five people. And he was at his own house at the time of the murders. Yet he awaits execution on Texas's death row because Robert Carter told a lie and said Graves had helped him.

The lack of any physical evidence against Graves, the fact that Carter repeatedly recanted, and even the sheer implausibility of the state's case no longer matter. When a defendant faces the death penalty, the burden is on the state to prove beyond a reasonable doubt that the defendant committed murder and deserves to be sentenced to death. Once the defendant is convicted and sent to death row, however, it is not enough to make the state's case disappear. He cannot get off unless he can prove that no reasonable juror would have voted to convict him. In other words, the burden of proof that a convicted death row inmate must sustain is substantially heavier than the burden of proof that the state must sustain at the trial. The implication of this asymmetry should be obvious: It is easier in our system to convict someone who did not commit a crime than to have that conviction set aside once we have evidence of the person's innocence.

Anthony Graves is a soft-spoken man who talks to me with exaggerated politeness. The Texas Innocence Network, which I direct, has been working with Graves's lawyers to establish his innocence. The dogged team of students is led by Nicole Casarez, a lawyer and journalism professor. They believe that the police and prosecutors lied and cheated. They are convinced that Graves is an innocent man.

I tell Graves what he already knows: that the students and Professor Casarez are turning every stone, but there is not going to be any DNA evidence. The investigators are not going to find the person who committed the crime and persuade him to confess, because that person—Robert Carter—already has confessed. There is no drama left.

I tell Graves that his case is not really about whether he committed the crime. He nods as if he understands, as if he understands the limitations that AEDPA places on the court, but I doubt he actually does, and in a moment, his questions will prove it. (Ninety percent of law school graduates, I would guess, do not understand AEDPA.) I tell Graves that we will do everything we can to establish his innocence, and he says he knows that, but I tell him that no matter what we find, it might not matter. It might not get us back into court. It might not impel a court to take another look at his case. He asks why, and I tell him the answer, which is a sterile explanation of federal law. I start to tell him about the idea of finality, that Congress and the federal courts want cases to end at a certain point. He looks at me quizzically, nodding slightly, but with a perplexed look in his eyes. How can it not matter that he is innocent? I do not even try to answer him. I just put my hand on the glass partition between us—which is how I shake hands with my clients—and tell him I will be back soon.

CHAPTER SIX

INTERLUDE:
WHY INNOCENCE MATTERS

I think the question, if I got it correctly, was do I think the death pen-alty is immoral because it will—I have to say it—it will inevitably lead at some point to the condemnation of someone who is innocent. Well, of course it will. I mean, you cannot have any system of human justice that is going to be perfect. And if the death penalty is immoral for that reason, so is life in prison. You think you're not going to have innocent people put in prison for life? It's one of the risks of living in an orga-nized human society. . . . I don't think that the system becomes immoral because it cannot be perfect. . . . I don't think you can judge the validity of any criminal law system on the basis of whether now and then it might make a mistake.

JUSTICE ANTONIN SCALIA

Our procedure has always been haunted by the ghost of the innocent man convicted. It is an unreal dream.

JUDGE LEARNED HAND

Justice Antonin Scalia does not support executing the innocent; he would not condone executing someone if he knew that the person was indeed innocent. He is simply willing to bite the bullet and say that he realizes we will make mistakes. The question Justice Scalia demands that we answer is this: Why does the fact that we will execute innocent people cause death penalty supporters to stop supporting the death penalty?

Judge Hand says: Executing an innocent person is a nightmare. But Judge Hand's visceral reaction, which Justice Scalia probably shares, is no answer at all. Law is not made up of visceral reactions. Law is about rules and principles. A good part of the first year of law school is spent teaching students to distinguish their feelings—their visceral reactions—from their analyses. To be sure, there is no rigid boundary between these domains: What we call "feelings" influences our ideas, and vice versa, but in legal discourse, it is never enough to express a feeling. Both Judge Hand and Justice Scalia agree that executing an innocent man *feels* wrong.

The question is whether that feeling undermines the legitimacy of capital punishment itself. What is the principle or rule that leads to that conclusion?[1] Justice Scalia does not see how it follows that the *occasional* execution of someone who is innocent entails that the death penalty is *always* wrong. He asks how that can be so. Judge Hand does not answer the question. Justice Scalia believes that there is no answer.

The question I would like to examine, therefore, is this: Why don't all supporters of the death penalty exhibit Justice Scalia's steely approach? Or, put somewhat differently: Why do some supporters of the death penalty turn against the punishment upon discovering that innocent people end up on death row? Is there a reason or a principle that underlies Judge Hand's visceral reaction, and if so, what is it?

In a famous law review article ("famous" by law review article standards, at any rate), former Judge Henry Friendly argued that whether a convicted prison inmate is actually innocent should have a significant impact on how an appellate court treats that inmate when he complains about the violation of his constitutional rights.[2] In other words, Judge Friendly argued, whether a judge should care about a violation of an inmate's constitutional rights —or, perhaps more precisely, whether a judge should be moved to act when confronted with a constitutional violation—should be influenced by whether the judge believes the inmate to be innocent. Judge Friendly shared the same visceral reaction that Judge Hand expressed; they were both bothered greatly by the specter of executing the innocent. Yet neither has answered Scalia: What makes "innocence" so special just because the punishment is death? If the fact that we execute innocent people has any legal or moral relevance, it must be for a reason that we have yet to articulate.

Recall that a death penalty trial is actually two trials. At the first trial, the jury decides whether the defendant committed the act that the state has accused him of doing. The word *innocent* works well in the context of this first trial. If the defendant did not do it, we say he is innocent. When an innocent man is found guilty of a crime he did not commit, we have made a mistake at the first trial.

Most mistakes, however, occur at the second trial, the trial that determines the punishment. Mistakes are rare at the first trial because most defendants did do what the state has accused them of doing; probably more than 90 percent of all criminal defendants did what the state said they did.[3] But that is only the beginning of the matter in death penalty cases. After the jury finds the defendant guilty, it has to decide whether the state should execute the defendant. At this second trial, the punishment phase, the defense does not contest the state's version of what happened; instead, it tries to show the jurors that the defendant is a human being who possesses qualities worth saving.

The Supreme Court has held that a state is not permitted to execute someone simply because that person has committed murder;[4] instead, the state must convince the jury that the defendant is among the worst of the worst. The idea that underlies the process of bifurcating capital trials into two separate proceedings is to ensure that, at the punishment phase, the jury singles out for execution the truly unreformable murderers. In the language of death penalty jurisprudence, the punishment phase performs a "narrowing function"; it reduces the total universe of murderers into a smaller subset of those murderers who are distinctively worthy of death.

When we make a mistake at the first trial and erroneously conclude that a defendant committed an act that he actually did not commit, we have convicted an innocent man. However, sometimes we make a mistake at the second trial by sentencing to death a defendant who does not warrant execution. This type of mistake occurs more frequently than the first type in death penalty cases, and it has nothing to do with innocence. But this type of mistake, I believe, is just as bad as executing the innocent.

Neither Johnny Martinez (whom we met in chapter 3) nor Carl Johnson (whom we discussed in chapter 1) was among the worst of the worst. Therefore, neither should have been sentenced to death. Both received the death penalty not because a jury considered all the details of their lives and deemed the men irredeemable, *but because their lawyers did not do their jobs.* When a jury sentences a defendant to death because the defendant's lawyer put on no evidence that would have persuaded the jury to spare the defendant's life, innocence is irrelevant. Both Martinez and Johnson did what the state said they did. The system did not make a mistake at their first trial. But the system did err at the second trial. It is quite reasonable to believe that had either of these men had the resources to hire a competent lawyer who would have conducted a thorough investigation into the defendant's background, or had the state paid an appointed lawyer enough money to conduct such an investigation, neither Martinez nor Johnson would have been executed. The same goes for hundreds of other men who have been executed over the last thirty years.[5]

Arguments about innocence fail to capture another group of death row inmates as well. On August 26, 2004, Texas executed James Allridge for a murder Allridge had committed nineteen years earlier. Allridge's case moved through the appellate process much more slowly than is possible in the years since AEDPA was enacted. During his long stay on death row, Allridge, who had grown up under the tutelage of habitual criminals, was fully rehabilitated.[6] He became a renowned artist, whose greeting cards were sold all over the world. He ministered to other inmates, both on death row and off. On more than one occasion, he intervened in conflicts between guards and prisoners, probably helping to save guards' lives. Prior to his execution, various prison guards signed affidavits urging that Allridge's death sentence be set aside. Yet it proved impossible to construct a winning legal argument based on Allridge's transformation. His lawyers could not identify a major constitutional error that had occurred at his trial; nor could they claim that he was innocent. Hence, despite the fact that he was manifestly and indisputably rehabilitated (which even the state conceded), Allridge was executed.

The key issue in most death penalty cases, then, is not whether the defendant *did* what the state said he did, but whether he should be executed. In most cases, therefore, the idea of innocence does not help us answer the question that truly matters.

There is another reason that innocence is a distraction. Innocent people die every day. The issue of innocence is a distraction because if the death penalty is valuable to society, it does not lose its value when innocent lives are lost. This, I believe, is the point that Justice Scalia was making. The cost of having the society we desire is the occasional loss of innocent life.

To be sure, the loss of innocent life may sadden us, but it is a price we have decided to pay in numerous contexts. For example, as a society we have chosen not to ban cigarettes even though innocent people die from inhaling secondhand smoke. We have decided not to ban alcohol even though innocent people die when drunk drivers cause traffic accidents. We have decided not to ban firearms even though innocent children and convenience store workers get fatally shot. We build interstate highways even though speeding vehicles will kill innocent workers. The list of things we tolerate despite their toll on human lives goes on and on. In all these cases, our reasoning is the same: Despite the obvious costs, we as a society have concluded that the price is justified, since the benefits outweigh the negatives.

Justice Scalia has performed the same calculus in the context of capital punishment. Like him, a death penalty supporter might conclude that the cost of executing the innocent is worth incurring. Why might we as a society have decided to pay that price in the context of the death penalty? To answer that question, we must know why someone would support the death penalty in the first place. In general, death penalty proponents believe at least one of the following propositions: (1) that executing someone is cheaper than life in prison, (2) that the death penalty deters other murderers and thereby saves lives,[7] or (3) that retribution demands that someone who takes a life pay with his own life. The first justification is economic, the second is the deterrence rationale, and the third is the retributive rationale.

None of these justifications is sound, but death penalty supporters take issue with that.[8] Death penalty supporters believe in at least one of these justifications or some combination of the three: economics, deterrence, and retribution. The question, therefore, is why someone who supports the death penalty for, say, economic reasons softens that support when confronted with the obvious fact that innocent people are convicted.

Justice Scalia points out that we as a society continue to believe in sending criminals to prison even though we at times mistakenly incarcerate an innocent person. We continue to imprison people who commit felonies because keeping criminals in prison makes society safer and serves as a legitimate punishment for people who commit serious crimes. Some people whom we sentence to prison wrongfully will never be able to prove their innocence and may well spend the rest of their lives in prison, and we must realize that that is true, but still we as a society do not turn against prison. Why, then, does support for the death penalty waver when death penalty supporters confront the fact that we as a society sometimes make mistakes?

One answer is simply that death is different. But this is not really an answer at all. Just as society makes the decision to use jury trials and prisons even though innocent people sometimes die in prison, society performs a similar calculus in numerous contexts. War is the most obvious case. When we go to war, we know that innocent civilians, both American and foreign, will die. We regret the loss of innocent life, but the fact that we know with certainty that innocent people will die does not cause us to abandon the war effort. The premise of Justice Scalia's view is that the war on crime is like the war on terror. Both wars aspire to worthy goals. Both wars are profoundly important. Both are necessary to making our society safer. Unfortunately, both involve the occasional loss of innocent life.

Of course, in theory, just wars are an example of self-defense, only on a much larger scale. Nevertheless, the uncomfortable truth is that we perform the same calculus and accept the same loss of innocent lives even in contexts where self-defense is entirely irrelevant. That is why we do not ban smoking and drinking. The simple fact of the matter is that we tolerate the loss of innocent life, even in areas where all we gain is convenience or comfort. That is what makes Justice Scalia's question so trenchant. If you think that the death penalty is cheaper, or that it deters murder, why would you be against the death penalty when you suddenly open your eyes to the obvious fact that innocent people die? If the death penalty is cheaper when it works perfectly, it is still cheaper when it misfires on occasion. If the death penalty deters a certain number of murders every time it is carried out, it still deters that same number, even if an innocent person is executed every once in a while. We do not ban tobacco. Why should we abandon the death penalty?

Why, in short, does the execution of an innocent person cause a visceral reaction that we do not feel when an innocent civilian dies in war or an innocent highway worker gets run over while smoothing asphalt? What is the legal principle hiding behind this "feeling"?[9]

The reason we react as we do when confronted with the execution of an innocent man is that we have done something we have promised not to do. The biblical rule of *lex taliones*, often cited (albeit erroneously) by death penalty supporters,[10] specifies an *eye for an eye*. Unless the defendant kills, we as a society are not permitted to take his life. In the case of war and highway construction, we say that we will try to avoid civilian casualties. We say we will try to avoid the loss of innocent lives. But road repair and warfare are not entirely predictable, and we can make no guarantees. That is not what we as a society say to criminal defendants. We say something quite different: We say that we will punish them for what they did, *and only for what they did*. This is the principle of just deserts. We tell suspected wrongdoers that in accordance with this principle, we will impose punishment only when we can prove beyond a reasonable doubt that they did something unlawful. Indeed, as a society we are so deeply committed to this principle of just deserts that we say we would prefer to let ten guilty people go free than punish even a single innocent person.[11] When we execute someone who has committed no crime, we are violating the principle of just deserts; we are breaking the social compact.

It is of course true that we likewise violate this principle when we imprison someone who has done no wrong, and Justice Scalia points out that we do not stop using prisons just because we sometimes incarcerate innocent people. Justice Scalia is obviously right about that, but there is a reason that we do not abandon prisons, and a reason that we do not have the same visceral reaction that accompanies the execution of an innocent person. That reason is that in the case of wrongful imprisonment, we have the opportunity to correct the mistake, to compensate someone for the injury caused by the violation of this principle; in the case of wrongful imprisonment, we remain hopeful that we can correct our mistakes. When we kill, we cannot mend the damage to our values; when we wrongfully execute, we are unable to right our wrong.

There is a difference between something that is *tragic* and something that is ethically and legally *wrong*. When an innocent civilian is bombed, when an innocent highway worker is struck and killed, the loss of human life is tragic. When an innocent inmate is executed, the tragedy is compounded by the violation of one of the foundational principles that make up our system of criminal justice. The difference between the innocent highway worker and the innocent execution victim is the difference between a tragedy and a broken promise. It is the difference between accidentally bombing a wedding party in Iraq while pursuing terrorists and the abuses at Abu Ghraib. It is the difference between a horrible accident and the failure of a principle.

When we execute someone who is innocent, we have violated a principle that lies at the very heart of our nation's criminal justice system, with no hope of repairing the damage. Judge Hand's visceral reaction turns out to be masking something else. When we execute an innocent man, we are betraying our principles.[12]

But there is nothing unique or special about the principle of just deserts. It is only one of several foundational principles that lie at the heart of our legal system, *and they are all of equal importance*, both legally and morally. For example, we have a principle that precludes the use of race as a decisional criterion. Suppose, however, that two defendants, one black and one white, rape and murder a young white college student. The jury finds both guilty and then sentences one to death and the other to life in prison. Upon investigation, we learn that the jury sentenced the black defendant to death while sparing the white defendant because the jury was made up entirely of racists who are especially repulsed by black-on-white rape. In other words, one defendant got death and the other got life *not* because the jury performed the constitutionally required "narrowing function," but because of simple racism. The Constitution, of course, forbids us from sentencing some defendants to death while sparing others simply because of their race (or the race of their victims), or from sentencing the poor to death while sparing the wealthy, but when this principle of equal treatment is violated—as it routinely is in death penalty cases—the language of innocence has no bearing.

The principle of just deserts says: People should not get punished if they do nothing wrong. The principle of equal protection says: People should not get punished on account of their race, the race of their victims, their religion, or their socioeconomic status. These principles are different, but they are of equal importance. (If anything, one could plausibly maintain that the equal protection principle is the single most important principle in the American legal culture, even more important than the principle of just deserts. But I am not interested in splitting hairs. For now I am content to say that both principles are important, neither one more than the other.) When we execute an innocent person, we violate one of the principles that we hold dear. But even when we execute someone who is not innocent, the strong likelihood is that we are violating some other principle that we hold equally dear.

When our actions violate our principles, our actions are wrong. It is wrong to execute innocent people because executing innocent people violates our principles. As counterintuitive as it may seem, it is equally wrong to execute guilty people because their executions, as we have seen, violate our principles as well, and in a way we can never correct. Our obsessive focus on innocence has so far prevented us from seeing that.

CHAPTER SEVEN

HOW THE RULE OF LAW
BECAME MOB RULE

Murders are more common in America than anywhere else on earth. Murder trials, therefore, unless they involve celebrities, are seldom noticed. There are obviously exceptions, especially in this age of media saturation and court TV. Trials of children who kill their parents (think of the Menendez brothers), or parents who kill their children (think of Andrea Yates), or husbands or wives who kill their spouses (think of Scott Peterson), and trials of celebrities, of course (think of O. J. or Robert Blake), do garner fairly wide attention. But the typical murder trial—the typical rape-murder or the ordinary convenience store killing, any of the trials I have discussed in this book—are largely ignored by the national media.

The trial of Richard Allen Davis is an exception. Davis murdered Polly Klaas, a beautiful twelve-year-old girl. Davis's murder trial received massive national attention for a variety of reasons, including Polly's youthful innocence; the fact that Davis had been released from prison shortly before the murder and his trial therefore became a window into the hows and whys of the parole system; and finally because Davis appeared cold, unremorseful, and cruel. With a taunting visage, he made people want to execute him. Whatever the causes, a good part of America was transfixed by the proceedings.

Thus it was that on Thursday, September 26, 1996, Davis sat in a California courtroom and, in a statement carried live by CNN and replayed later that night by the three major network news shows, vilely accused Polly's father, Marc Klaas, of having sexually molested young Polly. Moments earlier, Klaas had stood at a podium and angrily told Davis that he would meet Hitler in hell. When Davis spewed his grotesque final insult, Klaas, who during his frequent interviews throughout the trial often seemed on the precipice of completely losing control, lunged wildly at Davis and had to be dragged from the courtroom. After the bailiffs restored relative calm, the judge told Davis that he ordinarily found the imposition of a death sentence a difficult and solemn moment, but that Davis had made his job rather simple. I can personally relate to that comment. If I had to sentence someone to death, I would want that person to be vile and unrepentant until the very moment of my pronouncement. I would want that person to seem inhuman.

On the eve of Davis's despicable and hateful statement, a former student of mine, Gil Epstein, was murdered in a parking lot as he was returning to his car after his weekly pickup basketball game. The apparent motive was robbery. The irony of the motive is unspeakably tragic, for Gil would have given anyone who asked —anyone—the shirt off his back. He was an assistant district attorney, an ebullient and caring young man, a loving son and a wonderful human being, as generous as Gandhi. I learned of Gil's murder on the morning of the day I was scheduled to teach a seminar on the Supreme Court's decision in the case of *Gray v. Netherland*,[1] which at that time was the Court's most recent death penalty case—a decision that held, in short, that the prosecutor can lie to the defense attorney about the type of evidence he plans to introduce at the penalty phase of a capital trial and the fact of the lie will not necessarily constitute a violation of the defendant's rights. Gil would never have done what the prosecutors in the *Netherland* case had done, and he would not have found it forgivable. He was a prosecutor, and he was a man of principle. He did not believe that his job was simply to secure convictions. He believed that his job was to do justice.

Gil's murderers were prosecuted by the state, just as scores of other murderers are each year, and just as Richard Davis was. Yet I care far more about the trial of the thugs who killed my friend Gil than I do about most murder prosecutions. In other words, I understand deeply that violent crime—and above all crimes like rape and murder—are brutally individual matters; people care more about some murders than they do about others. That is natural, and there is nothing wrong with it. We care more about murder victims who are not anonymous; we care more about victims we love than victims we detest. I cared more about Gil's murder than about the murder described in the case I was teaching that afternoon. Marc Klaas cared more about the prosecution of the man who took away his daughter than about the trial of the men who took away my friend. This fact is neither wrong nor right; it is simply a fact. Human beings are not connected equally to all human beings, and so we feel special pain when those to whom we are connected are injured or extinguished.

Yet justice is not supposed to be a personal matter. When someone commits a crime, that person has acted against all of society, against the entire state. Nothing conveys this powerful fact better than the very style of a case itself: the state versus Ted Bundy, for example, or the people versus O. J. Simpson, or the United States versus Timothy McVeigh. Of course it is true—it would be extraordinary if it were not—that the parents of the young girls whom Ted Bundy murdered cared more about the pursuit of justice in Bundy's case than they did in other murder cases. None of us cares equally about all crimes. The state, however, is supposed to. It is not supposed to care more when the murdered girl is the daughter of a rich man rather than the child of a single mother. My friend Gil would have prosecuted the murder of a homeless man as vigorously as he would have prosecuted the murder of the mayor.

In 458 BC, Aeschylus wrote *The Oresteia*, a trilogy of plays which the great classicist Robert Fagles, in his introduction to the Penguin edition, called "our rite of passage from savagery to civilization" (1984). In *The Oresteia* the state takes over from aggrieved individuals the task of pursuing justice. Athena realizes that the cycle of violence will be infinite if murdered family members act out on the urge to avenge their loved ones' murders. If Gil Epstein's family and friends pursue and punish Gil's murderers, then the family and friends of those we punish will pursue us. And our families and friends will pursue them. And so on, endlessly and forever. Justice cannot be personal, because if it is, it will never be done. That was Athena's insight. That is what it means to be a nation of laws.

The English word *state* is related to the Latin and Greek words *stater* and *statikos*, both of which pertain to weighing. *Statike* in Greek is the science of weighing. The state is a weigher. Legislators weigh pros and cons of various proposals and then enact statutes (the word comes from the same root). Likewise, in meting out justice in individual cases, the judge, the agent of the state, holds a scale in front of her hooded eyes.

Just as the scale implies weighing, the blindfold implies the irrelevance of the identities of the individuals standing before her. The state weighs, and it must do so blindly. This, I think, is Aeschylus's central point: Justice is modern only when the identities of the persons in the courtroom are irrelevant, only when actions alone, and not personalities, are placed on the scales of justice.

Until a decade ago, this Greek ideal had been nearly achieved in America. Criminal trials generally, and murder trials too, were managed not by the victims of the crime (or the relatives of a murder victim), but by the state. To be sure, not everything the state has done in the name of justice has been irreproachable. Many more death sentences are sought, for example, against those who murder whites than those who murder blacks. In addition, the state has sometimes seemed indifferent to the injury done to the immediate victims of criminals: those whose homes are robbed, those whose loved ones are taken. Nevertheless, even if certain aspects of the state's decision making seemed objectionable, the system as a whole still partook of the majestic ideal identified by the Greeks, which was absent on the frontier: the replacement of the blood feud with justice pursued by the state.

But in the early 1990s everything began to unravel in America. Americans had grown weary and frustrated with increasing crime rates (or at least the perception of increasing crime). Crime victims began to organize and complain that the state cared more about criminals than it did about them; and the state, rather than explain the concept of constitutional protections to a frustrated and angry audience, decided instead to let the victims vent. It decided, in other words, to endorse the personalization of violence rather than to explain the difference between anger and justice. And finally, the dam broke in the 1991 case of *Payne v. Tennessee*, when the Supreme Court lent its weight to this personalization of justice.

To convey just how radical a capitulation *Payne* was, I want to describe three scenarios and how the American legal system has traditionally responded to them.[2] First, suppose that Harry comes home from work one evening and finds a note from his wife saying that she has left him. He grabs a bottle of whiskey and his shotgun and goes out to the back porch, drinking whiskey and firing his gun until his anger leaves him. He damages quite a few trees, but nothing more. Second, suppose that Harriet arrives home and learns that her husband has left her. Like Harry, she grabs a bottle and a gun and steps outside to drink and shoot until she feels better. Like Harry, she damages some trees. Unfortunately, that is not all. She also kills a homeless man named Darryl, who was sleeping in the woods. Finally, suppose that everything is as it was in scenario number 2, except that instead of killing Darryl, Harriet kills the Reverend Thomas Olsen, an amateur entomologist who was searching for a rare beetle in the woods behind Harriet's house.

The legal and philosophical literature pays a great deal of attention to the distinction between scenario 1, on the one hand, and scenarios 2 and 3, on the other.[3] The reason for this attention is not difficult to understand, for there is a very real sense in which Harry and Harriet have *done* the same thing. By drinking and shooting their guns randomly, both acted recklessly in exactly the same way. The difference was one of luck. Harriet happened to kill somebody, whereas Harry did not. Yet the law takes consequences into account when meting out punishment. That is why a drunk driver who runs a red light and kills someone will be punished more severely than a driver who runs a red light and totals someone's car without killing anyone. In every jurisdiction in America, Harriet will be subject to a more severe punishment than Harry will.

But does the fact that we distinguish between Harry and Harriet also mean that we should distinguish between scenarios 2 and 3? Put differently, does the fact that the legal system attributes relevance to the consequences of one's reckless actions also mean that the legal system should draw distinctions among victims of crime when deciding how severely to punish people who are reckless? Should we punish Harriet more severely when she kills Olsen instead of homeless Darryl? Until 1991, the answer was no. In the case of *Booth v. Maryland*,[4] which the Supreme Court decided in 1987, the Court ruled that the suffering experienced by the surviving family members of a murder victim is a factor that the jury cannot consider when deciding whether to execute someone. Extending the reasoning of *Booth*, the Court ruled two years later, in the case of *South Carolina v. Gathers*,[5] that the prosecutor cannot ask the jury to sentence someone to death by focusing narrowly on the personal characteristics of the murder victim. The logic of these decisions is easy to see: When someone like Johnny Martinez stabs a convenience store clerk, he does not know anything about the characteristics of the person he is stabbing. He does not know whether his victim hopes to enter the ministry or whether he is working at a convenience store as a front to sell narcotics. His crime is that he has *murdered* somebody, not that he has murdered a person with certain *characteristics*. His crime is the same, regardless of whether the murder victim was the nicest man you have ever known or a surly misanthrope.

The difference between Darryl and Olsen is not that one is more human than the other. The difference is that more people know Olsen, more people love him. There are more people to whom the murder of Olsen *matters*. From the standpoint of the state, however, these two murders are equally bad. Both Darryl and Olsen were law-abiding citizens whose lives were taken from them wrongfully. And yet, precisely because more people know Olsen, more people clamor for justice in his case. These are the voices to which the Supreme Court succumbed in *Payne v. Tennessee*[6] when it overruled *Booth* and *Gathers* and held that during a capital murder prosecution, the state could introduce testimony from relatives of the murder victim pertaining to how the murder of their loved one had affected their personal lives. No longer would the focus be solely on the fact that one human being had murdered another, which is the quintessential focus when justice is blind; rather the focus would again be on personal qualities and identities. Harriet would be treated leniently if her victim was Darryl because Darryl had no loved ones—no parents, no children, no spouse, no friends—who could attend the trial and talk about how they had been affected by his death. Yet Harriet would be treated severely if she inadvertently killed Olsen because his wife and children, his friends and congregants, could appear and tell the jury how grievously they had suffered. As individuals, we care more about some people than we care about others. But in the eyes of the state, we are all the same, we are all individual human lives. When law distinguishes between Darryl and Olsen, it is no longer blind. Aeschylus's justice is emphatically impersonal, but in *Payne* the Supreme Court rejected Athena's model and embraced a return to the blood feud.

In truth, and to be entirely fair, the Supreme Court did not so much cause the problem as legitimize it. For even prior to the Court's decision, prosecutors and especially judges, most of whom are elected officials, had already begun to depart from Athena's ideal. Most significantly, state trial judges in a number of states had been permitting relatives of murder victims to address the convicted murderer at the culmination of the proceedings. (*Payne* held that they could do so *during* the proceedings.) Inevitably, these highly charged moments would be broadcast on local news coverage (they do make for riveting viewing), and in more than a handful of instances families of the murder victim and of the murderer would exchange taunts if not blows in the corridors of the courthouse. When Richard Davis and Polly Klaas's father, Marc, hurled venom at each other in a California courtroom, the state was no longer running the justice system; it was standing back and watching a dogfight.

Justice is, at least in part, about control. Individuals feel passion, but the role of the state is to be dispassionate. Indeed, part of what it means to be civilized is to understand that our personal emotions, our individual lives, should not dictate the state's pursuit of justice. Our individual urges to lash out are precisely what the state's act of weighing must supplant. Grief, emptiness, frustration, and even rage are perfectly appropriate human responses to murderous violence. These are the emotions that we humans experience, and I for one would not want *not* to feel them. But these responses are not justice, and they ought not to be vented in the courtroom, which is justice's hall. When we confuse justice with revenge, we revert to savagery.

Becoming savage is one manifestation of the demise of the rule of law in death penalty cases, but in truth this demise has many iterations. Barely half a century ago, many states assigned children to schools based on their race. The practice of racial segregation was so deeply embedded in the culture of the South that when the Supreme Court declared racial segregation unconstitutional in 1954,[7] many southern states simply chose not to adhere to the Court's command. States acted lawlessly. Local politicians and state court judges flouted the rule of law. They declared their opposition to the Court's decision. They claimed not to be subordinate to the Court or federal law. They announced they would thwart the federal courts' efforts to implement desegregation. They pandered to their constituents' worst instincts.

Yet the federal government would have none of it. First President Eisenhower, and later Presidents Kennedy and Johnson, made it clear that federal troops would be used to enforce the Supreme Court's orders. The Court was steadfast, issuing a series of unanimous opinions that sent the clear message that even though the justices may have disagreed about the particulars of certain decisions, they were united in rejecting the dangerous proposition that states could disregard the Court's authority. In doing their part to desegregate American society, the justices of the Supreme Court realized that the Court's currency is not control over the purse or the sword; its currency is its judgment. When the people lose faith in the Court's judgment, the Court itself—and with it, the institution of judicial review—will be mortally wounded. It is for precisely this reason that so many observers were scornful of the Court's decision to intervene in the presidential election of 2000. And yet, as astonishing and as unprecedented as the Court's intrusion into the election was, the case of *Bush v. Gore* [8] did not even compare with the more recent case of *Kelly v. South Carolina*[9] in terms of a threat to the Court's very legitimacy.

Kelly, decided by the Supreme Court in 2002, was brought by a death row inmate in South Carolina. This inmate argued that his rights had been violated because the jury that sentenced him was not told that he would spend the rest of his life in prison, with no possibility for parole, if he were not sentenced to death. What is extraordinary about the *Kelly* case is that it was not the first time this issue had come up in South Carolina. As a matter of fact, it was not even the second time. In 1994, in a case involving a death row inmate named Simmons, the Supreme Court ruled, by a lop-sided vote of seven to two, that a death penalty defendant who will spend the rest of his life in prison if he is not sentenced to death has a right to have the jury know that fact.[10]

The South Carolina Supreme Court, however, responded just as the southern states had during the desegregation era. In the next case that came along raising essentially the same issue, the state supreme court ignored federal law and upheld the death sentence. The inmate, Wesley Shafer, took his case to the Supreme Court, where he too prevailed by the same seven-to-two margin. In its *Shafer* decision,[11] the U.S. Supreme Court flatly explained that South Carolina had attempted to limit the *Simmons* decision—something lower courts are not permitted to do.

But just as southern racist governors and other politicians continued to resist federal orders to desegregate a generation ago, South Carolina prosecutors and judges were not chastened by the Supreme Court's action in *Shafer*. Prosecutors and judges, and even the state supreme court, continued to ignore the Constitution. They kept doing the same thing they had already twice been told they could not do. The Supreme Court was therefore compelled to intervene a third time, in this instance in the case of death row inmate William Kelly. Like Simmons and Shafer before him, Kelly was sentenced to death without the jury's knowledge that he would spend the rest of his life in prison if he were not sent to death row. In a blunt repudiation of the state court's decision, the Supreme Court held that the state court's decision in Kelly's case was unrealistic and "flatly at odds" with the law.

But this is not just a story, or even primarily a story, about the lawlessness of the South Carolina Supreme Court. It is mostly a story about death penalty law and the legitimacy of the Supreme Court of the United States. In the *Simmons* case, the first South Carolina case to reach the Supreme Court, Justice Scalia, joined by Justice Thomas, dissented. Scalia characterized Simmons's lawyers, and death penalty lawyers in general, as guerrillas bent on subverting the rule of law. What is so extraordinary about this libel, aside from the outburst itself, is precisely that Simmons prevailed by such a decisive vote.

Justice Scalia's view in *Simmons* was a minority view, but there is nothing unusual about a dissent by Justice Scalia in a case where a death row inmate prevails. What is far more notable than his view of the merits of the case is the refusal by Justices Scalia and Thomas to join the majority in sending a message to the South Carolina Supreme Court when the issue arose for the second time. It is one thing for Supreme Court justices to continue to adhere to their views even when those views do not command a majority of the Court; it is quite another to insinuate, by deed or by silence, that lower courts, including state courts, are permitted to follow a dissenting opinion. Yet that is exactly what Justice Scalia did. Justice Scalia, a practicing Catholic who has criticized the doctrinal soundness of the church's opposition to capital punishment, winked at the South Carolina Supreme Court. By refusing to join his colleagues in telling South Carolina that, like it or not, the state must follow federal law, Justice Scalia, along with Justice Thomas, fomented South Carolina's lawlessness. And stunningly, when the issue arose for a third time in a span of eight short years, two other justices lost their resolve.[12] Whereas *Simmons* and *Shafer* were decided by votes of 7 to 2, Kelly prevailed by a vote of only 5 to 4 (with Chief Justice Rehnquist and Associate Justice

Kennedy joining Justices Scalia and Thomas).[13] If the Court had been composed of judges like these in the 1950s and 1960s, blacks and whites would still be eating lunch at separate counters.

In no other area of law would this type of lawlessness by a state court be countenanced, much less encouraged. Murder is undoubtedly among the ugliest of crimes, but it is beyond ironic when our response to horrific crimes is to embrace the lawless tactics of the vigilante. One's view of the merits of the *Simmons* case is beside the point. We have a nation of laws. These laws apply to state courts, and even accused murderers can claim their protection. When the Supreme Court loses sight of these rather elementary propositions, it despoils the very rule of law.

In the same way that children mime the actions and attitudes of their parents, the lower federal courts watch and emulate the Supreme Court. They watched the Court brook disdain in the South Carolina cases. They perceived impatience with constitutional rights and values when those rights were being invoked by residents on death row. And so it comes as little surprise that the indifference to legal rules and principles that has grown prevalent on the nation's highest court has seeped into the entire federal system.

No court epitomizes this indifference, and even hostility, to the rule of law better than the Fifth Circuit, which is responsible for reviewing death penalty cases from Texas, Louisiana, and Mississippi. And no episode of litigation better illustrates the Fifth Circuit's attitude than a series of challenges to the chemical mixture used in carrying out executions in late 2003 and early 2004.

On Tuesday, December 9, 2003, the state of Texas played Russian roulette with Billy Vickers. Early that afternoon, prison authorities removed him from his cell on death row, at the Polunsky unit in Livingston, Texas, and drove him to the Walls unit, sometimes known as the death house, in Huntsville. They placed Vickers in a holding cell outside the execution chamber, where he would spend his final hours, in anticipation of a six o'clock execution. Vickers ate his last meal, thanked his lawyer, and said his good-byes. It was five o'clock. Every time Vickers heard a commotion, he thought the executioners were coming for him. He paced back and forth in his tiny cell, chain-smoking cigarettes that the guards, ignoring prison regulations, had provided. It was eight o'clock, and then nine. Vickers was ready for it to be over. Then midnight arrived, and Vickers was still alive. The death warrant had expired.

The guards outside the holding cell and prison officials knew before eight o'clock that there would be no execution on that day, but they decided not to tell Vickers. They deliberately tortured him by withholding this information. Finally, shortly after midnight, the guards laughed and told him they knew he would not be executed that night. Prison authorities loaded Vickers into the back of a van and returned him to his sixty-square-foot cell on Texas's death row.

A month and a half later, on Wednesday, January 28, 2004, shortly after 6 p.m. local time, the state of Texas finally executed the convicted murderer. He was the fourth person to be executed in Texas in 2004, and the 317th since the death penalty had resumed in 1982.

Vickers was a so-called career criminal, not a sympathetic character. Prior to being convicted of capital murder and sentenced to death in 1993 for murdering Phillip Kinslow during a robbery, Vickers had been twice convicted of burglary, twice convicted of being a felon in possession of burglary tools, and once convicted of arson and conspiracy to commit arson. The evidence that he killed Kinslow was substantial. On the gurney on the evening of January 28, Vickers took responsibility for as many as a dozen other murders. His motive for confessing to additional murders is perhaps difficult to understand, but we can say with a high degree of confidence that Vickers was not a good person. He committed at least one murder, and maybe quite a few more. His case has nothing to do with actual innocence. Instead, it lays bare the way the legal system deals with a man whose guilt is not in question.

Vickers's case is that proverbial suitcase full of money that we find when we pick up the wrong bag on the airport carousel. We know what we are supposed to do with it. We know it is not ours to keep. But it is a lot of money. The temptation tests our principles. Vickers tested our principles, and our principles failed.

Inmates on death row can file two different types of legal proceedings. If they are challenging the legality of either their conviction or their sentence, they must use the writ of habeas corpus.[14] Indeed, the only purpose of the writ of habeas corpus is to compel the government to defend its detention of an inmate (or its intention to carry out a certain sentence). For that very reason, the federal habeas corpus statute provides that a federal court may grant a writ of habeas corpus on behalf of a state prisoner "*only* on the ground that he is in custody in violation of the Constitution or laws or treaties of the United States."[15] But there are other problems death row inmates might want to complain about. If guards beat them, if they are kept in squalid conditions, or if they are given no food, they are entitled to file a lawsuit to complain about their treatment. The fact that we are going to execute someone does not mean that we can treat him any way we wish prior to the execution.

But challenging one's treatment is not the same as saying that one's conviction is invalid. An inmate whom the guards beat can concede that the state is permitted to execute him yet also complain about the fact that he was beaten. How must such an inmate proceed? If an inmate concedes that the state may punish him as it intends (by executing him, for example) yet wants to avoid being tortured in the interim, how does he do so? The appropriate device is a "1983 action"—named after the section in the statute (section 1983) that authorizes such suits. Actions brought under section 1983 are a type of civil rights litigation. Although the law pertaining to 1983 litigation is arcane and complex, prisoners who challenge the conditions of their confinement routinely use it.

Before he was executed in May 2002, Johnny Martinez (the subject of chapter 3) filed a suit under section 1983. As we saw earlier, he was executed without ever having had a federal court evaluate the merits of various legal challenges he brought, because the lawyer appointed by the state in prior legal proceedings had taken steps that caused Martinez's rights to be forfeited. As we also saw, the fate that befell Martinez was not unique; many death row inmates in Texas suffered the same forfeiture of their rights because of the ineptitude of their lawyers, all of whom were appointed by the state. Consequently, in the late spring of 2002, Martinez and two other death row inmates, Napoleon Beazley and Gary Etheridge, sued the state of Texas, contending that the state had effectively denied them access to the federal courts by appointing incompetent lawyers during state court proceedings. The inmates were making the simple claim that the state had cleverly insulated its unconstitutional behavior from federal court review by saddling the death row inmates with poor lawyers who took steps in state court proceedings to cause the inmates' rights to be waived for purposes of federal court review.[16] These inmates were not challenging the legality of either their convictions or their sentences. Instead they were claiming that the state could not cynically force them to be represented by incompetent lawyers whose incompetence would ensure that they could never have a federal judge determine the constitutionality of their death sentences.[17]

Because these inmates were not challenging either the legality of their conviction or their sentence, they did not bring this lawsuit as a habeas corpus proceeding. Instead, they filed a civil rights suit. They lost, and all were executed in the summer of 2002. In rejecting their suit, however, the federal courts did not address the merits of their complaint. Rather, the Fifth Circuit held that a suit under section 1983 was not available to these inmates.[18] The court's language in *Martinez* was broad. Essentially, the court held that a death row inmate could not challenge any aspect of his sentence through an action under section 1983; the sole procedural vehicle that could be used was the writ of habeas corpus.

The position of the Fifth Circuit obviously made no sense. The inmates were not claiming that their conviction or sentence was invalid. They were claiming that they were entitled to have a federal court *consider* whether their conviction or sentence was invalid, and the state of Texas had erected a byzantine statutory scheme that denied them access to federal courts. Because all these inmates had already filed a habeas corpus petition—the very reason they brought the civil rights suit was that they had filed a habeas corpus petition that the federal courts had been unable to consider on the merits because of the failures of the state habeas corpus lawyers—they were unable to file another habeas action.[19] Hence, if they could not bring their complaint as a civil rights action, there was no way to bring it at all. The ultimate consequence of the Fifth Circuit's decision in the *Martinez* case was that death row inmates, unlike other prisoners, have no legal vehicle that they can use to complain about conditions that they are constitutionally entitled to complain about. The state can disregard their rights with impunity because there is nothing the inmates can do.

In November 2003, about a year after the court issued the *Martinez* decision, lawyers representing death row inmates in Texas and several other states reached the conclusion that the combination of chemicals that many states were using to carry out executions violated the Eighth Amendment's prohibition on cruel and unusual punishments.[20] Evidence had come to light suggesting that the combination of chemicals used in Texas was not working exactly as intended.[21] There was reason to believe that the sedative administered wore off and that the chemical used to induce cardiac arrest was causing the inmates to suffocate to death. Witnesses to executions routinely report that execution victims appear to be going to sleep, but lawyers representing death row inmates came to believe that this appearance was misleading. The inmates appeared to be going to sleep, rather than suffering excruciating pain, not because the death was painless, but because another drug administered as part of the lethal cocktail paralyzes skeletal muscles and prevents the inmates from expressing any pain.

One group of inmates in Texas did not want to be tortured. Billy Vickers was one of them. Vickers conceded that the state could go forward with his planned execution, but he wanted the state to modify the chemical combination it planned to use. His problem was that he had no avenue to enter federal court. He could not file a habeas petition because he was not challenging the legality of his conviction or sentence. And he could not file an action under section 1983 because of the Fifth Circuit's decision in the *Martinez* case.

Then, on December 1, 2003, a week and one day before his scheduled execution, the Supreme Court decided to entertain an appeal on behalf of an Alabama death row inmate named David Nelson. Nelson had been a heavy drug user prior to arriving on death row. Alabama officials had therefore determined that they might need to employ a so-called cut-down procedure in order to gain access to one of Nelson's veins. Nelson did not want untrained people to slice him open—with no general anesthesia—to find a suitable vein. But his challenge was not a habeas action because he was not asking for relief from the conviction or sentence. He filed an action under section 1983. When the Supreme Court agreed to hear his appeal on December 1, it indicated that it would resolve the following question: "Whether a complaint brought under 42 U.S.C § 1983 by a death-sentenced state prisoner, who seeks to stay his execution in order to pursue a challenge to the procedures for carrying out the execution, is properly recharacterized as a habeas corpus petition under 28 U.S.C § 2254?"[22]

Obviously, the Supreme Court's resolution of the question presented in *Nelson* would do Martinez, Beazley, and Etheridge no good; they had long since been executed. But it did give new hope to Vickers, for it suggested that he could challenge the lethal injection cocktail under section 1983 after all.[23]

In one of the most important Eighth Amendment cases of the twentieth century, Chief Justice Warren explained: "The basic concept underlying the Eighth Amendment is nothing less than the dignity of man.... The Amendment must draw its meaning from the evolving standards of decency that mark the progress of a maturing society."[24]

The essence of the claim that Vickers wanted to litigate was straightforward. The Eighth Amendment prohibits punishments that are "cruel and unusual." The question whether a punishment is cruel can perhaps be answered in the abstract, but whether a punishment is "unusual" is a purely empirical issue. If many jurisdictions do something, then whatever they do is not unusual; it is common. If few jurisdictions do something, then it is unusual. Consequently, whether something is unusual is a dynamic question. A practice may be common today yet unusual a month from now if jurisdictions that currently use the practice gradually abandon it. This basic strand of death penalty law—that something can become unusual—is known as the "evolving standards of decency" norm. A society's standards evolve, and as they do, a practice that was formerly common may become less so, and eventually it may become unusual.[25]

The lawyers representing the death row inmates who wanted to challenge the legality of the chemical combination planned to argue that society's standards of decency had evolved in such a way as to prohibit the use of certain chemicals. Although death penalty lawyers had been familiar with the physiology that underlay the lethal injection claim for many years,[26] an important development caused those lawyers to believe that perhaps society's standards had indeed evolved such that the use of the drug combination was no longer permissible. In particular, most states had passed laws prohibiting veterinarians from euthanizing pets using the same protocol. Vickers argued that a chemical that a state had deemed unsuitable for killing stray dogs was also unsuitable for executing human beings.[27]

No central authority sets execution dates in Texas. Instead, the presiding judge of the court where the death row inmate was convicted sets the date, usually upon being asked to do so by the district attorney for that county. Until the mid-1990s, execution warrants quaintly directed the warden to carry out an execution "before sunrise" on a given date, meaning that executions occurred between midnight and dawn. In 1995 Texas began to carry out executions after 6 p.m. Thus, execution warrants in Texas now direct the warden to carry out the execution "after 6:00 p.m." on a given day. Whereas prior to 1995 prison authorities could carry out an execution in the roughly six-hour window between midnight and dawn, currently prison authorities must carry out the execution between 6 p.m. and midnight.

Texas had scheduled three executions for the week of December 8. Billy Vickers was scheduled to be executed after 6 p.m. on Tuesday, December 9, 2003. Kevin Zimmerman was scheduled for execution on Wednesday, December 10, and Bobby Hines was scheduled to be executed on Thursday, December 11. On Monday, December 8, 2003—just one week following the grant of *certiorari* in *Nelson*—Vickers, along with Zimmerman and Hines, filed a lawsuit in federal district court, pursuant to 42 U.S.C. § 1983, seeking to enjoin the use of a particular array of chemicals for executing death-sentenced inmates in Texas. The district court dismissed the action on December 8, one day before the scheduled execution.

Vickers appealed to the Fifth Circuit. He made two principal arguments in that appeal. First, he said, *Martinez* was not controlling because he was *not* challenging the mode or method of his execution; he was *not* claiming that lethal injection is categorically cruel and unusual punishment. Second, even if the court of appeals felt that *Martinez* was relevant, the Supreme Court's grant of *certiorari* in *Nelson* had cast serious doubt upon the validity of *Martinez*. "Do not execute me," Vickers said, "while the Supreme Court is figuring out whether I am entitled to bring this action."

At 1:30 on the afternoon of December 9, the date of the scheduled execution, the Fifth Circuit issued an unusual opinion.[28] The court of appeals stated that it was "keenly aware that the Supreme Court has under consideration the procedural question whether § 1983 is available as a vehicle for mounting attacks such as this; but until a different rule is announced, we continue to follow the procedure described by the district court."[29] Moreover, with respect to the merits of the underlying Eighth Amendment claim, the Fifth Circuit's opinion was also far from dismissive. The court noted: "Substantively, [Vickers has] submitted evidence that appears to be facially stronger than that which has supported prior complaints of this nature; but we are not in a posture to deal further with it under our present precedent."[30]

As I and Vickers's other lawyers read the panel's opinion, the court was signaling that it found the merits of the challenge intriguing but was precluded by circuit precedent from examining the merits.[31] The panel also noted that the Supreme Court's grant of *certiorari* in *Nelson* did seem to implicate the very circuit precedent that prevented it from inquiring further into the merits. The Fifth Circuit issued its opinion at approximately 3:30 p.m. on

December 9, 2003, the day of Vickers's scheduled execution. Although Vickers's lawyers had originally planned to seek immediate review in the Supreme Court, the language of the panel's opinion seemed to invite counsel to request en banc review—a procedure whereby a party can ask the entire court of appeals (which, in the case of the Fifth Circuit, comprises seventeen judges)[32] to review the decision of a three-judge panel. Consequently, at around 4 p.m. on December 9, Vickers's lawyers filed a motion seeking that the Fifth Circuit take the case en banc.

The Fifth Circuit is accustomed to deciding death penalty cases under the pressure of execution deadlines. Indeed, in the not-so-distant past the state of Texas used execution dates to drive death penalty litigation. By setting an execution date, the state coerces the courts to adjudicate cases faster than they might otherwise. This practice has provoked condemnation from some judges on the Fifth Circuit, including those not typically solicitous to claims brought by death row inmates.[33] The short of it is that the Fifth Circuit is a well-oiled machine when it comes to disposing of death penalty cases quickly to permit an execution to proceed on schedule. Yet at 5 o'clock there was still no decision on the motion for en banc review. The execution warrant directed the warden to execute Vickers after 6 p.m. Six o'clock arrived, and still there was no word from the court. Then it was 6:30, and 7, and still nothing. Vickers's lawyers concluded that the Fifth Circuit had to be on the verge of granting an en banc review, and that someone was writing a dissenting opinion, which was causing the delay. There was no other explanation for the silence. It was 7:30, then 8. Nothing. Then, at shortly past 8, more than two hours into the execution window, the clerk of the court phoned Vickers's lawyers and the attorney general's office. The clerk announced that the Fifth Circuit would be taking no further action on the case that evening. Everyone on the phone, Vickers's lawyers and the state's lawyers as well, were utterly nonplussed. The warden was holding a valid execution warrant directing him to carry out the execution before midnight, and the Fifth Circuit judges were going home. Vickers's lawyers asked the clerk whether a motion could be filed with the panel, requesting that the panel stay the execution until the en banc court issued an order the following day. The clerk's response was that Vickers could file anything he wanted, but the Fifth Circuit would be taking no further action that day. The clerk reminded counsel that because there was no stay in effect, the state was free to go forward with the execution.

At the same time that Vickers's lawyers had requested an en banc review in the Fifth Circuit, they had lodged a stay motion with the Supreme Court. Under this practice, lawyers can provide the clerk of the Supreme Court with pleadings that they will later file, so that the pleadings are already at the Court and are ready for distribution to the justices' chambers. Following the conference call, counsel for the parties engaged in a series of discussions regarding the appropriate course of action in light of the court of appeals' unprecedented action. The attorney general's office agreed that it would be inappropriate to execute Vickers under the circumstances. The attorney general informed Vickers's counsel that she would advise her client, the warden, not to carry out the execution. Vickers's lawyers asked whether she would put that in writing, but she declined.[34] Vickers's lawyers then asked whether she could assure them that the warden would heed her advice. She told them she could not. Finally, Vickers's lawyers attempted to speak directly with the warden, to ask him whether he intended to follow the advice of his lawyers in the attorney general's office, but Vickers's lawyers were denied permission to speak directly to the warden.

By that time it was 10 p.m. Vickers's lawyers had two choices: to do nothing or to inform the clerk at the Supreme Court that they wished to file the stay motion that they had lodged with the Court earlier that day. The advantage of filing the stay motion was that if the Court granted it, everyone could go home for the evening; the disadvantage was that if the Court denied it, the warden might perceive that he had been authorized to go forward with the execution. Vickers's counsel took a deep breath and decided to do nothing. Two hours later, the execution had not been carried out, and the execution warrant expired. Vickers was returned to death row.

A week after the Fifth Circuit took no action in Vickers's case, the state of Virginia set an execution date for James Reid. Lawyers for Reid in Virginia filed an action under 42 U.S.C. § 1983, challenging not only the specific chemical mixture that would be used to carry out the execution, but also the legality of the so-called cut-down procedure—the procedure that had been implicated in the *Nelson* case from Alabama. A panel of the Fourth Circuit stayed Reid's execution on December 17. The Fourth Circuit observed that the jurisdictional issue presented by Reid was similar if not identical to the issue the Supreme Court was going to decide in *Nelson*, and that it was therefore appropriate to stay the Reid execution pending *Nelson*. In other words, the Fourth Circuit, in contrast to the Fifth, ruled that it would be unjust to execute Reid while the Supreme Court was considering a case that would determine whether Reid was entitled to raise the challenge he was attempting to raise. The Virginia attorney general asked the Supreme Court to vacate the Fourth Circuit's stay, but, on December 18, the Supreme Court refused.[35] Like Vickers, Reid survived. Unlike Vickers, he did not owe his survival to sheer luck; it resulted from a sound decision by a federal court.

January 2004 was a busy month for executioners. On January 6, 2004, Texas executed Ynobe Matthews. Matthews had been— in the argot of death penalty lawyers—a volunteer, having refused to authorize any appeals to be filed on his behalf. The first scheduled execution in Texas for a nonvolunteer was the impending execution of Kenneth Bruce, set to die on January 14. In the meantime, the state of North Carolina had executed Raymond Rowsey on January 9, 2004. North Carolina is in the same judicial circuit as Virginia, where the Reid case was from. The federal court of appeals issued an order halting Rowsey's execution, just as a different panel of the same court had stopped Reid's execution.[36] However, when the North Carolina attorney general asked the Supreme Court to intervene, the Supreme Court dissolved the stay of execution by a vote of five to four. The Supreme Court had left the stay of execution in place in the Reid case, but not in Rowsey's case. To death penalty lawyers, it was not immediately clear what distinguished *Nelson* and *Reid*, in which stays of execution had remained in place, from Rowsey's case, where the stay had been dissolved. As death penalty lawyers would soon learn, most cases would turn out to be like Rowsey's rather than Reid's.

Thus, the state of Oklahoma executed Tyrone Darks on January 13, 2004. Darks had received a stay from the Tenth Circuit on grounds similar to the stay issued by the Fourth Circuit in the *Reid* case. The Supreme Court dissolved the stay by a vote of 5 to 4. On January 14, 2004, the state of Ohio executed Lewis Williams. A panel of the Sixth Circuit, by a vote of 2 to 1, had declined to follow the Fourth Circuit's lead in *Reid*. The dissenting judge argued that it was inappropriate for the execution to go forward in a case where the inmate had raised the precise procedural question that the Supreme Court would review in *Nelson*. Williams's lawyers asked the Supreme Court for a stay. It was denied by a vote of 5 to 4.

Of the first fifteen people executed in the United States in 2004, eight—more than half—were put to death after they lost a final effort to halt their executions by a vote of 5 to 4. As a death penalty lawyer, if your client is seeking to gain relief on the basis of an issue that no Supreme Court justices seem interested in, then it can be difficult to continue fighting the war. But when inmate after inmate is losing by a vote of 5 to 4, the slimmest conceivable margin, then lawyers feel the need to do everything they can to pick up the one additional vote that will save their client's life. If a lawyer needs to convince five justices, then the task is hopeless. But when all you need to do is change one person's mind, then there is a desperate search to locate the right phrase, the right precedent, the right argument that will convince that judge.

Bruce was set for execution in Texas on the same day Williams was executed in Ohio. He was to be the first of three inmates in Texas to be executed on consecutive Wednesdays: Bruce on the 14th, Kevin Zimmerman on the 21st, and Vickers on the 28th. Although Bruce, Vickers, and Zimmerman each had independent counsel,[37] the same set of lawyers represented all of the inmates in connection with the lethal injection litigation. For perhaps obvious reasons, the lawyers unbundled the cases of the three Texas inmates set for execution in January. Their plan was to use lessons learned from litigating one case when litigating the next. If one inmate got a stay, the tactics employed to obtain it would be repeated; if the inmate was executed, the tactics would be modified. The approach of the lawyers was a reaction to the pattern of five-to-four denials. It was possible that the stay that had stood up in *Reid* was an anomaly, without any significant analytical distinctiveness. But it was also possible that there was a coherent explanation, albeit an elusive one. If there was some coherent theory that explained *Nelson* and *Reid*, on the one hand, versus the five-to-four denials from Oklahoma, Ohio, and North Carolina, on the other, then the fates of Vickers, Zimmerman, and Bruce hinged on the ability of their lawyers to figure out what that theory was.

Bruce was executed on January 14, 2004. The lawyers tried a subtly different approach for Zimmerman. It also did not succeed. Zimmerman was executed on January 21. Vickers was next, scheduled to die on January 28. Before Zimmerman's execution, the most plausible theory was that the Supreme Court thought there was something distinctively problematic with the so-called cut-down procedure. But Zimmerman had also been a long-term drug user whose veins were compromised, and he had been complaining about the risk of a cut-down procedure for many years. When he too lost in the Supreme Court by the same five-to-four vote, the hypothesis that the cut-down issue was doing the work lost favor. Vickers's lawyers were at a loss; they had no good theory as to why Reid's stay had held up while all the others were denied. One thing was clear, however: If Vickers went to the Supreme Court with nothing other than the question of whether he could challenge the lethal injection protocol with an action under section 1983, he would lose by a vote of five to four. To get a fifth vote, he needed a new argument.

And indeed he had one. Vickers's case *was* different from all the others that had preceded his because of the surreal events of December 9. On that day, he had become the only person in the history of the death penalty in Texas not to be executed despite the existence of a valid death warrant that was neither rescinded nor stayed. The lethal injection claim was not going to get him a fifth vote for a stay, but Vickers's lawyers decided that perhaps one justice might be persuaded by a claim arising out of the facts of December 9,[38] and that justice, in combination with the four who had been dissenting in all the lethal injection cases over the preceding month and a half, would be sufficient to keep Vickers alive until the Supreme Court decided the jurisdictional question in *Nelson.*

The gist of the claim arising out of the events of December 9 was that the state's failure to inform Vickers that it was not going forward with the execution for more than three hours after it had made the decision constituted cruel and unusual punishment, and that the state's new attempt to carry out his execution amounted to double jeopardy. In ordinary English, the state had intentionally engaged in psychological torture, pretending it was going to execute Vickers, even though it had decided not to go forward with the execution. A strand of Eighth Amendment jurisprudence that is more than a century old holds that although the state is permitted to execute its citizens, it is not allowed to torture them, physically or mentally.

Vickers had new substantive arguments as a result of the debacle on December 9, but he faced a procedural dilemma. At the time of his execution, the highest Texas state criminal court, the Texas Court of Criminal Appeals (CCA), adhered to a doctrine it calls the two-forum rule. Under this rule, the CCA refuses to adjudicate any case in which an identical or closely related issue is pending in federal court.[39] Vickers was concerned that if he filed his action in federal court immediately, the state courts would refuse to adjudicate it. But Vickers's lawyers thought it would be unwise to forfeit the chance to have the state courts review his suit because the federal courts had already been so inhospitable to his claims. So Vickers's lawyers decided that even though going to state court would ultimately mean that the federal court would have less time to review the case (assuming the case got that far), it was simply a risk they had to take. Hence, on Friday, January 23—less than two days following the Zimmerman execution, Vickers's lawyers asked the state courts to spare him from the death sentence on the grounds that the state had already conducted a mock execution two weeks earlier. By midday the following Monday, the state court had still not resolved the case. Vickers's lawyers decided they could wait no longer and filed their papers in federal court.[40]

By mid-afternoon on Tuesday, one day before the scheduled execution, the federal district court dismissed the suit. Although Vickers's counsel did not immediately receive a copy of the district court's order, the court clerk led them to assume that the district court simply did what it had done a month earlier and dismissed the § 1983 action as a habeas petition. (This is also what the district courts had done in the *Bruce* and *Zimmerman* cases.) The clerk of the Fifth Circuit called counsel to ask whether they would be filing anything in the court of appeals, and counsel told her that they planned to do so. The clerk informed the lawyers that the court would close for the day at 5 p.m.

Because Vickers's lawyers assumed that the district court had disposed of the case in the same way that the lower courts had in the two previous cases, they had already written the appeal. The lawyers modified that appeal, tailoring it to Vickers's case, and, at approximately 4:30, sent it via e-mail to the clerk's office. Minutes later, counsel finally received a copy of the district court's order. As it happened, the district court had *not* disposed of the case in the same way the federal district court had done in the prior § 1983 litigation in December 2003; nor had the court acted in the same way as had the district courts in the *Bruce* and *Zimmerman* litigation. Instead, the district court followed a practice that had not previously been used in Texas. The technical details of this practice are rather esoteric,[41] but what the district court had done was extremely significant because it made the Vickers case unlike the Zimmerman and Bruce cases in one critically important respect. Specifically, the lower court had disposed of the appeal in such a way that Vickers's lawyers believed that the Fifth Circuit might not even have the authority to review it, and if the Fifth Circuit could not review it, there was no way to get the issue before the Supreme Court.

Upon at last seeing the district court's order, I and Vickers's other lawyers immediately realized that we had to file an appeal significantly different from the one we had sent to the clerk's office only moments earlier. Consequently, counsel immediately phoned the clerk for the Fifth Circuit and informed her that they did not wish to file the appeal that they had sent via e-mail minutes earlier. She informed counsel that the document would not be filed, and she asked when an appeal would in fact be sent. Vickers's lawyers assured her that it would be sent first thing the following morning, Wednesday, January 28, 2004.

Vickers's lawyers got to work. At shortly before 8 p.m. the fax machine rang, and an order started to arrive from the Fifth Circuit. The lawyers assumed this was good news. No appeal had been filed, and the only thing an order could be doing, therefore, was staying the execution. As it happened, that was not what the Fifth Circuit did. Even though the federal statute specifies that these cases must be decided by three judges, a two-judge quorum issued an order that disposed of all "anticipated" filings by Vickers. The judges on the court of appeals had predicted the arguments Vickers's lawyers planned to make, and then resolved those arguments against Vickers. Vickers lost in the court of appeals before he even arrived at the door of the courthouse. Vickers had now set two precedents in Texas: He had become the first person to have an execution warrant expire, and he now became the first person to have the Fifth Circuit deny his appeal before that appeal was even filed. (The court also ordered that any motion for rehearing be physically filed by 10 a.m. central time the following day, an astonishing order in view of the fact that Vickers had still not filed his original appeal.)

Vickers's lawyers knew futility when they saw it, and they elected not to seek further review in the Fifth Circuit. Early the following morning, Vickers sought relief in the Supreme Court. At approximately 5:50, the Court denied the stay by a vote of five to four. Vickers was executed several minutes later. He was pronounced dead shortly after 6.

Four months after he was executed, the Supreme Court decided David Nelson's case. By a vote of nine to nothing, the Court ruled that Nelson could use § 1983 to challenge the state's use of a cut-down procedure.[42]

Many death row inmates probably committed the crimes that led a jury to sentence them to death. Many death row inmates, in other words, are not innocent. This creates a dilemma for judges. A murderer is asking these judges to protect his constitutional rights. At the same time, although there are exceptions, friends and family members of the murder victim are demanding vengeance, claiming that since the murderer did not care about the victim's rights, they cannot care about his. Demagogic politicians join the chorus. They read the polls. No one picks up votes defending a convicted murderer's constitutional rights when there is an innocent dead body in the picture. That is the context of most death penalty appeals. Imagine being asked to grant Ted Bundy a new trial. Imagine being asked to declare that Timothy McVeigh's death sentence must be set aside.

It cannot be easy. It cannot be easy to be a federal judge who must preside over the habeas corpus appeal of a death row inmate whom the judge believes to be guilty, and perhaps even a despicable human being. It cannot be easy, with the victim's family sitting in the courtroom, to say that the death row inmate deserves a new trial. A death row inmate's lawyers *know* that inmate; they see him with his mother and father, with his brothers and sisters, with his wife and children. They know more about him than the fact that he committed a despicable crime. They have seen him cry, they have seen him scared, they have seen him full of sorrow. The inmate's lawyers know their client as a human being. The rest of us, and the judge who must preside over his case, know him for the horrible thing he has done and nothing more.

And that is the biggest part of the problem. We pretend that death row inmates are murderous machines. We pretend that they are not human beings. This delusion is rather easy to maintain because death row inmates are locked away where we need not confront them. They are frequently functionally illiterate and often inarticulate. They could not express themselves with eloquence even if they had a forum. These inmates do not have the power or the skills to thrust their humanity before our very eyes, to make us see them as human beings. There are perhaps six people alive who read the letter that Billy Vickers wrote the day after the night that the state pretended it was going to execute him, perhaps six people who know something of the excruciating pain he felt as the state was toying with him. It is easy for me to understand death penalty supporters who say that although Vickers might have suffered, his victims suffered too, and therefore he should die. It is easy for me to understand them, because when I started representing people like Billy Vickers, that was my view as well. As I mentioned, when I began representing men on death row, all I knew was their names and the worst things they had done. That is why I was not against the death penalty: these inmates were simply murderers, not people. Now I know my clients —not just their names, but who they are. Death penalty lawyers like me are against the death penalty for the same reason you would be against the execution of your son, your father, or your brother even if your son or your father or your brother had committed an atrocious crime: because you know that person as a human being.

Judges do not know inmates as human beings because they do not want to. They could not send them to their deaths if they did. That is why it is not easy for a judge to rule that because the inmate's rights were violated, he must receive a new trial, be removed from death row, or released from prison altogether. And yet that is what judges ought to do. It is what judges *must* do, not just because it is their job, not just because they have sworn an oath to uphold the Constitution, but because the fate of our legal and political system depends upon their doing the right thing even when it is difficult. These very difficulties are the price of principle. They arise because we are a nation of laws, where the rule of law prevails over a particular sentiment. No matter how deeply the federal judges who presided over the case of Billy Vickers might have reviled him, their duty was to separate their revulsion from their dedication to the enforcement of constitutional norms. Their duty was to enforce the law.

We do not need the *Vickers* case—or any other case I have discussed in this book—to teach us that there is murder and evil in our midst; that we sadly already know. We do need the *Vickers* case, and cases like it, to remind us that these inmates are in fact human, and to illuminate a tragic phenomenon that we remain loath to concede: In death penalty cases, we have abandoned our principles. We have replaced our lofty ideals with crass expedience. The tragedy of contemporary death penalty litigation is not simply that innocent victims were murdered; the further tragedy is that we use those murders as excuses to violate our constitutional values. We defile ourselves and innocent victims by using the victims as pretexts. By willfully ignoring that death row inmates are human beings, we say that the "animals" deserve to die; and since it is only an animal after all, the ends justify the means. Death penalty law is not law at all. It is the rule of the mob.

A PERSONAL NOTE

During the Albigensian Crusade, around the year 1210, the iron-
ically named Pope Innocent III, when asked by the crusaders how
they might avoid killing Catholics and focus their efforts on the
impious infidels, is said to have replied that the crusaders should
kill everyone. God would sort it out.[1] Our death penalty jurisprudence aspires to less haphazardness. As we have seen, in this
aspiration, our law falls far short.

There is no such thing as an ordinary murder. Every murder
takes a human life; every murder leaves behind a victim's family
and friends. Every murder is wrong. But the fact that there are no
ordinary murders does not mean that all murders are the same.
When the Supreme Court struck down the death penalty in 1972,
it did so because the system was arbitrary: People who committed
less horrible crimes were being punished more severely than people who committed more horrible crimes. States responded by
enacting new death penalty laws that sought to eliminate this arbitrariness, severely limiting the number of crimes that would
render someone susceptible to the death penalty and then asking

juries to examine the individual lives of capital murder defendants in great detail. States obviously wanted the death penalty, but for it to be constitutional, it had to be reserved for the most despicable and heinous crimes and for the most unredeemable, unremorseful, and unforgivable defendants.

When representing men like the ones whose cases I have recounted in this book, I realized that the death penalty we have today is as arbitrary as it was a generation ago when the Supreme Court briefly condemned it as unconstitutional. We do not have a fair system, and when you try over a period of thirty years to make a system fair and still you fail, it is time to conclude that the system cannot be made fair. I have argued in this book that the system is unfair and incapable of being made fair, which is reason enough to abolish capital punishment. But I have also come to believe that even if we could perfect the death penalty apparatus, we should still do away with it, and so I want to spend a few moments in this afterword explaining how I came to that view.

When we execute condemned murderers, we desperately try to avoid acknowledging the fact that we are executing a human being. Newspaper photos of death row inmates are almost always mug shots—grainy pictures that could make the world's most handsome model look sinister. We hear virtually nothing about the lives of these inmates in any complexity. I understand the instinctive belief that by humanizing the inmate we are somehow betraying the victim. Before I knew any inmates, before I saw them with their families, I thought that myself.

Unlike many death penalty lawyers, I did not start representing death row inmates because I was opposed to capital punishment. During my first years of representing these men, I tried to spend as little time as I could with them because I did not want to know them. I did not want to become close to men I would not be able to save. But once you begin to do this work, you can't not meet your clients. You meet them, and inexorably you begin to know them. Knowing death row inmates does not make you forgive them for the terrible thing they have done; it does, however, cause you to realize that the terrible thing they have done is not the entirety of who they are.

In 1994 four young men, members of a gang, broke into the home of an elderly woman named Martha Lennox. James Henderson, one of the gang members, shot her in the head and killed her. He handed the gun to his cousin Willie Pondexter, who shot her in the jaw. At Henderson's trial, the prosecutor said that Henderson killed Lennox. The jury sentenced Henderson to death. At Pondexter's trial, the prosecutor said that, actually, Pondexter had killed Lennox. The jury sent him to death row as well.

When I met Willie Pondexter for the first time, I did not know why he was on death row. A lawyer who had been appointed to represent him planned to stop practicing law, and he asked me whether I could take over the habeas corpus appeal. I told him I would if Pondexter wanted me to.

While I was waiting for Pondexter to come out from his cell, the guard who watched over the death row visiting area told me that Pondexter was her favorite inmate on the row, and that if she had her druthers, she would turn him loose. She told me that she believed in the death penalty but that she had no doubt that Pondexter had matured and would not return to the gang, which is what had put him on death row to begin with. I nodded, not knowing exactly what to say, since I still did not know what Pondexter had done.

Lennox was probably already dead when Pondexter shot her. The prosecutor got it right the first time when he told the jury that Pondexter's cousin James Henderson had killed her. Although that point perhaps has great legal significance, it may have very little moral relevance. Pondexter did something hideous and cruel. But on the day that I arrived at the prison, he was not the same person who had participated in the murder. That is what the guard knew and told me even before I ever met him.

The reason we know that Lennox was probably already dead when Pondexter shot her is that Pondexter's habeas lawyers hired a pathologist. Unfortunately for Pondexter, his trial lawyer had not bothered to do that, even though there were good reasons for him to believe that Lennox was already dead when Pondexter fired a shot. One of those reasons is that a jailhouse informant who testified for the state gave a statement saying that Pondexter had told him that the woman was already dead when he shot her. The lawyer probably never read that statement, however; and he never bothered interviewing the informant. Undoubtedly Pondexter participated in a heinous crime. But he is on death row because his lawyer did not do his job, and if the state one day executes Willie Pondexter, it will kill a man who is not the same person who broke into Lennox's home.

Some weeks later I went back to the prison to visit Pondexter again. By this time I had studied his case and worked on the appeal. As I started to tell him what to expect, the guard came over and teased him about something. I told Pondexter the issues I had identified as worth pursuing. I told him that the case was comparatively strong but that the courts would be looking for a way to rule against him because, even though Martha Lennox might already have been dead, Pondexter had shot her. "On paper," I told him, "you are not someone that a judge is going to want to save; and unfortunately," I continued, "the only place the judge is going to see you is on paper."

Pondexter nodded and said nothing for a moment. When he looked up, he seemed close to crying. I tried to soften what I said, to tell him not to give up hope, that we had a number of arrows left in our quiver and he was not going to die anytime soon. He said that that was not what was bothering him. He was upset because his father was sick and close to death. I had thought he was feeling sorry for himself. In fact, he detested himself for not being able to go to his father's funeral.

*   *   *

I once had an image of death row inmates as cold, loveless, and cruel. If you do not know anyone who has committed a murder, if all you have seen are grainy black-and-white mug shots of inmates and defendants sitting in stony silence at their trials, it will be hard for you to replace that image.

Two months before he died, Donald Aldrich wanted to talk to me. Aldrich's lawyer had reached the end of the appellate road; he told Aldrich that there was nothing left to do. His lawyer asked me whether my office would take over Aldrich's appeals if Aldrich decided to pursue any further legal proceedings.

Before going to the prison, I looked into his case. I read that Aldrich had killed a man just because the man was gay, so I already did not care for him. Aldrich entered the visiting cage. He had thinning hair and arms covered with tattoos. He was neither muscular nor fat. You would not notice him if he had not been wearing a white prison jumpsuit stenciled with the letters "DR" on the back. If, when you imagine a typical death row inmate, you picture Charles Manson or Hannibal Lecter, you are already forming a faulty image. What is arresting about nearly all murderers is how ordinary they are, how unremarkable they appear.

The first thing Aldrich told me is that his crime was not a hate crime. He told me he robbed gay men because they were in the closet, and they would not report to the police that they had been robbed in the parking lot of a gay bar. Aldrich did not try to hide from me that he was a career robber or that he had participated in a murder. He just did not want me to think that he hated homosexuals. He told me about the gay prisoners he had shared cells with during his previous time in prison for robbery. He told me the names of gay men on death row I could talk to about him. He gave me a list of references to prove that although he had participated in a murder, he wasn't a bigot. Then he looked me in the eye and asked me whether I was a Christian. I said no. He said, "Oh, well, that's all right. It just means that you might not understand this when I tell you that I have accepted my fate. I did something wrong. I know that. There are guys in here who are innocent. I did not intend to commit murder that night, but I was there. That means that I am not innocent. I am a thief, not a murderer, and I'm no bigot, but I am not innocent."

Aldrich was a career criminal, and he probably needed to spend the rest of his natural life in prison. But he did not have a history of violence prior to being involved in the murder that landed him on death row. Yet he was sentenced to death anyway for a single reason: A psychiatrist testified that if he were not executed, Aldrich would kill again.[2]

In the 1983 decision of *Barefoot v. Estelle*,[3] the Supreme Court ruled that juries at death penalty trials are permitted to give weight to these predictions of future dangerousness. Even though the American Psychiatric Association had insisted that such predictions were scientifically unsound and were a form of medical quackery, the Court trusted juries to assess the evidence. In its faith in juries, the Court assumed that indigent defendants would be represented by competent trial lawyers who could vigorously cross-examine so-called psychiatric experts. That faith, however, was misplaced. As a result, some defendants were sentenced to death because of the testimony of men like Walter Quijano, who in at least seven cases involving Hispanic defendants testified that they were likely to be dangerous in the future just because they were Hispanic. They were sentenced to death also because of the testimony of men like James Grigson, who would spend fifteen minutes administering a Rorschach exam to inmates and then spend several hours telling the jury that these inmates would undoubtedly kill again if not sentenced to death. Twenty years later, a report suggested that these psychiatric predictions are wrong around 95 percent of the time,[4] and indeed, in Aldrich's case, the prediction had proven spectacularly unsound. Aldrich's prison disciplinary record was essentially spotless.

We wanted to try to get back into federal court to challenge the reliability of the key piece of evidence that had led to his being on death row—the erroneous prediction of future dangerousness —but there were daunting procedural obstacles. We developed a theory to try to deal with these obstacles, but despite our confidence in the soundness of our legal position, we did not hold out much hope of success. As I have argued, courts do not care much about the rule of law in death penalty cases. I did not want to mislead Aldrich. I told him that his case had potential claims we could raise, but that the odds that we would prevail were exceedingly remote. I told him he should prepare himself for execution.

After the lower courts rejected our appeals, I went back to the prison to tell Aldrich that we had nearly reached the end of the road. He thanked me for our efforts but seemed not to be paying attention to me. His eyes were looking over my shoulder, darting back and forth. I assumed that he had held out some small reservoir of hope and he was having difficulty assimilating what I was telling him. I was wrong. He told me he was distracted because he was looking for his son. I had not known he had children. He told me he had four boys: twenty-one-year-old twins named Ronald and Donald, a nineteen-year-old named Aaron, and a seventeen-year-old named Sam. He had not seen any of them for more than five years. When Aldrich first went to prison, Sam, who was a toddler, did not know that his dad was on death row. Sam went to visit Aldrich and asked when his daddy would come home. Aldrich had to tell his seven-year-old boy that he was on death row, that he wouldn't come home at all. Sam became hysterical. A guard carried him away from the visiting area.

Aldrich's eyes were wet as he told me the story, but his expression suddenly changed. One of his twins had entered the visiting area with his wife. Aldrich had never met his daughter-in-law, but he instantly recognized his son. Aldrich and I were in an attorney booth. To talk to his son, he had to be relocated to the general visiting area. I introduced myself to his family while the guards moved Aldrich from one cage to another. Once Aldrich was relocated, I told him good-bye. I handed the phone to his son and tried not to listen as he told his father that he loved him.

At fifteen minutes past five on the day of the execution, the Supreme Court turned down our final appeal. I called Aldrich, who was in the holding cell next to the execution chamber, to tell him the news. He thanked me for representing him, and he reminded me that I had told him we would lose and that he should prepare to die. He told me he had done that, and he said that he hoped I had learned something from his case that might help someone else. Aldrich was executed on October 12, 2004.

One of the reasons it is so jarring to see death row inmates as loving fathers, husbands, or sons is that their own family histories are so devoid of love. If you show me a death row inmate, I will tell you his biography. People on death row are poor. They were abused as children, emotionally or physically. They are uneducated. They came from homes so dizzyingly broken that describing them with the word *dysfunctional* is not even remotely adequate. They grew up abusing alcohol, drugs, or people. Proponents of the death penalty say that not everyone who grows up with an abusive father turns into a murderer, and that is thankfully true, but it is also true that abuse breeds abuse, and that is why the victims of abuse continue to surprise me.

At the age of seventeen, Randy Arroyo helped steal a car. The car's owner, an air force officer, was shot and killed. Arroyo admits he was in the car but says he was not there at the time of the shooting. We have not been able to prove that.

Arroyo is a slight, boyish-looking man with widely gapped teeth and thick eyeglasses. He is very bright. The first time I met him, before we had agreed to represent him, he asked questions about his case that were as insightful as the ones I would expect from a law student. I went to see Arroyo to tell him about some developments in his appeal. Although he was usually very interested in the details of the legal arguments, this time he asked no questions. Instead he looked at me and said, "Are you a Jew?" I laughed, and he asked me what was so funny. I told him that on my last trip to the prison, Aldrich had asked whether I was Christian, and so I was wondering whether the next guy was going to ask me whether I'm Muslim or Hindu.

On a previous visit, he had told me that he had gotten a disciplinary write-up for refusing to shave. I asked why he didn't want to shave; he replied that he is not supposed to shave during Ramadan. Arroyo was raised a Catholic. "You observe Ramadan?" I asked him. He said that of course he did. He told me that he had taken the name Abdullah and that he had converted to Islam. I said, "You are the first Muslim I've ever met named Arroyo."

When I laughed at his question, Arroyo thought he had insulted me. He said that he didn't mean anything by it, that his best friend on the row is Jewish. Arroyo was asking about my religion because he had been thinking about forgiveness. I had once told Arroyo about the meeting between Johnny Martinez and his victim's mother. Arroyo told me he didn't think he had that kind of forgiveness in him.

Arroyo and I spent some time talking about religion. He said, "I see that you're hopeless, so I won't waste any more of our time trying to convert you." He said he was going to start telling people that I am an infidel. The conversation was serious yet playful, a conversation two college students might have had. He asked, "Do we have to talk about my case today?" I told him we did not, and he got to the point. Arroyo had no relationship with his father, yet he was still tormented by the prospect of severing that bond. He told me what I already knew from having investigated the case: His father had been absent and abusive when Arroyo was a child. Yet Arroyo could not help continuing to reach out. He would write his dad and beg him to visit. Three times Arroyo's dad had said that he would, and three times he had not shown up.

Arroyo knew that my wife and I have a son. I had become his lawyer and a father figure as well. He wanted to know whether I thought he had been a bad son. He asked, "What if your son was like me?" I told him that I would still love him, that I might not know how to relate to him if he was on death row, but that I would still love him, and that I was sure his dad felt the same. Arroyo shook his head, unpersuaded.

Then he said, "I wish I wasn't here, but death row has not been all bad for me. This is going to sound like a funny thing to say, but some good has come from this. My mom died before I knew how to tell people I love that I love them. Being here has taught me how to do that. I never told my mom that I loved her. But I did. I still do. Now I know what love is. I know how to tell people that I love them." He asked about students of mine who were working with me on his case. He told me he had plans to write to them soon. He wanted me to send them his regards and to ask them to pay him a visit. I promised to do that.

As I was concluding my visit with him, Arroyo nodded toward an inmate who was sitting in the cage behind me. "Do you know that guy?" I asked. Arroyo said, "Yeah, the dude's crazy. He showers with his boots on." I told Arroyo that I knew that.

Arroyo was talking about Scott Panetti. In September 1992, Panetti, dressed in army combat fatigues, walked into the home of his former in-laws. He was looking for his estranged wife and their three-year-old daughter. His wife's parents, Joe and Amanda Alvarado, confronted him, and Panetti shot them with a sawed-off shotgun. He then took his wife and daughter to a cabin, where he held them until police surrounded the place. Panetti released them, changed into a suit and tie, and surrendered. A jury that was charged with deciding whether Panetti was competent to stand trial could not agree on a conclusion, so a second jury was empaneled. That jury deemed Panetti mentally competent, and so the state pursued capital murder charges in 1995.

Panetti wanted to represent himself, and, astonishingly, the trial judge allowed him to. At his trial, he dressed in a cowboy outfit, complete with chaps and a holster—empty, of course, since he was not permitted to appear in court with a sidearm. He asked the judge to issue subpoenas for John F. Kennedy, Anne Bancroft, and Jesus. Panetti's reason for wanting Jesus to testify on his behalf was that Jesus would tell the jury that Panetti had murdered the three people at Jesus's request. During his closing argument, he said to the jury, "If you sacrifice one sheep, two destroy the wolf; that does not make that sheep guilty." He was of course convicted and sentenced to death. In time, the state set a date for his execution.

The Supreme Court had previously ruled, in the 1987 case of *Ford v. Wainwright,*[5] that the state cannot execute someone who is mentally incompetent. Panetti's lawyer went to court to argue that, under *Ford,* the state could not execute Scott Panetti. On Tuesday, February 3, 2004, two days before Panetti's scheduled execution, I and a licensed psychologist, at the request of Panetti's lawyer, visited Panetti to form an opinion as to his competence.

When we arrived at the prison, Panetti was visiting with his parents—who had driven to Texas from Wisconsin—his brother, his sister-in-law, and a chaplain. Panetti looked eerily like the character Jim Carrey played in the movie *Me, Myself, and Irene,* a film in which Carrey makes fun of multiple personality disorder. Panetti did not suffer from MPD, however; he had a single, pathological identity. By the time he murdered his ex-in-laws, Panetti had been placed in a mental hospital fourteen times. Two weeks before the murders, Panetti's ex-wife had asked police officials to confiscate his weapons.

Just as it does not take a rocket scientist to look at a paper airplane and conclude that the vehicle cannot escape the earth's gravity, it did not require a trained mental health professional to conclude that Panetti is deeply and severely disturbed. In response to the psychologist's questions, Panetti would quote biblical passages, seemingly at random. The passages he quoted had nothing to do with the questions. He could not carry on a conversation for more than a moment or two. He would answer one or two questions (for example, "How old are you?" "Where do your parents live?"), and then veer off into a discussion of some collateral issue, like a conversation he had had with a fellow inmate several weeks previously or with a guard years before.

His brother had purchased three sandwiches for him, which Panetti had disassembled into their constituent parts and then placed in separate piles, so he had a pile of bread, a pile of processed cheese, and a pile of lunch meat. He would move from pile to pile to pile, first placing an entire piece of bread in his mouth, then a slice of cheese, then a piece of meat. While chewing, he would not his head vigorously, as if answering some question with an emphatic yes, though no one had asked him anything. He explained that he was Jesus's agent, that the people who wanted him dead were heathens and philistines. While telling us this, he would lower his voice to a barely audible whisper so that the guards would not overhear him. He believed that the guards might try to murder him in advance of his impending execution date, because they knew that Jesus might intervene and prevent the chemicals from killing him.

Panetti is crazy, but that does not mean he is incompetent under *Ford*. To determine *Ford* competency, the courts inquire as to whether the inmate knows why he was convicted and whether he comprehends his sentence. By this standard, Panetti's case was by no means clear. He knew whom he had killed. His purported reasons for carrying out the murders were demented, but arguably the only salient issue—as far as the *Ford* standard is concerned—is that he knew what he had done. Similarly, Panetti knew that the state planned to execute him. He expressed cautious optimism that Jesus would intervene directly on his behalf to prevent the lethal chemicals from killing him, but he could not be certain this would happen. Along with Cesar Fierro (whose case I discussed in chapter 2), Scott Panetti is among the most disturbed people I have ever met, but "deeply disturbed" and "*Ford* incompetent" are very different things. The Supreme Court has ruled that it is unconstitutional to execute the mentally retarded; it has not yet held that it is unconstitutional to execute the insane.

Our interview ended. Panetti's parents and brother thanked the doctor and me profusely. We told them that there was little we could do. They said they knew that, but that they were happy they were not the only ones who worried about their son. On my way out of the prison, a guard said to me, "Scott's crazy. We call the guy 'preacher' around here. Do what you can." Both the psychiatrist and I prepared affidavits, reporting our observations. Two days later a federal judge stayed Panetti's execution and set a date for a hearing to determine his mental competence.

Several months later, when I was at the prison visiting Arroyo, Panetti saw me. He told the young woman he was visiting with to come get me, and she did. I picked up the phone. Panetti squinted at me as if staring at the sun. He said, "I know you. I know why you did what you did." I did not know exactly what he meant and said simply that we were working hard for him. He said: "I see Jesus Christ inside you." He squinted again. "I see you, Jesus," he said.[6]

The difference between Scott Panetti and a sane person is that Panetti meant that literally.

When I say that if you show me a death row inmate, I will tell you his biography, I am not suggesting that these facts about death row inmates—about my clients—are an excuse for what they have done. There are no excuses for murder. But there are explanations. Murderers are made, not born. They are born as human beings. On death row, almost all of them—not every one of them, but most—exhibit the entire range of characteristics that make a person human. They grow up in homes and in neighborhoods where their humanity is quashed and assaulted, but they routinely heal on death row. Many of these men are too dangerous to be let out of prison, too vulnerable to whatever it is about them that is broken. But in prison, they pose no danger to us. In prison, they are human beings. Guards and wardens see this, but society does not, because these men are on death row, in prisons that are far away—geographically, emotionally, and in every sense of the word—from where we live.

If we could see how human beings who have committed the quintessentially criminal act of taking a human life exhibit basic human qualities, we would not be able to delude ourselves into thinking that we are exterminating insentient beings. No case better illustrates this proposition than the execution of Karla Faye Tucker, whose moment of fame erupted not just because George W. Bush was running for president, but because people who ordinarily support capital punishment with nary a qualm looked at Tucker and paused.

In June 1983 Tucker and a companion brutally murdered two people, Jerry Dean and Deborah Thornton. Tucker's companion, Daniel Garrett, beat Dean on the head with a hammer, and Tucker struck him repeatedly with a pickax. Dean and Thornton had more than twenty stab wounds apiece. Tucker reportedly said that she had orgasms as she was striking her victims. On February 3, 1998, she became the first woman to be executed in Texas since the Civil War.

The days leading up to the execution were a circus. Homicide detectives, prosecutors, and even Newt Gingrich spoke up for Tucker. People for whom death penalty discussions typically begin and end with some reference to the Bible's "eye-for-an-eye" language became, at least momentarily, abolitionists. Pat Robertson appeared on the *Larry King Live* show and appealed for her life to be spared. The death penalty, Robertson said, is not about vengeance, and Tucker, he believed, had reformed.

And she probably had, as have hundreds of other death row inmates. Yet neither Gingrich nor Robertson is championing any of the rest of them. Neither was in Texas when James Allridge, a black man whom I discussed in chapter 6, was executed in August 2004. Tucker was white, attractive, articulate, female, and Christian. People who watch television shows such as *Friends* and *NYPD Blue* paid attention to the Tucker story because she *looked* like someone they could relate to. She sounded like people they know. She was not unique in this regard. What was unusual is that people who did not know Tucker got to see her visage, to hear her voice. Two years later, on February 24, 2000, the state of Texas executed another woman, Betty Lou Beets. There were no national media, no protests from Pat Robertson. Where Tucker was a voluble and an effervescently reborn Christian, Beets was sullen and laconic. Tucker was pretty, Beets was not. I did not know either woman, but I feel that I knew Tucker because she was on television frequently. All I know about Beets is what I read in the paper, which was very little. People cared about the Tucker execution for the same reason they cared about Princess Diana's car crash: They thought they knew her. They were indifferent to Betty Beets's death for the same reason they are not moved to tears when they see footage of a fatal car crash on the nightly news.

Long before the rest of us in society become indifferent to the looming execution of a convicted murderer, a jury has sentenced that murderer to death. How does that happen? Is it that the twelve men and women on the sentencing jury do not apprehend that the person whose fate they control is in fact a person? Or is it that they do not care?

I think that cases like Karla Faye Tucker's answer that question for us. Prosecutors succeed in obtaining death sentences when they can make the defendant seem inhuman.[7] If even lawyers like me, lawyers who represent death row inmates, are caught by surprise by mundane moments of tenderness between men who murder and the people they love, those moments must be unimaginable to people who know death row inmates only from the details of the worst thing they have done.

The proof of how hard it is to execute someone we think of as human can be found in one of the most disturbing episodes in American legal and cultural history. On October 3, 1995, every major network interrupted its regular programming to broadcast live the jury's verdict in the O.J. Simpson murder trial. In California white pedestrians in an upscale shopping mall watched the verdict on large-screen TVs in stunned silence, while two thousand miles away, black students watching in a college auditorium erupted in spontaneous jubilation.

Today, a decade later, the racial chasm captured by these images remains, with 90 percent of whites believing that Simpson was guilty and an equal percentage of blacks believing he was not. Part of the explanation for this disturbing divide lies on death row itself. More than 17,000 executions have taken place in the United States. Of that number, fewer than 40 have involved a white murderer and a black victim. In Texas, on a death row of more than 400 men, there was not a single white murderer whose victim was black until two men who chained James Byrd to the back of a pickup and dragged him to his death arrived there in 1999.

In some ways, Texas is unique, but not when it comes to race. In Georgia, for example, blacks represent 60 percent of all homicide victims, yet 80 percent of those executed are executed for killing a white person. In Kentucky, more than 1,000 blacks have been murdered since 1977, but of the 28 people on death row, not a single one is there for killing a black person. These data have been known for many years. Over a decade ago, a group of researchers, led by David Baldus, examined more than 2,000 homicides in Georgia and, as part of the examination, analyzed more than 200 different variables: race of victim, race of offender, economic status of victim and offender, details of the crime, and so on. They determined that although black murderers were significantly more likely than white murderers to be sentenced to death, the truly dramatic variable was the race of the victim: Murderers of whites were between four and five times as likely to be sentenced to death as murderers of blacks. This essential finding has been replicated in every state where the study was conducted.[8]

Nationwide, whites make up slightly less than half of the total number of murder victims, but more than 80 percent of those executed are executed for killing a white person.[9] Not all scholars agree that the race of the accused plays a significant role in determining which defendants are sentenced to death; nevertheless, it is fair to say that a broad consensus acknowledges the impact of the race of the victim.[10] Not even the Supreme Court has denied this fact. Nevertheless, in 1987, in the case of *McCleskey v. Kemp*,[11] the Court denied relief to McCleskey, a black man sent to death row for murdering a white victim, on the grounds that McCleskey's statistical showing did not demonstrate that racism had operated *in his particular case.* The dissenting justices complained that the burden the majority placed on McCleskey could never be met; all a death row inmate can show are statistics. At some point, those statistics must be permitted to speak for themselves.

The death penalty regime retains vestiges of our nation's sordid history of race discrimination. There is simply no getting around that fact. The reaction to the Simpson verdict is tied up in a complicated and depressing way with that history. But an important decision occurred in the Simpson case many months before the jury's explosive verdict. On September 9, 1994, the Los Angeles county district attorney decided not to seek the death penalty against him. On paper, this was a surprising decision. Confronted with a black man who was connected by DNA to the brutal murder of a young, attractive white man and a young, attractive white mother of two small children, the state of California, with close to five hundred people on its death row, chose not to seek death. Why?

A simple thought experiment will help answer that question. If you are a white person, the statistics suggest that you think O. J. Simpson murdered Ron Goldman and Nicole Brown. Now try to imagine executing Simpson. It is unimaginable, isn't it? You can imagine O. J. in prison for the rest of his life, but you cannot imagine him sitting hooded in the electric chair or strapped to the gurney. Simpson was acquitted because he had the resources to hire superb lawyers. But even if he had been broke and forced to rely on appointed counsel, Simpson's case would still be different. It would be different because the entire country knew him. The district attorney did not seek the death penalty against Simpson because the district attorney knew that he would not get it. The prosecution could argue that Simpson committed an animalistic act, but it would never be able to persuade the jury that Simpson was an animal. It would not succeed in erasing the images of O. J. carrying the football or bantering with Howard Cosell during *Monday Night Football*. O. J. Simpson was somebody the jury already knew.

Two weeks before the major television networks interrupted prime time programming to broadcast the famous Ford Bronco chase, the state of Texas executed Denton Crank (on June 14, 1994). Along with his half-brother, Crank murdered a man named Terry Oringderff after holding him hostage all night and then robbing the store that Oringderff managed. Though his brother received a life sentence, Crank was sentenced to death. Like Simpson, Crank had two young children, two girls named Amanda and Cherie. When their dad was executed, Amanda was twelve and Cherie was thirteen. For the ten years leading up to the execution, they visited him once a week, driving more than an hour each way from their home north of Houston to Texas's death row. They would talk to their dad across thick, wire-laced, bulletproof glass. They never hugged him, kissed him, or held his hand. In his final statement, Crank told his family that he loved them.

Like all murderers, Crank committed a vile, despicable act. Unlike O. J. Simpson, he had no money to hire first-rate lawyers. Great lawyers probably would not have had him acquitted, but they would have kept him off death row. If you are a celebrity, people think they know you. If you are poor and inarticulate, they do not, and your only hope if you face a trial for your life is to change that. The defendants who end up on death row are the ones whose lawyers did not try to humanize them, or who tried and failed.

A federal district judge ruled in our favor in Willie Pondexter's case. The court concluded that Pondexter's trial lawyer had been ineffective. However, the state appealed to the Fifth Circuit Court of Appeals. I went to the prison to report on the status of the case and to let Pondexter know what to expect.

"I doubt we will hold on to the victory," I told him. Even though the district court judge reached what I believe is the correct legal conclusion, the Fifth Circuit would take it away. Several months later my pessimistic forecast proved correct. I went back to the prison to convey the news. "Our problem," I told Pondexter, "is that the judges on the court of appeals focus heavily on what you did, not on whether your rights were violated. All they know about you—all they care about knowing—is what you did that one night. Who you are now does not interest them."

I told Pondexter that I believed I was a competent lawyer, but what he needed at that point was a poet, someone who could make the judges realize that he was a remorseful and redeemed human being, someone who could make them care about that. "I don't think I have that talent," I told him. "Even if we win again in the lower courts, I am not hopeful that it will be any different next time around." But I told him that we would keep trying, that we would keep fighting until there were no more arrows left in our quiver. He said that he knew that, and he said thank you. I touched the glass between us and told him I'd be back soon. As I walked out of the prison, a guard lightly touched my arm and whispered good luck.

ACKNOWLEDGMENTS

My friend Jim Marcus, a former student of mine, is the executive director of the Texas Defender Service, an organization dedicated to improving the representation of people who face the death penalty. I have told Jim more than once that the difference between him and me is that when one of my clients is executed, I put my kayak on my truck, kiss my wife and son good-bye, tell them that I will see them tomorrow, and then go find some moving water somewhere. When one of Jim's clients is executed, he goes back to the office the next day to work on behalf of someone else.

This book would not exist if I did not know people like Jim. It draws on more than fifteen years of working with some of the finest death penalty lawyers in the country. Not all the people I name on the right side of the colon still represent death row inmates on a full-time basis, but most of them did and most of them still do. I have been privileged to work with and learn from each of them. I am grateful to: Tony Amsterdam, Sandra Babcock,

Bryce Benjet, John Blume, Steve Bright, Dick Burr, Mark Gruber, Andrew Hammel, Eden Harrington, Scott Howe, Kathryn Kase, Andrea Keilen, George Kendall, Lynn Lamberty, Maurie Levin, Jim Liebman, Robin Maher, Jim Marcus, Joe Marguelies, Rob McDuff, Robert McGlasson, Morris Moon, Brent Newton, John Niland, Mark Olive, Rob Owen, Danalynn Recer, Meredith Roundtree, Raoul Schonemann, Clive Stafford-Smith, Jordan Steicker, Naomi Terr, Jean Terranova, Jared Tyler, Mandy Welch, and Greg Wiercioch. I have also benefited on more occasions than I can recount from the willingness of habeas and death penalty lawyers across the county to respond to queries I have placed on the habeas listserv run by Professor Eric Freedman at Hofstra.

I benefited greatly from the opportunity to present portions of the argument to my colleagues at the University of Houston, to faculty and students in Jane Cohen's classes at the University of Texas, to faculty and students in Phil Broadhead's classes at Ole Miss, and to a group of lawyers and judges at a seminar put on by the Center for Justice and the Rule of Law. The University of Houston Law Center and the Law Center Foundation provided valuable financial support. My own students at the Law Center provided constant moral support and inspiration.

I owe especial thanks to my agent, Simon Lipskar, and my editor, Gayatri Patnaik. Simon took this project on because he believed in it, and Helene Atwan and Beacon Press took it on for the same reason. Everyone at Beacon Press—editors, copyeditors, production staff, publicity personnel—has been a pleasure to work with. It is sometimes hard to get much useful assistance when one is preaching to the converted, but that has not been the case with Simon and Gayatri. The book is immeasurably better for their involvement and for Helene's meticulous reading. If there are Platonic forms for agents, editors, and publishers, they undoubtedly resemble Simon, Gayatri, and Helene.

I dedicate this book to my parents, who raised their five sons not just through exhortation, but through example; to my brother Mark, who read and improved virtually every page; to my wife, Katya, and son, Lincoln, who inspired me to write it; and to Whitney and Winona, who made me into someone who could.

NOTES

Introduction: Beyond Innocence

1. Throughout this book I use the masculine pronoun when I refer to people on death row. I do so because approximately 98.5 percent of the death row population in America is male.

2. 408 U.S. 238 (1972).

3. *Id.* at 309–10 (Stewart, J., concurring) (citations and footnotes are omitted in the extract).

4. 408 U.S. at 358 (Douglas, J., concurring).

5. 408 U.S. at 268–71 (Brennan, J., concurring).

6. *Id.* at 297.

7. For Justice Brennan, see *id.* at 298–99 and nn. 52, 53; for Justice Marshall, see at 340–42.

8. 347 U.S. 483 (1954).

9. 381 U.S. 479 (1965).

10. *Goodridge et al. v. Department of Public Health*, 440 Mass. 309 (Mass. 2004).

11. A summary of survey data can be found in David Niven, *Bolstering an Illusory Majority: The Effects of the Media's Portrayal of Death Penalty Support*, 83:3 Social Science Quarterly 671 (2002).

12. The Court upheld the laws in Texas, Georgia, and Florida while striking down those in Louisiana and North Carolina. See *Gregg v. Georgia*,

428 U.S. 153 (1976); *Proffitt v. Florida*, 428 U.S. 242 (1976); *Jurek v. Texas*, 428 U.S. 262 (1976); *Roberts v. Louisiana*, 428 U.S. 325 (1976); *Woodson v. North Carolina*, 428 U.S. 280 (1976).

13. James S. Liebman, *The Overproduction of Death*, 100 Colum. L. Rev. 2030 (2000).

14. 428 U.S. 153 (1976).

15. *Id.* at 188 (1976) (Stewart, J., joined by Powell and Stevens, J.).

16. In *California v. Ramos*, 463 U.S. 992, 998–99 (1983), the Court explicitly ruled that the fact that death is different means that the federal courts must be especially attentive to constitutional violations in death penalty cases.

17. See, for example, *Simmons. v. South Carolina*, 512 U.S. 154, 185 (1994) (Scalia, J., dissenting) (writing, "The heavily outnumbered opponents of capital punishment have successfully opened yet another front in their guerilla war to make this unquestionably constitutional sentence a practical impossibility"); *Bell v. Lynaugh*, 858 F.2d 978, 985–86 (5th Cir. 1988) (opinion of Jones, J.) (characterizing the tactics of Bell's lawyer as "inexcusable").

18. This figure is based on data I collected, which I will present in a paper at a November 2005 conference on AEDPA.

19. 536 U.S. 304 (2002).

20. 492 U.S. 302 (1989).

21. The "evolving standards of decency" idea was articulated for the first time in *Trop v. Dulles*, 356 U.S. 86 (1958). The proposition is deeply rooted in contemporary death penalty jurisprudence. See, for example, *Furman v. Georgia*, 408 U.S. 238 (1972); *Coker v. Georgia*, 433 584 597 (1977); *Atkins v. Virginia*, 536 U.S. 304, 311–20 (2002).

CHAPTER I. THE EXECUTION OF CARL JOHNSON

1. The epigraph is from Joe Cannon, who represented Carl Johnson at trial, as quoted in Paul Barrett, "On the Defense," *Wall Street Journal*, September 7, 1994, at 1.

2. Alex Kozinski and Sean Gallagher, "For an Honest Death Penalty," op-ed page, *New York Times*, March 8, 1995, at A21. Judge Kozinski has objected to my characterization of his opinion, but his editorial in the *Times* speaks for itself.

3. Edith Jones, *Death Penalty Procedures*, 53 Texas Bar Journal 850 (1990).

4. See, for example, *Collins v. Byrd*, 510 U.S. 1185 (1994) (Scalia, J., dissenting).

5. In one vitriolic opinion, Judge Jones chastised a lawyer for "playing

chicken" with the court by waiting until the eleventh hour to file the inmate's habeas petition. *Bell v. Lynaugh*, 858 F.2d 978, 986 (5th Cir.), *cert. denied*, 492 U.S. 925 (1988).

6. I do not always work on these cases for free. In perhaps four or five cases I have submitted vouchers for my work. Vouchers are almost always slashed, often dramatically. It is not uncommon for the courts to pay death penalty lawyers less than half of what they are due.

7. See David R. Dow, *Panel Discussion: The Death of Fairness? Counsel Competency & Due Process in Death Penalty Cases*, 31 Hous. L. Rev. 1105, 1114–18 (1994).

8. Many years ago I collected data comparing conviction rates of defendants in various jurisdictions. See David R. Dow, *Teague and Death: The Impact of Current Retroactivity Doctrine on Capital Defendants*, 19 Hastings Const. L. Q. 23 (1991). Since that time, the number of capital murder defendants sentenced to death has declined somewhat, although the percentage of convictions has not appreciably declined. See Adam Liptak, "Fewer Death Sentences Being Imposed in U.S.," *New York Times*, September 15, 2004. The article is based on a report prepared by the Death Penalty Information Center; the report attributes the decline to popular concerns about innocence. See http://www.deathpenaltyinfo .org/article.php?scid=45&did=1149. A more likely explanation is that trial lawyers representing capital defendants now receive much more sophisticated training in how to present evidence that supports a life sentence rather than a death sentence.

Federal death penalty prosecutions are a different matter entirely. In federal cases, the defendant is sentenced to death only one time out of ten. See http://www.deathpenaltyinfo.org/article.php?scid=29&did= 147#race.

9. See, for example, *McFarland v. Scott*, 512 U.S. 849 (1994); *Graham v. Collins*, 506 U.S. 461 (1993); *Herrera v. Collins*, 506 U.S. 390 (1993); *Sawyer v. Whitley*, 505 U.S. 333 (1992); *Coleman v. Thompson*, 501 U.S. 722 (991); *Butler v. McKellar*, 494 U.S. 407 (1990); *Murray v. Giarratano*, 492 U.S. 1 (1989). Perhaps the most important habeas case of the last decade, however, was a non—death penalty case, *Teague v. Lane*, 489 U.S. 288 (1989), the essential holding of which was quickly applied to death penalty appeals in *Penry v. Lynaugh*, 492 U.S. 302 (1989).

10. Both the O.J. Simpson trial and the trial of the Menendez brothers in California have contributed to the public interest. See David R. Dow, Letter ("Trial by Jury"), *Commentary* 6–7 (July 1994), responding to Walter Berns, "Getting Away with Murder," *Commentary* (April 1994).

11. David R. Dow, *Teague and Death*, 19 Hastings Const. L. Q. 23 (1991).
12. See Mark Ballard, *Gideon's Broken Promise*, Texas Lawyer, August 28, 1995, at 1.
13. *Id.*
14. No one disputes that the lawyer dozed off on several occasions. When Johnson first told me that his lawyer had fallen asleep, I took his comment with the usual large grain of salt. But all it took was a phone call to the co-counsel to confirm that the story was indeed true. This lawyer has since been deemed constitutionally ineffective in a different case.
15. *Strickland v. Washington*, 466 U.S. 668 (1984).
16. For a truly harrowing discussion of endemic ineptitude in the representation of indigent capital defendants, see Stephen B. Bright, *Counsel for the Poor*, 103 Yale L. J. 1835 (1994).
17. The lawyer is described in Paul Barrett's "On the Defense," *Wall Street Journal*, September 7, 1994, at A1. After representing Johnson, the lawyer had two of his clients escape death row, though it is not clear whether this was the lawyer's doing or the state's decision. The lawyer is now deceased.
18. After the Supreme Court's decision in *Penry v. Lynaugh*, 492 U.S. 302 (1989), the Texas statute was changed. The jury still determines whether the defendant acted deliberately and whether he will be dangerous. But if the jury answers affirmatively, then it must determine whether, based on all the mitigating evidence, the defendant should be sentenced to death or to life in prison. See Tex. Code Crim. Proc. art. 37.071(b), (e).
19. The objection was ill founded because even if state evidentiary rules supported the exclusion, which Johnson argued was not the case, the Constitution clearly requires that such testimony be admissible in a capital case. See, for example, *Lockett v. Ohio*, 438 U.S. 586 (1978); *Eddings v. Oklahoma*, 455 U.S. 104 (1982); *Green v. Georgia*, 442 U.S. 95 (1979).
20. See Exhibit 17 of Johnson's "Petition for Writ of Habeas Corpus," filed in the United States District Court for the Southern District of Texas, December 23, 1993.
21. *Id.*
22. *Jurek v. Texas*, 428 U.S. 262 (1976).
23. *Id.* at 273; see also *Franklin v. Lynaugh*, 487 U.S. 164, 178 (1988).
24. *Johnson v. State*, 629 S.W.2d 731 (Tex. Crim. App. 1981).
25. See generally 28 U.S.C. 2254.
26. The exhaustion requirement is now codified as part of the procedural

rules pertaining to habeas corpus procedures in the federal courts. See 28 U.S.C. 2254(b). But the requirement first appeared in case law as early as 1886. See *Ex parte Royall*, 117 U.S. 241 (1877). The doctrine is now firmly established. See, for example, *Vasquez v. Hillery*, 474 U.S. 254 (1986); *Rose v. Lundy*, 455 U.S. 509 (1982). The scholarship pertaining to exhaustion is legion. See generally James Liebman, 1 *Federal Habeas Corpus Practice and Procedure* 37–56 (1988); Paul Bator, *Finality in Criminal Law and Federal Habeas Corpus for State Prisoners*, 76 Harv. L. Rev. 441 (1963); Gary Peller, *In Defense of Federal Habeas Corpus Relitigation*, 16 Harv. C.R.-C.L. L. Rev. 579 (1982).

27. 492 U.S. 302 (1989).

28. The notion that the Constitution, in assessing a sentence, requires the sentencer to take into account all mitigating evidence proffered by the capital defendant was delineated in *Lockett v. Ohio*, 438 U.S. 586 (1978). The Supreme Court has revisited one of the issues it decided in the *Penry* case and has held that the Constitution categorically forbids the execution of the mentally retarded. See *Atkins v. Virginia*, 536 U.S. 304 (2002).

29. *Selvage v. Collins*, 816 S.W.2d 390 (Tex. Crim. App. 1991).

30. 874 F.2d 954 (5th Cir. 1989).

31. When cases are disposed of on the summary calendar, the lawyers do not have an opportunity to appear before the judges to present an oral argument; instead, the court issues a ruling based entirely on the written briefs filed by the lawyers.

32. *James v. Collins*, 987 F.2d 1116 (5th Cir.), *cert. denied*, 509 U.S. 947 (1993).

33. When appellate courts decide cases, they issue opinions that announce the result and at times lay out the reasoning that underlies the result. If the court believes the opinion is important, or involves a significant issue, it will have the opinion published in an official report; if the court does not think the case is important, it will not publish the opinion. With the advent of the Internet, even so-called unpublished opinions became frequently available; however, until quite recently, an unpublished opinion was essentially unknown to anyone other than the parties to the case. In Texas, unpublished opinions are still essentially invisible because the state courts do not even make them available electronically.

34. See Tex. Code. Crim. Proc. art. 43.14 (West 1995).

35. As it became clear that the Supreme Court would not rule before sun-

rise, Sam Houston Clinton, a judge on the Texas Court of Criminal Appeals, issued a stay. Leonel Herrera, a Texas death row inmate, was eventually executed after the Supreme Court reached the merits of his case in *Herrera v. Collins*, 506 U.S. 390 (1993); but he had come within moments of death a year earlier, when the Court had denied him temporary relief; see *Herrera v. Texas*, 502 U.S. 1085 (1992).

36. Rule 39, Sup. Ct. Rules.

37. Death row has since been moved to the Polunsky unit, in Livingston, Texas.

38. For a more technical discussion of the issues I raised before the Supreme Court, see David R. Dow, *The State, the Death Penalty, and Carl Johnson*, 37 Boston College Law Review 691 (1996).

39. *McCoy v. Lynaugh*, 874 F.2d 954, 968 (5th Cir. 1989) (Williams, J., concurring).

40. They also might be wrong. For instance, polls routinely suggest that most Americans would not want to know in advance the date and time they will die.

41. That is, there is no reliable evidence that capital punishment generally deters others from committing capital crimes. See Michael L. Radelet and Margaret Vandiver, *Capital Punishment in America* (NY: Garland, 1988).

42. Footnote 1 of the Fifth Circuit's opinion in Johnson's case included this familiar boilerplate: "Local Rule 47.5 provides: 'The publication of opinions that have no precedential value and merely decide particular cases on the basis of well-settled principles of law imposes needless expense on the public and burdens the legal profession.' Pursuant to that Rule, the Court has determined that this opinion should not be published."

43. *Callins v. Collins*, 510 U.S. 1141 (1994).

44. Indeed, in the 1976 cases that reinstated the death penalty in America, Justice Blackmun voted with Justice Rehnquist in favor of sustaining each of the five challenged statutes. Justices Stewart, Powell, and Stevens were the centrists responsible for the result whereby the mandatory death penalty statutes of North Carolina and Louisiana were stricken down, whereas the statutes of Georgia, Texas, and Florida survived. See *Gregg v. Georgia*, 428 U.S. 153 (1976); *Proffitt v. Florida*, 428 U.S. 242 (1976); *Jurek v. Texas*, 428 U.S. 262 (1976); *Woodson v. North Carolina*, 428 U.S. 280 (1976); *Roberts v. Louisiana*, 428 U.S. 325 (1976).

45. Quoted in Anthony Lewis, *Panel Discussion: The Death of Fairness? Coun-*

sel Competency & Due Process in Death Penalty Cases, 31 Hous. L. Rev. 1105, 1111 (1994). The case was *McFarland v. Scott,* 512 U.S. 1256 (1994), which held, with Justice Scalia in dissent, that a capital defendant need not file a habeas petition in order to invoke his right to qualified representation and to establish a federal court's jurisdiction to grant a stay of execution.

46. Actually, federal death penalty cases are somewhat different. But all state cases proceed in the manner that Johnson's did.

47. This schedule applied to the old statute, which set executions for after midnight. Inmates are now executed between 6 p.m. and midnight.

CHAPTER 2. CESAR FIERRO'S COERCED CONFESSION

1. The epigraph to this chapter is from Judge Baird, dissenting, in the case of Cesar Fierro, 934 S.W.2d at 383.

There is actually some question about whether the report was produced to Fierro's trial lawyers. Fierro's current lawyers believe that it was not. Even if it was, however, it was given to those lawyers in a context where they would not have paid attention to the inconsistency between its contents and the testimony of Medrano.

2. 499 U.S. 279 (1991).

3. The idea of harmless error review is examined at greater length in David R. Dow and James Rytting, *Can Constitutional Error Be Harmless?* 2000 Utah Law Review 483. It is actually impossible to determine whether a trial error has influenced the jury's verdict, and most constitutional errors should therefore be treated as fundamental.

4. 499 U.S. at 309.

5. See James S. Liebman., *The Overproduction of Death,* 100 Columbia L. Rev. 2030 (2000).

6. 28 U.S.C. section 2244 provides as follows:

(a) No circuit or district judge shall be required to entertain an application for a writ of habeas corpus to inquire into the detention of a person pursuant to a judgment of a court of the United States if it appears that the legality of such detention has been determined by a judge or court of the United States on a prior application for a writ of habeas corpus, except as provided in section 2255.

(b)(1) A claim presented in a second or successive habeas corpus application under section 2254 that was presented in a prior application shall be dismissed.

(2) A claim presented in a second or successive habeas corpus application under section 2254 that was not presented in a prior application shall be dismissed unless—

(A) the applicant shows that the claim relies on a new rule of constitutional law, made retroactive to cases on collateral review by the Supreme Court, that was previously unavailable; or

(B)(i) the factual predicate for the claim could not have been discovered previously through the exercise of due diligence; and

(ii) the facts underlying the claim, if proven and viewed in light of the evidence as a whole, would be sufficient to establish by clear and convincing evidence that, but for constitutional error, no reasonable factfinder would have found the applicant guilty of the underlying offense.

(3)(A) Before a second or successive application permitted by this section is filed in the district court, the applicant shall move in the appropriate court of appeals for an order authorizing the district court to consider the application.

(B) A motion in the court of appeals for an order authorizing the district court to consider a second or successive application shall be determined by a three-judge panel of the court of appeals.

(C) The court of appeals may authorize the filing of a second or successive application only if it determines that the application makes a prima facie showing that the application satisfies the requirements of this subsection.

(D) The court of appeals shall grant or deny the authorization to file a second or successive application not later than 30 days after the filing of the motion.

(E) The grant or denial of an authorization by a court of appeals to file a second or successive application shall not be appealable and shall not be the subject of a petition for rehearing or for a writ of certiorari.

(4) A district court shall dismiss any claim presented in a second or successive application that the court of appeals has authorized to be filed unless the applicant shows that the claim satisfies the requirements of this section.

(c) In a habeas corpus proceeding brought in behalf of a person in custody pursuant to the judgment of a State court, a prior judgment of the Supreme Court of the United States on an appeal or review by a writ of certiorari at the instance of the prisoner of the decision of such State court, shall be conclusive as to all issues of fact or law with respect to an asserted denial of a Federal right which constitutes ground for discharge in a habeas corpus proceeding, actually adjudicated by the Supreme Court therein, unless the applicant for the writ of habeas corpus shall plead and the court shall find the existence of a material and controlling fact which did not appear in the record of the proceeding in the Supreme Court and the court shall further find that the applicant for the writ of habeas corpus could not have caused such fact to appear in such record by the exercise of reasonable diligence.

(d)(1) A 1-year period of limitation shall apply to an application for a writ of habeas corpus by a person in custody pursuant to the judgment of a State court. The limitation period shall run from the latest of—

(A) the date on which the judgment became final by the conclusion of direct review or the expiration of the time for seeking such review;

(B) the date on which the impediment to filing an application created by State action in violation of the Constitution or laws of the United States is removed, if the applicant was prevented from filing by such State action;

(C) the date on which the constitutional right asserted was initially recognized by the Supreme Court, if the right has been newly recognized by the Supreme Court and made retroactively applicable to cases on collateral review; or

(D) the date on which the factual predicate of the claim or claims presented could have been discovered through the exercise of due diligence.

(2) The time during which a properly filed application for State post-conviction or other collateral review with respect to the pertinent judgment or claim is pending shall not be counted toward any period of limitation under this subsection.

7. 372 U.S. 385 (1963).
8. 492 U.S. 302 (1989).
9. 28 U.S.C. section 2254 provides as follows:

> (a) The Supreme Court, a Justice thereof, a circuit judge, or a district court shall entertain an application for a writ of habeas corpus in behalf of a person in custody pursuant to the judgment of a State court only on the ground that he is in custody in violation of the Constitution or laws or treaties of the United States.
>
> (b)(1) An application for a writ of habeas corpus on behalf of a person in custody pursuant to the judgment of a State court shall not be granted unless it appears that—
>
> (A) the applicant has exhausted the remedies available in the courts of the State; or
>
> (B)(i) there is an absence of available State corrective process; or
>
> (ii) circumstances exist that render such process ineffective to protect the rights of the applicant.
>
> (2) An application for a writ of habeas corpus may be denied on the merits, notwithstanding the failure of the applicant to exhaust the remedies available in the courts of the State.
>
> (3) A State shall not be deemed to have waived the exhaustion requirement or be estopped from reliance upon the requirement unless the State, through counsel, expressly waives the requirement.
>
> (c) An applicant shall not be deemed to have exhausted the remedies available in the courts of the State, within the meaning of this section, if he has the right under the law of the State to raise, by any available procedure, the question presented.
>
> (d) An application for a writ of habeas corpus on behalf of a person in custody pursuant to the judgment of a State court shall not be granted with respect to any claim that was adjudicated on the merits in State court proceedings unless the adjudication of the claim—
>
> (1) resulted in a decision that was contrary to, or involved an unreasonable application of, clearly established Federal law, as determined by the Supreme Court of the United States; or

(2) resulted in a decision that was based on an unreasonable determination of the facts in light of the evidence presented in the State court proceeding.

(e)(1) In a proceeding instituted by an application for a writ of habeas corpus by a person in custody pursuant to the judgment of a State court, a determination of a factual issue made by a State court shall be presumed to be correct. The applicant shall have the burden of rebutting the presumption of correctness by clear and convincing evidence.

(2) If the applicant has failed to develop the factual basis of a claim in State court proceedings, the court shall not hold an evidentiary hearing on the claim unless the applicant shows that—

(A) the claim relies on—

(i) a new rule of constitutional law, made retroactive to cases on collateral review by the Supreme Court, that was previously unavailable; or

(ii) a factual predicate that could not have been previously discovered through the exercise of due diligence; and

(B) the facts underlying the claim would be sufficient to establish by clear and convincing evidence that but for constitutional error, no reasonable factfinder would have found the applicant guilty of the underlying offense.

(f) If the applicant challenges the sufficiency of the evidence adduced in such State court proceeding to support the State court's determination of a factual issue made therein, the applicant, if able, shall produce that part of the record pertinent to a determination of the sufficiency of the evidence to support such determination. If the applicant, because of indigency or other reason is unable to produce such part of the record, then the State shall produce such part of the record and the Federal court shall direct the State to do so by order directed to an appropriate State official. If the State cannot provide such pertinent part of the record, then the court shall determine under the existing facts and circumstances what weight shall be given to the State court's factual determination.

(g) A copy of the official records of the State court, duly certified by the clerk of such court to be a true and correct copy of a finding, judicial opinion, or other reliable written indicia showing such a factual determination by the State court shall be admissible in the Federal court proceeding.

(h) Except as provided in section 408 of the Controlled Substances Act, in all proceedings brought under this section, and any subsequent proceedings on review, the court may appoint counsel for an applicant who is or becomes financially unable to afford counsel, except as provided by a rule promulgated by the Supreme Court pursuant to statutory authority. Appointment of counsel under this section shall be governed by section 3006A of title 18.

(i) The ineffectiveness or incompetence of counsel during Federal or State collateral post-conviction proceedings shall not be a ground for relief in a proceeding arising under section 2254.

10. 28 U.S.C. section 2244(d).

11. The chief justice was Rose Bird.

12. The defeated judge was a Republican. He was also a former marine who had served in Vietnam. His law-and-order credentials were impeccable—save for the one case referred to in the text.

13. Frank Newport, "Support for Death Penalty Drops to Lowest Level in 19 Years, Although Still High at 66%," Gallup News Service, February 24, 2000; Phoebe C. Ellsworth and Samuel R. Gross, *Hardening of the Attitudes: Americans' Views on the Death Penalty*, 50 J. Soc. Issues 19, 20 (Summer 1994), at 19, 20.

14. 518 U.S. 152 (1996).

15. 506 U.S. 390 (1993).

16. *Lindh v. Murphy*, 521 U.S. 320 (1997); see also *Kiser v. Johnson*, 163 F.3d 326 (5th Cir. 1999).

17. *Ford v. Wainwright*, 477 U.S. 399 (1986).

CHAPTER 3. JOHNNY JOE MARTINEZ'S FATAL FIVE MINUTES

1. *Roberts v. Louisiana*, 428 U.S. 325 (1976); *Woodson v. North Carolina*, 428 U.S. 380, 303–4 (1976).

2. *Zant v. Stephens*, 462 U.S. 862, 879 (1983).

3. 428 U.S. at 333–34.

4. Although the Supreme Court has not directly addressed the question, despite having had numerous opportunities, the lower courts have found no infirmity with permitting the state to tell the jury, during the punishment phase of a death penalty trial, that the defendant is a sus-

pect in other crimes. See, for example, *Williams v. Lynaugh*, 814 F.2d 205, 208 (5th Cir.), *cert. denied*, 484 U.S. 935 (1987); *Beazeley v. Johnson*, 242 F.3d 248 (5th Cir.), *cert. denied*, 534 U.S. 945 (2001).

5. *Murray v. Giarratano*, 492 U.S. 1 (1989); *Coleman v. Thompson*, 501 U.S. 722 (1991).

6. Of states with significant death row populations, Alabama is the most prominent exception; in Alabama, state death row inmates are not guaranteed counsel. All other states with more than a dozen people on death row do guarantee a lawyer during state habeas proceedings.

7. Tex. Code Crim. Proc. article 11.071 § 2(d).

8. *Id.* § 3(a).

9. The amended application for state habeas relief, of whose existence Martinez did not appear to know, had been filed on his behalf almost six months earlier. Apparently state habeas counsel never sent Martinez a copy of the habeas petition filed on his behalf.

10. *Ex parte Torres*, 943 S.W.2d 469, 474 (Tex. Crim. App. 1998).

11. Tex. Code Crim. Proc. Ann. art. 11.071(5)(a) (emphasis added).

12. Federal Court Hearing (Exhibit 3) at 14–18. The District Court later remarked: "I don't know what's holding up the State of Texas giving competent counsel to persons who have been sentenced to die." *Id.* at 19.

In the years since the Texas legislature passed article 11.071, several instances have come to light of inexperienced or incompetent 11.071 counsel committing serious blunders and of the CCA providing no remedy to the affected inmates. Former CCA judge Charles Baird— who shared responsibility for appointing state habeas corpus lawyers when counsel for Martinez was appointed—has admitted that the court "appointed some absolutely terrible lawyers. I mean lawyers that nobody should have, much less somebody on death row on his last appeal." Staff writers, "Defense Called Lacking for Death Row Indigents: But System Supporters Say Most Attorneys Effective," *Dallas Morning News*, September 10, 2000, at 1A.

13. *Strickland v. Washington*, 466 U.S. 668 (1984).

14. *Ex parte Graves*, 70 S.W.3d 103 (Tex. Cr. App. 2002).

15. 70 S.W.3d at 113.

16. *Id.* at 114.

17. *Williams v. Taylor*, 529 U.S. 362, 396–97 (2000) (citing 1 ABA Standards for Criminal Justice 4–4.1, commentary, pp. 4–55 [2d ed. 1980]).

18. Chavera, Martinez's mother, had long ceased all drug and alcohol abuse by the time of Martinez's trial. Chavera Aff. at ¶6; D. Martinez Aff. at ¶6.

19. 28 U.S.C. section 2254(i).
20. 501 U.S. 722 (1991).
21. *Charlotte Observer*, October 16, 2002 (summarizing a report released by the Common Sense Foundation, a Raleigh-based think tank).
22. *Dallas Morning News*, September 10, 2000.23. Liebman, *Overproduction*, at n. 178.
24. See *Lethal Indifference*, published by the Texas Defender Service (2002).
25. "Troubled Lawyers Still Allowed to Work Death Cases," *Tennessean*, July 25, 2001.
26. "Unequal, Unfair and Irreversible: The Death Penalty in Virginia," a 2000 study by the ACLU of Virginia. The report is available at http://members.aol.com/acluva/DPSTUDY.doc. The specific information appears at pages 16–17 and associated footnotes.
27. Stephanie Saul, "When Death Is the Penalty: Attorneys for Poor Defendants Often Lack Experience and Skill," *New York Newsday*, November 25, 1991, p. 8.
28. Data for many southern states can be found in Marcia Coyle, Fred Strasser, and Marianne Lavelle, *Fatal Defense: Trial and Error in the Nation's Death Belt*, National Law Journal, June 11, 1990, pp. 30, 44,
29. "Capital Defense on the Cheap," *Seattle Post-Intelligencer*, August 6–8, 2001.
30. "Death Row Justice Derailed," *Chicago Tribune*, November 14, 1999.
31. The authoritative study is that of Liebman. He collects much of the data on the disciplinary history of lawyers who represent capital defendants in *The Overproduction of Death*, 100 Colum. L. Rev. at 2102–6 and n. 178.
32. *Ex parte Graves*, 70 S.W.3d at 118.
33. Following the Supreme Court's decision that the Eighth Amendment forbids the states from executing the mentally retarded, states have been forced to implement mechanisms to determine whether a given inmate is in fact mentally retarded. See *Atkins v. Virginia*, 536 U.S. 304 (2002). Once an inmate is found to be so afflicted, he must be moved off death row.

Chapter 4. Some Are Released, Others Are Executed

1. As of September 1, 2004, 926 inmates have been executed in the United States. Over the same period, there were 105 exonerations. In addition, 9 were exonerated while the death penalty was dormant (from 1972 through 1976), bringing the total number of exonerees to 114. An additional 18 people have been removed from death row or released from

prison altogether because they appeared to be innocent. Latest data are available at the Death Penalty Information Center, http://www.death penaltyinfo.org/.

2. For data on erroneous convictions generally, the authoritative source is Samuel R. Gross et al., *Exonerations in the United States, 1989–2003*, available at http://www.law.umich.edu/NewsAndInfo/exonerations-in-us.pdf. Of course, generalizing about the error rate involves a certain amount of guesswork, but some reliable guesses are discussed in Daniel Givelber's *Meaningless Acquittals, Meaningful Convictions: Do We Reliably Acquit the Innocent?* 49 Rutgers L. Rev. 1317 (1997) (discussing data that suggest general error rates ranging from 3 percent to nearly 8 percent). Givelber also remarks that the data point to a higher error rate in death penalty cases. See also Samuel R. Gross, *Loss of Innocence: Eyewitness Identification and Proof of Guilt*, 16 J. Legal Stud. 395 (1987) (comprehensively surveying exonerations in the twentieth century), and Arye Rattner, *Convicted but Innocent*, 12 Law and Hum. Behav. 283 (1988); James Liebman et al., A Broken System: Error Rates in Capital Cases, 1973–1995, www.justice.policy.net/cjedfund/jpreport (2000); Hugo Adam Bedau and Michael L. Radelet, *Miscarriages of Justice in Potentially Capital Cases*, 40 Stan. L. Rev. 21 (1987). On the low end, one study surmises an error rate of 1 percent in death penalty cases. See C. Ronald Huff et al., *Convicted but Innocent: Wrongful Conviction and Public Policy* (Thousand Oaks, CA: Sage Publications, 1996). This low estimate seems far too conservative in view of the recent spate of exonerations in capital cases.

3. Givelber, *Meaningless Acquittals*, at 1185–86.

4. The extrapolation to death row assumes a national death row population of 4,000 (see DPIC). Three percent of 4,000 equals 120 people; 6 percent equals 240. See also Samuel R. Gross, *The Risks of Death: Why Erroneous Convictions Are Common in Capital Cases*, 44 Buffalo L. Rev. 469 (1996).

5. Current exoneration information where the exoneration is based on DNA can be found at www.innocenceproject.org.

6. *Id.*

7. Tex. Code Crim. Proc. § 37.071.

8. 492 U.S. 302 (1989).

9. Tex. Code Crim. Proc. § 37.071.

10. *Fuller v. State*, 829 S.W.2d 191 (Tex. Cr. App. 1992).

11. *Branch v. Texas* was the companion case from Texas when the Court

held, in *Furman v. Georgia*, that the death penalty, as then applied, was unconstitutional; 408 U.S. 238 (1972).

12. More recently, a study of more than one hundred Texas death penalty cases involving so-called expert testimony concerning future dangerousness has established that these predictions are wrong 95 percent of the time. See Deadly Speculation: Misleading Texas Capital Juries with False Predictions of Future Dangerousness (2004). A copy of the report, prepared by the Texas Defender Service, an organization that provides assistance to death row inmates, can be located at http://www.texas defender.org/publications.htm.

13. 577 S.W.2d 717 (Tex. Cr. App. 1979).

14. 391 U.S. 510 (1968).

15. Tex. Penal Code § 12.31 (repealed).

16. *Adams v. Texas*, 448 U.S. 38 (1980).

17. *Adams v. State*, 624 S.W.2d 568 (1981).

18. *Ex parte Adams*, 768 S.W.2d 281 (Ct. Cr. App. 1989).

19. A detailed account of the Graham litigation, written by his habeas counsel, Dick Burr and Mandy Welch, can be found in David R. Dow and Mark Dow, *Machinery of Death: The Reality of America's Death Penalty Regime* (NY: Routledge, 2002).

20. The Sixth Amendment entitles a person accused in a criminal prosecution to obtain the effective assistance of counsel. The Fourteenth Amendment makes this protection applicable to state criminal prosecutions.

21. "Cause" is defined as "some objective factor external to the defense [that] impeded counsel's efforts to comply with the [rule requiring that all claims be raised in the first petition]"; *Murray v. Carrier*, 477 U.S. 478, 488 (1986).

22. See *Kuhlmann v. Wilson*, 477 U.S. 436, 444 n. 6, 454 (1986); *McCleskey v. Zant*, 499 U.S. 467, 494 (1991).

23. The reason for this is that "cause" is defined as something "external" to the defense—for example, a corrupt prosecutor who withholds the evidence. If the evidence is there, right in front of the lawyer, and the lawyer simply does not see it, the death row inmate cannot satisfy the cause standard.

24. *Graham v. Collins*, 829 F.Supp. 204 (S.D. Tex. 1993).

25. *Graham v. Johnson*, 94 F.3d 958, 971 (5th Cir. 1996).

26. The court declared only the following, without any explanation: "We have examined the application and find it fails to satisfy Art. 11.071, §

5, and accordingly dismiss the application as an abuse of the writ"; *Ex parte Graham*, No. 17,568-05 (November 18, 1998). Article 11.071 of the Texas Code of Criminal Procedure provides, in pertinent part, as follows:

> (a) If a subsequent application for a writ of habeas corpus is filed after filing an initial application, a court may not consider the merits of or grant relief based on the subsequent application unless the application contains sufficient specific facts establishing that: (1) the current claims and issues have not been and could not have been presented previously.

27. *Graham v. Johnson*, 45 F.Supp.2d 555 (S.D. Tex. 1999); *Graham v. Johnson*, 168 F.3d 762 (5th Cir. 1999); *Graham v. Johnson*, 120 S. Ct. 1830 (2000).

CHAPTER 5. INNOCENCE IS NOT ENOUGH

1. *Herrera v. Collins*, 502 U.S. 1085 (1992). According to the Court's order, "The motion for leave to proceed in forma pauperis and the petition for a writ of certiorari are granted. The order of this date denying the application for stay of execution of sentence of death is to remain in effect."

2. *Ex parte Herrera*, 828 S.W.2d 8 (Tex. Crim. App. 1992).

3. *Herrera v. Collins*, 506 U.S. 390 (1993).

4. *Id.* at 404–5.

5. See, for example, *United States v. Quinones*, 196 F.Supp. 416 (S.D.N.Y. 2002); Seth Kreimer and David Rudovsky, *Double Helix, Double Bind: Factual Innocence and Postconviction DNA Testing*, 151 U. Pa. L. Rev. 547 (2002).

6. 506 U.S. at 446 (Blackmun, J., dissenting).

7. Transcript of an oral argument before the Supreme Court in *Herrera v. Collins*, 506 U.S. 390 (1993). Herrera was finally executed in 1993. In his final statement he said: "I am innocent, innocent, innocent. Make no mistake about this; I owe society nothing. . . . I am an innocent man, and something very wrong is taking place tonight. May God bless you all. I am ready." The evidence of his innocence was not particularly strong, in my judgment, although that hardly seems the point.

The irony of the colloquy between Justice Kennedy and the assistant attorney general is that Justice Kennedy's hypothetical was not a hypothetical at all. From the very dawn of the modern death penalty era, Texas has embraced the notion that executing the innocent was a tolerable cost. Thus, Charlie Brooks, the first man executed in Texas in the modern era, may have been innocent. Jack Strickland, the prosecutor who sent Brooks to death row, intervened at the eleventh hour in an effort to halt Brooks's execution. Strickland developed doubts about whether Brooks was the triggerman, and after Brooks was put to death, Strickland lamented: "It may well be, as horrible as it is to contemplate, that the state executed the wrong man." See Brian Wice, *Capital Punishment Texas Style*, Texas Bar Journal 386, 388 (April 1992).

8. See Daryl A. Mundis, *Current Developments at the Ad Hoc International Criminal Tribunals*, 1 Journal of International Criminal Justice 197 (2003, citing *Prosecutor v. Kunarac, Kovac, and Vukovic*, Judgment, Case Nos. IT-96-23-A and IT-96-23/1-A, June 12, 2002).

9. Tex. Code Crim. Pros. Art. 38.14; *Cook v. State*, 1993 Westlaw 99906 (Tex. Crim. App. 1993).

10. Even before DNA testing was sufficiently advanced to permit individual hairs to be associated with a particular person, hair analysts could determine whether a hair came from a person of Caucasian, as distinguished from Negroid or Asian, heritage. For a useful overview of hair analysis, which includes an extensive bibliography, see http://www.fbi.gov/hq/lab/fsc/backissu/jan2002/houck.htm.

11. See *Ex parte Brandley* 781 S.W.2d 886 (Tex. Crim. App. 1989). A lurid but detailed account of the incident appears in Nick Davies, *White Lies: Rape, Murder, and Justice Texas Style* (New York: Pantheon, 1991).

12. After being released, DNA evidence established conclusively that Cook was not guilty, but this evidence was unknown when his conviction was set aside.

13. Only six-year-old Brittany had smoke in her lungs, so the others were probably already dead when the house was set on fire.

14. Aside from the theory's being absurd, it was also factually inaccurate. According to Wanda Lattimore, a supervisor at the Brenham State School who was called as a witness by Graves's counsel, Bobbie Davis and Graves's mother, Doris Curry, were good friends and Davis was not "taking anything from Curry" by being promoted.

15. The four lawyers were Mary Hennessy, Bill Whitehurst, Patrick McCann, and Roy Greenwood.

16. The residents of death row were Alvin Kelly, who has since been executed, and Kerry Max Cook, who has since been released from death row on the grounds that he is innocent of the crime for which he was convicted and sentenced to death.

17. The letter was dated January 14, 1998.

18. In a recorded television interview broadcast by NBC on September 10, 2000, Sebesta admitted that Carter told him before he testified that Graves was innocent and that Carter had acted alone. Sebesta told Geraldo Rivera, the interviewer, "And, yes, at that point he did tell us that, 'Oh, I did it myself. I did it.' He did tell us that." Similarly, Sebesta told Austin journalist Susan Solar in 2000 that "Carter did in fact that night tell us . . . he did it all himself." Graves's defense counsel insist that Sebesta did not inform them that the state's primary witness had exonerated Graves only hours before taking the witness stand.

19. Sebesta added that he did not believe Carter. That seems unlikely in view of the steps Sebesta took to coerce Carter to testify against Graves.

20. Affidavit of Hezekiah Carter, 2003.

21. Affidavit of Roy Rueter, dated November 22, 2003 detailing a conversation with E. K. Murray, Sebesta's lead investigator. The next morning, Murray told Rueter that Rueter's testimony would have to be delayed because Carter "had gotten wet feet about giving testimony against Graves."

    The state had good reason to think that Cookie was indeed involved. The night before Carter was scheduled to testify against Graves, the state had Carter undergo a polygraph examination. District Attorney Sebesta stated during a state habeas corpus evidentiary hearing on November 15, 1998, that during this polygraph examination, Carter informed Sebesta that Carter's wife, Cookie, was present at the crime scene and was an active participant in the killings. The district attorney stated at the hearing that "Carter admitted to us that . . . yes, Cookie was there; yes, Cookie had the hammer." And there was in fact physical evidence to support the theory that Cookie was the second participant. In a 2003 interview, 1992 Somerville police chief Jewel Fisher stated that at the time of her arrest, Cookie also had a small burn on her neck; however, she told officers she had burned herself with a curling iron (statement to Nicole Casarez).

22. Arthur Curry, Graves's brother, testified that Graves was at home on the night of the murders with their sister, Dietrich Curry, and Graves's girlfriend, Yolanda Mathis, and so could not have participated in the crimes.

23. Affidavit of Rick Carroll, November 24, 2003.

24. Interview, July 24, 2003.

25. Affidavit of Yolanda Mathis, 2003.

26. Statement to Nicole Casarez. Wright came forward in 2003.

Chapter 6. Interlude: Why Innocence Matters

1. For Justice Scalia's quote in the epigraph, see http://pewforum.org/
   deathpenalty/resources/transcript3.php3. For Judge Hand's quote, see
   United States v. Garsson, 291 F. 646, 649 (S.D.N.Y. 1923). I have elsewhere discussed at some length the relationship between so-called
   emotions (or feelings) and the development of legal norms. David R.
   Dow, *When Words Mean What We Believe They Say*, 76 Iowa L. Rev. 1
   (1990).

2. Henry J. Friendly, *Is Innocence Irrelevant? Collateral Attack on Criminal
   Judgments*, 28 U. Chi. L. Rev. 142 (1970). Drawing on Jewish law, my
   colleagues, Irene Rosenberg and the late Yale Rosenberg, have written
   a spectacular rejoinder to Judge Hand. See Irene Merker Rosenberg and
   Yale L. Rosenberg, *Guilt: Henry Friendly Meets the MaHaRaL of Prague*,
   90 Mich. L. Rev. 604, 620–22 (1991).

3. This means that even if the state secured convictions 100 percent of the
   time, it would have an error rate of only 10 percent. As I have suggested
   in chapter 4, the actual error rate is probably around 5 percent.

4. *Woodson v. North Carolina*, 428 U.S. 280 (1976); *Roberts v. Louisiana*, 428
   U.S. 325 (1976); *Gregg. v. Georgia*, 428 U.S. 153 (1976). In *Woodson* and
   Roberts, the Court struck down statutes that would have automatically
   imposed a death sentence on any defendant convicted of first-degree
   murder. *Gregg* upheld the Georgia statute, which required the jury to
   examine the defendant's personal characteristics before sentencing him
   to death. Similar statutes in Texas and Florida were also upheld in the
   1976 cases that reinstated the death penalty. See *Jurek v. Texas*, 428 U.S.
   262 (1976); *Proffitt v. Florida*, 428 U.S. 242 (1976).

5. In *Sawyer v. Whitley*, the Supreme Court held that someone who is
   guilty but who cannot constitutionally be executed is "innocent" of the
   death sentence; 505 U.S. 333 (1992). Accordingly, as part of death penalty jurisprudence, there is in fact a concept of being "innocent" of the
   sentence. Yet even in the context of doctrinal discussion, this locution
   is awkward, and for purposes of a nonspecialized discussion, it just does
   not work. In ordinary English, and even for most lawyers unfamiliar
   with death penalty doctrine, it makes no sense to say that someone who
   committed the act he was accused of is "innocent."

6. Allridge was as fully reformed as Karla Faye Tucker, whose case received
   much more attention than Allridge's prior to her execution in 1999.
   Tucker's case is discussed in the Afterword.

7. The idea that executing one murderer dissuades someone else, a third

party, from committing murder is known as general deterrence. The idea that executing a murderer prevents that very murderer from killing again is known as specific deterrence (or incapacitation). In the text, I mean for the second rationale to encompass either or both of these iterations of deterrence.

8. At this point, permit me to interject an observation about these justifications: None of them is sound. With respect to economics, it is cheaper to keep someone in prison for life than to carry out a death penalty. Contrary to popular belief, death penalty cases cost a great deal not because of appeals but because the trials are expensive. They are significantly more expensive than noncapital trials for a variety of reasons. One is that a death penalty trial is two trials, not one. Another is that the second trial, the punishment trial, inevitably entails enormous investigative expense. A third is that jury selection in capital trials involves questioning jurors individually, and picking a jury in a death penalty case therefore takes weeks if not months (rather than mere days). A fourth reason is that two lawyers are ordinarily appointed to represent indigent defendants. None of these factors is affected by expediting the appellate process. All in all, reliable estimates suggest that it costs in the neighborhood of $2 million to carry out a single death penalty. In contrast, housing a prison inmate in a maximum security facility costs in the neighborhood of $25,000 per year. Hence, keeping an inmate behind bars for forty years costs $1 million—half the price of a death penalty case.

The costs obviously vary from state to state, but death sentences are consistently more expensive than life sentences. In Kansas, a study found that death penalty cases, from indictment through execution, cost $1.26 million, whereas nondeath cases cost $740,000 from indictment through sentence. In New York, according to one estimate, each death penalty case costs more than $20 million. See http://www.deathpenaltyinfo.org/article.php?did=108&scid=7#From%20DPIC. In Los Angeles County, according to one study, death penalty cases cost approximately $700,000 more than nondeath cases. See http://justice.uaa.alaska.edu/death/issues.html#cost. A summary of the data can be found in Hugo Adam Bedau, The Case against the Death Penalty, located at http://archive.aclu.org/library/case_against_death.html#incarceration.

With respect to deterrence: The only studies that even remotely suggest a deterrent effect are those conducted by people who believed in deterrence prior to publishing the study. It is fair to say that the overwhelming scholarly consensus, among death penalty supporters as well as opponents, is that deterrence is chimerical. The literature is voluminous, but the most recent contribution, which provides citations for all the major studies, is by Richard Berk, of UCLA. His paper "New Claims about Executions and General Deterrence" can be found at http://preprints.stat.ucla.edu/396/JELS.pap.pdf.

Finally, with respect to the final rationale: Retribution is not an argument at all; it is simply a conclusion. Someone who supports the death penalty on retributive grounds is simply saying that a person who kills should die. (Of course, even if that were so, there is a wide chasm between the premise that "someone who kills should die" and the conclusion that "the state should therefore carry out the execution." I return to the idea of retribution in chapter 7.)

9. Let's dispense with one distraction. The answer has nothing to do with the notion of consent. Though some might argue that innocent civilians in Iraq or Vietnam or Afghanistan have somehow "consented" to the risk that they might accidentally be killed—either because they have not taken the chance to flee the country or because they might have supported a corrupt regime—that argument pushes the definition of *consent* beyond any reasonable bounds. What if the innocent civilians are children? What if they tried to flee or are too elderly to flee? Have they "consented"? The absurdity of the question is its own answer. Even in the case of the highway worker, it makes no more sense to say that he has consented to the risk that he might run into and be killed than to say that someone who chooses to live in a state with the death penalty has consented to the risk that he might be the innocent person who is one day put to death.

10. As I have argued elsewhere, the rule of *lex taliones* is actually a moderating principle. Executions were exceedingly rare under biblical law because the procedural safeguards required in death penalty cases made capital punishment practically impossible. I discuss these issues at somewhat greater length in *The Death of Fairness*, 31 Houston L. Rev. 1105 (1994). See also Irene Merker Rosenberg and Yale L. Rosenberg, *Of God's Mercy and the Four Biblical Methods of Capital Punishment*, 78 Tulane l. Rev. 1169 (2004); Irene Merker Rosenberg and Yale L. Rosenberg, *Lone Star Liberal Musings on "Eye for Eye" and the Death Penalty*, 1998 Utah L. Rev. 505.

11. Sir William Blackstone, 4 Commentaries on the Laws of England 358.

12. Justice Scalia points out that we do not stop using prisons just because we sometimes incarcerate innocent men, and he is obviously right

about that, but we do not experience the visceral reaction that accompanies the execution of someone who is innocent because, in case of wrongful imprisonment, we remain hopeful about correcting our mistakes. When we kill, we cannot mend the damage to our values.

CHAPTER 7. HOW THE RULE OF LAW BECAME MOB RULE

1. 518 U.S. 152 (1996).
2. These scenarios are variations of scenarios I discuss in a longer article that addresses the legal and philosophical issues in *Payne*. See David R. Dow, *When Law Bows to Politics*, 26 U.C. Davis Law Rev. 157 (1992).
3. For citations to this literature, see *id.*.
4. 482 U.S. 496 (1987).
5. 490 U.S. 805 (1989).
6. 501 U.S. 808 (1991).
7. *Brown v. Board of Education*, 347 U.S. 483 (1954).
8. 531 U.S. 98 (2000).
9. 534 U.S. 246 (2002).
10. *Simmons v. South Carolina*, 512 U.S. 154 (1994).
11. *Shafer v. South Carolina*, 532 U.S. 36 (2001).
12. *Kelly v. South Carolina*, 534 U.S. 246 (2002).
13. To be sure, there are differences among the three South Carolina cases, but they are trivial and simply do not bear on the basic principle of *Simmons*, which is that a defendant who stands to be executed is entitled to have his jury know that the alternative to the death penalty is life without parole.
14. Throughout, I use the masculine pronoun simply to reflect that the vast majority of death row inmates are men.
15. 28 U.S.C. § 2254. See, for example, *Heck v. Humphrey*, 512 U.S. 477, 486–87 (1994). See also Brian M. Hoffstadt, *How Congress Might Redesign a Leaner, Cleaner Writ of Habeas Corpus*, 49 Duke L.J. 947, 966–67 n. 79 (2000); *Habeas Relief for Federal Prisoners*, 91 Geo. L.J. 862 (2003). This provision has been construed to encompass challenges to the legality of the conviction as well as the legality of the sentence; *Sawyer v. Whitley*, 505 U.S. 333 (1992).
16. On procedural default, see *Wainwright v. Sykes*, 433 U.S. 72, 90–91 (1977). For a discussion of the problem of default in capital cases, see Andrew Hammel, *Diabolical Federalism*, 39 Am. Crim. L. Rev. 1, 12–13 and nn. 98, 99 (2002); John H. Blume and Pamela A. Wilkins, *Death by Default: State Procedural Default Doctrine in Capital Cases*, 50 S.C. L. Rev. 1, 40–42 and nn. 214–17 (1998).

17. The plaintiffs also relied on state law, which guarantees death row inmates the right to be represented by "competent" counsel in state habeas corpus proceedings. See Tex. Code Crim. Proc. Art. 11.071, § 2(a). But see *Ex parte Graves*, 70 S.W.3d 103 (Tex. Crim. App. 2002), holding that statutory guarantee of "competent" counsel does not guarantee a certain level of performance.

18. See *Martinez v. Texas Court of Criminal Appeals*, 292 F.3d 417, 423 (5th Cir. 2002).

19. For the difficulties of filing a subsequent federal habeas petition, see chapter 2 (the discussion on Fierro).

20. Many lawyers contributed to the development of this challenge, but the person most responsible was Gary Clement, of the Louisiana Capital Assistance Center.

21. Texas carries out lethal injections by administering a combination of three chemical substances: sodium thiopental, or sodium pentothal (an ultrashort-acting barbiturate); pancuronium bromide, or pavulon (a curare-derived agent that paralyzes all skeletal or voluntary muscles but has no effect on awareness, cognition, or sensation); and potassium chloride (which activates the nerve fibers lining the person's veins, causes great pain, and can interfere with the rhythmic contractions of the heart, thus leading to cardiac arrest).

22. 124 S.Ct. 835 (December 1, 2003).

23. The issue had received some attention in the scholarly literature for a number of years prior to the commencement of litigation. See, for example, Deborah W. Denno, *Getting to Death: Are Executions Constitutional?* 82 Iowa L. Rev. 319 (1997); Julian Davis Mortenson, *Earning the Right to Be Retributive*, 88 Iowa L. Rev. 1099 (2003).

24. *Atkins v. Virginia*, 536 U.S. 304, 311–12 (2002), quoting *Trop v. Dulles*, 356 U.S. 86, 100–101(1958).

25. The phrase "evolving standards of decency" originated in a non–death penalty case. *Trop v. Dulles*, 356 U.S. 86 (1958) (opinion of Warren, C.J.). The idea underlying this phrase, however, has been present in death penalty jurisprudence since the dawn of the modern death penalty era. See, for example, *Furman v. Georgia*, 408 U.S. 238, 388–89 (1972) (Burger, C.J., dissenting); *Gregg v. Georgia*, 428 U.S. 227 (1976); see also *Witherspoon v. Illinois*, 391 U.S. 510, 520 and n. 15 (1968).

26. *Chaney v. Heckler*, 718 F.2d 1174 (D.C. Cir. 1983), *overturned on other grounds, Heckler v. Chaney*, 470 U.S. 821 (1985), observing that "drugs used in lethal injections pose a substantial threat of torturous pain to persons being executed."

27. One could perhaps argue that animals that are euthanized are "innocent," in some philosophic sense, and deserve better than a convicted murderer. That argument would of course be a position on the merits of the Eighth Amendment issue. However, in the litigation pursued by Vickers, as well as Kevin Zimmerman and Kenneth Bruce, two other Texas death row inmates, no discussion of the merits ever occurred.

28. *Hines v. Johnson*, 83 Fed. Appx. 592 (5th Cir. 2003).

29. 83 Fed. Appx. at 592–93.

30. *Id.* at 93.

31. Even in death penalty cases, the Fifth Circuit follows the practice of all the federal circuits whereby a panel of the court is bound by a prior panel's resolution of the legal issue presented. See, for example, *Goodwin v. Johnson*, 132 F.3d 162, 175–76 (5th Cir. 1997).

32. There are seventeen active judges plus an additional three who have taken senior status.

33. See David R. Dow, *The State, the Death Penalty, and Carl Johnson*, 37 Boston College Law Review 691 (1996), at 705 and n. 42 (discussing the criticism of the state's practice by Judges Reavley and Jones).

34. It was not terribly unreasonable for the attorney general's office to be reluctant to indicate in writing that it had advised its client to defy a court order, even though defiance of that order undoubtedly was appropriate.

35. *Johnson v. Reid*, 124 S.Ct. 980 (December 18, 2003).

36. See, for example, *Breard v. Pruett*, 134 F.3 615, 621 (4th Cir. 1998).

37. Each of the inmates scheduled for execution in January was also represented by appointed counsel. Bruce was represented by Mike Charlton, of Santa Fe, New Mexico. Vickers was represented by Keith Hampton, of Austin, Texas. Zimmerman was represented by Richard Ellis, of San Francisco, California. These three lawyers also worked on the lethal injection litigation, simultaneously pursuing avenues unrelated to the lethal injection challenges.

38. Vickers did not argue that the state of Texas should have executed him on December 9, when the Fifth Circuit refused to rule on his pending motion for en banc review. He did argue, however, that the state of Texas had an obligation to inform him that it had decided not to go forward with the execution as soon as that decision was reached, and that the state's action—pretending as if the execution would go forward for more than three hours after a decision to the contrary had been reached—amounted to unconstitutional torture.

39. The doctrine has been recently modified, but not in a way that would

have had any impact on the lethal injection litigation. See *Ex parte Soffar*, 120 S.W.3d 344 (Tex. Crim. App. 2003); *Ex parte Soffar*, 2004 WL 245190 (Tex. Crim. App. 2004).

40. A more detailed examination of the timing issues can be found in Dow et al., *The Extraordinary Execution of Billy Vickers*, William and Mary Bills of Rts Journal (forthcoming, 2005).

41. Whereas the district courts in the *Bruce* and *Zimmerman* litigation had dismissed their cases, the court in the *Vickers* litigation purported to transfer the case under 28 U.S.C. section 1631. Consequently, whereas it was clear in the *Bruce* and *Zimmerman* cases that the court of appeals had appellate jurisdiction, this was not clear in the *Vickers* case. See generally *Abdur'Rahman v. Bell*, 226 F.3d 696 (6th Cir. 2000), *cert. granted*, 535 U.S. 1016 (2002), and cert. dismissed as improvidently granted, 537 U.S. 88 (2002).

42. 124 S.Ct. 2117 (2004).

AFTERWORD: A PERSONAL NOTE

1. I have also read that it was actually King Ulrich of France who gave this reply. If that is true, the sentiment would date from the later crusades, during the fourteenth century.

2. Under the current statute, if the jury concludes that the defendant will be a future danger, then the defendant is sentenced to death unless the jury also concludes that the mitigating evidence introduced by the defendant warrants a sentence of life in prison rather than death.

3. 463 U.S. 880 (1983).

4. Deadly Speculation: Misleading Texas Capital Juries with False Predictions of Future Dangerousness (2004), available at http://www .texasdefender.org/deadlysp.pdf. See also Bruce J. Ennis and Thomas R. Litwack, *Psychiatry and the Presumption of Expertise*, 62 Calif. L. Rev. 693 (1974); Christopher Slobogin, *Dangerousness and Expertise*, 133 U. Pa. L. Rev. 97 (1984); Randy K. Otto, *On the Ability of Mental Health Professionals to Predict Dangerousness*, 18 Law & Psychol. Rev. 43 (1994).

5. 477 U.S. 399 (1986).

6. At a hearing in September 2004, a federal judge found that although Panetti might be insane, he is not incompetent to be executed under the legal standard articulated in *Ford*.

7. Too often, prosecutors face little resistance. When Jesus Romero was on trial for his life in Texas, his court-appointed lawyer gave a closing argument that contained fewer than thirty words. Although a federal district court found that Romero's constitutional right to be represented

by competent counsel had been violated, and that his death sentence was therefore unlawful, the court of appeals reversed that decision, and the state of Texas executed Romero on May 20, 1992. At Anthony Westley's trial in 1985, his court-appointed lawyer exaggerated the defendant's criminal record and told the jury that there was no way his client would be rehabilitated. Westley was executed on May 13, 1997. At the 1984 trial of Jose Guzmon, Guzmon's trial attorney referred to Guzmon as a wetback. The jury sentenced him to death. And at James Russell's trial, Russell's lawyer showed up drunk. Russell was executed on September 19, 1991.

8. See David C. Baldus, *Racial Discrimination and the Death Penalty*, 83 Cornell L. Rev. 1638 (1998); John H. Blume, *Post-McClesky Racial Discrimination Claims in Capital Cases*, 83 Cornell L. Rev. 1771 (1998); see also U.S. Gen. Acc't Office, Death Penalty Sentencing 6 (1996) (summarizing data from more than twenty studies); Stephen P. Garvey, *The Emotional Economy of Capital Sentencing*, 75 N.Y.U.L. Rev. 26 (2000).

9. Current statistics, as well as links to death penalty sites, both pro and con, can be found at the Web site of the Death Penalty Information Center, www.essential.org/dpic.

10. See, for example, John C. McAdams, *Racial Disparity and the Death Penalty*, 61 Law & Contemp. Problems 153 (1998).

11. 481 U.S. 279 (1987).

INDEX